Flight from Innocence

A Memoir
1927–1947

Flight from Innocence
A Memoir
1927–1947

JUDSON JEROME

THE UNIVERSITY OF ARKANSAS PRESS

FAYETTEVILLE   LONDON   1990

Designer: *Ellen Beeler*
Typeface: *Linotron 202 Goudy Old Style*

The paper used in this publication meets the minimum
requirements of the American National Standard for
Permanence of Paper for Printed Library Materials
Z39.48-1984. ⊗

LIBRARY OF CONGRESS CATALOGING-IN-PUBLICATION DATA

Jerome, Judson.
    Flight from innocence : a memoir, 1927–1947 / Judson Jerome.
        p.   cm.
    ISBN 1-55728-152-1 (alk. paper). — ISBN 1-55728-153-X (pbk. :
alk. paper)
    1. Jerome, Judson—Biography—Youth.   2. Authors, American—20th
century—Biography—Youth.   I. Title.
PS3519.E814Z465   1990
811'.54—dc20
    [B]   89-27252
                                                                          CIP
                                                                          Rev

Jacket/cover photo by Carl Mydans (courtesy of the Library of Congress)

Acknowledgments

"Abhorrent Acts" is reprinted by permission of *Negative Capability* and appeared in vol. 7, no. 3 & 4, 1987.

"King of the Mountain" originally appeared in *Cedar Rock* vol. 2, no. 2, Spring 1977.

"A Sense of Sin" is reprinted by permission of *The Beloit Poetry Journal* and appeared in vol. 8, no. 4, Summer 1958.

"On Mountain Fork" is reprinted by permission of *Poetry* and appeared in vol. 113, no. 2, Nov. 1967.

"Noodling" is reprinted by permission of *Shenandoah* and appeared in vol. 9, no. 2, Spring 1958.

"Deer Hunt" originally appeared in *Poetry*, May 1955.

"Memory of Grey Fox" is reprinted by permission of *Kindred Spirit* and appeared in Spring 1988. Originally published in *The Sparrow Magazine*, Nov. 1956.

"Vera's Blaze" is reprinted from *Prairie Schooner*, by permission of University of Nebraska Press. Copyright 1957 University of Nebraska Press.

"Diver" originally appeared in *Coastlines* vol. 3, no. 3, Autumn 1958.

"The Unchosen" originally appeared in *Cedar Rock* vol. 11, no. 1, Winter 1976.

"Revival" is reprinted by permission of *Epoch* and appeared in vol. 11, no. 1, Winter 1961.

"A Handful of Grit" is reprinted by permission of *Negative Capability* and appeared in vol. 7, no. 3 & 4, 1987.

"Gull at Play" originally appeared in *The Colorado Quarterly* vol. 6, no. 3, Winter 1958.

"Alcoholic" is reprinted from *Prairie Schooner*, by permission of University of Nebraska Press. Copyright 1960 University of Nebraska Press.

"Window Painters" originally appeared in *The Red Earth* vol. 1, no. 2, Mar.-Apr. 1944.

"Descent of Man" originally appeared in *Coastlines* vol. 4, no. 4, Autumn 1960.

"Elegy: Barefoot Boy" is reprinted by permission of *Kindred Spirit* vol. 7, no. 1, Spring 1987. Originally published in *The Colorado Quarterly* vol. 9, no. 1, Summer 1960.

"Janet" is reprinted by permission of *Epoch* vol. 9, no. 4, Spring 1959.

Significant portions of an essay, "Go East Young Man," are reprinted by permission of *Chicago Review* and appeared in Winter 1965.

Significant portions of an essay, "Alcoholic," originally appeared in *The Colorado Quarterly* Winter 1965.

Contents

1

Glancing Blows

Tulsa: 1928

I grab the bars of my crib and pull myself to my feet in the dark. I cannot open my eyes: my lids are sealed, and sight suffocates inside them. I scream. A light comes on. I sense it through lids glued shut, hear Mother's consoling voice. She has come to me from the bed where she and Daddy sleep on the other side of the small room. I feel a warm washcloth dissolving the dry seal. At last my eyelids peel open. I see Mother's soft face in the slice of light from the open bathroom. She is wearing nothing but a silky nightgown. My father is a dark shape under covers on the bed behind her. Some exudation has seeped out of my eyes and dried into a crust, night after night. . . . My sobbing subsides in the comfort of her dry kisses, her smooth bare arms, her bosomy embrace.

I wake to blindness and am given light by love.

✦   ✦   ✦

I stand in the little pool with goldfish circling around my knees, the water to my waist. Mother, wearing a one-piece blue wool swimsuit and standing beside the pool, tells me to hold my breath and to put my face in the water. Now she climbs in with me and puts her hand under my chest, which is covered by my wool swimsuit with a net top, and tells me to kick. She teaches me to put my face in the water, and then to twist my face to the side and take a breath, then to let it out in the water, making bubbles flow around my cheeks. I swim across the pool. She lifts me to the birdbath, where I squat and laugh. She leaves me squatting there, a grinning frog, and takes my picture with our family's box Kodak.

I look triumphant in the photo. I have conquered. I have been praised and adored.

In the background are signs of a house under construction. It will be home for me most of my first five years, one of a pair of brick houses, mirror images of one another, to be built on either side of a drive that divides to go around the central fishpond, then on back to a large barn-like garage—houses designed by my father and his brother Glen, who bought the land together. Mother and Daddy were to move out of his parents' house to begin their family in this new home.

I have never since seen roof edges like the ones on those houses. The shingles, probably asphalt, were curled under in fat semicircles as though around large horizontal poles. Each house would soon have a radio aerial—a tall pole with a metal globe at the top. Tulsa and Oklahoma City were forests of such globes in those days, just as there are forests of television aerials today. Uncle Glen and Aunt Agnes at first lived in the house on the left, but they soon moved into a house-trailer they could take with them to Glen's jobs in the oil fields. Then my father's parents and sisters moved in.

✦   ✦   ✦

During my childhood my mother was a very pretty dark-haired woman, a day shy of twenty when I was born. She had finished high school in Tulsa at sixteen, started work as a secretary, and in 1926 married my father, who was two years older. Like many other children all over the world, I was raised by children. Dad had left high school without graduating to join *his* father as an oil royalty broker. Both the Stewarts, my mother's family, and the Jeromes had come to Oklahoma from Missouri in the era of the "runs" (1893–1901), when land expropriated from the Indians was offered free to settlers from the States who raced to stake out claims. The Indians—against the wishes of many of them—were given compensating individual land grants when the communal tribal land was broken up.

John Stewart, my mother's father (my Stewart grandparents both died in 1925), worked on a farm near Haskell. The Jeromes settled near Yale, Oklahoma. Bampaw, as I called Frank Jerome, my other grandfather, had accompanied his family when they left Hannibal, Missouri, to "make the run" in 1899. With no more than five years of schooling, before he was twenty, he entered the oil business, first as a driller, then as a lease buyer for Tom Slick. About 1913 he moved to Tulsa and became a friend and business associate of Col. C. B. Lynch, eventually forming the Keno Oil Company (so called, he said, because it was a gamble). He was reputedly a millionaire when, in 1921 (my father being sixteen at the time) Frank, for reasons of health, moved his family to Neosho, Missouri. Undoubtedly that fortune was made by exploiting the Indians, who had been given land grants when moved off their tribal lands and who did not understand the law well enough to protect their mineral interests.

The earliest photo I remember of my father is in the Ozark Mountains near Neosho. Dad, in his teens, is standing somberly on a ledge on a cliff face wearing jodhpurs and high-laced boots. I thought he looked heroic in that photo, like Jungle Jim. Aunt Marie (one of the few still alive of my older relatives) says they were very happy in Missouri, but the business, left under the control of one of Frank's brothers, fell apart. They returned to Tulsa in 1924, and, for cash to live on, they had to sell their expensive piano, many of the paintings, and much of the fine leather-bound library Frank had collected in his prosperous days. A few of the books were still in the family during my childhood. Books. Precious artifacts in glass-faced shelves, the most elegant furniture in a shabby living room. My memories are of relative poverty, but not of hardship, through the Dust Bowl and Depression years.

✦　✦　✦

My parents' bed. I am lying still on top of the covers on a hot afternoon. Now the bed tilts—a slow heaving upward of the side toward the window like a drawbridge opening. I clutch the covers to stay on it. I scream with fright, yelling out the open window, across the wide divided driveways, toward Aunt Agnes's house, where Mother has gone to visit.

Mother is soon at my side as I cling to the tilted bed. Cool cloth on my face. Her round cool cheek on my forehead, her soft long curls tenting us. She assures me that the bed is not tilted. It is my fever. She holds me to her breast, kissing my hot forehead.

✦　✦　✦

I have been allowed to go outdoors and now am sitting immobile on the grass in my shorts, barefooted, my legs crossed at the ankles, beside the large flowering spirea bushes called bridal veil that line the front porch's brick railing. For no reason that I know of, I gently leave my body and float upward. I rise about fifteen feet in the air and slowly somersault. The me in the air still has crossed ankles, and below, as I turn upside down and over, I see the physical me still sitting calmly on the lawn. I see the vacant field across the street. I see the brown asphalt-shingled roofs of the twin houses. I feel soft spring air under me and around me. And as peacefully as I lifted out of myself I settle back into my body.

I am not frightened, but mystified. I stand up and go inside, the screen door slapping shut behind me. Mother, wearing a flowered print dress, her hair now fashionably bobbed, is ironing in the living room, listening to dance music on the radio. I tell her matter-of-factly that I floated in the air, but that I could still see myself down on the ground. She smiles down at me and goes on ironing. She tells me it is the fever. She doesn't want me to go back into the yard today. She says I will get better soon.

4

When I mentioned these experiences to her in her later years she could not remember my tilting bed, my somersault in the air. But they are vivid memories. I see these events from the outside: things happening to a little wooden boy. Happening *to* him. He is strangely passive and passionless, surrendering himself to the ministrations and instructions of adults, accepting circumstances with tacit wonder. At the same time he is quietly figuring out how to survive in the context in which he finds himself. I seem to have observed a great deal, but to have recorded it objectively, passionlessly. My memories seem safely packaged, insulated from fear and pain.

✦   ✦   ✦

I wandered freely between Mammaw and Bampaw's house and ours. There was a little box of a store at the corner where I was sometimes sent to buy bread (a nickel a loaf) and butter (a nickel a stick), and sometimes bought penny candy from a vast display of orangey things and red things and yellow things, and, my favorite, long black ropes of licorice. I was deliciously free out there in my own world, an outlaw world—beyond the rule of the tall tribe of adults.

✦   ✦   ✦

1931. I am four. An alligator is following my mother in the water. Uncle Charley, who is rowing our boat, hasn't seen it. I tell him, as though I weren't sure whether this was a normal event for Florida or not, that there is an alligator swimming out there, and I point. He yells at Gwen, my mother. She takes a half-dozen swift strokes in her smooth crawl and pulls herself up the side of the boat. I watch the water slide down her tan thighs.

Uncle Charlie's house was on a lake near Orlando. Whenever I hear mention of Orlando I think of that quiet boat ride in the still, glass-clear water under the beards of Spanish moss hanging from surrounding oaks.

We visited two of Bampaw's brothers in Florida that summer. Uncle Henry was living with an artist, a woman who wore a blotchy smock and painted pictures of palm trees and hibiscus blossoms on a canvas on a large tripod. We slept on a wide screened porch. I remember sleeping with Bonita, who was twelve, my youngest aunt. After dark she told me that she was too hot to wear her nightgown. I remember the warm squash of her developing breasts against my bare back when she snuggled. She was hot all right, but it felt good. Intimacy, comfort, and sensuality are tangled in my memories from my earliest years.

On that same trip I saw the ocean for the first time—at Daytona Beach. I remember someone holding my hand and trying to persuade me to enter the water. Perhaps that was Tubby, the middle of that set of aunts. She would have been fourteen-and-a-half that summer and not tubby at all, a well-developed freckle-faced redhead, but maybe she had been fat when she was younger. Her real name was Lucille. A wave crashed around my shins, and I screamed. I was too frightened to go into the water, so they let me play in the sand on the beach. Mother held a conch shell to my ear so I could hear the ocean inside it. Why did it roar like that? Did it roar when it was lying on the sand and nobody was listening?

✦ ✦ ✦

The Jerome sisters were all teenagers during my early years. Marie was always the one of my father's sisters who held the family together. I remember her as very thin, rather sharp featured, her straight blonde hair snitched back. She had a high nasal voice, was exceedingly emotional and quick to tears, but nonetheless responsible, reliable, sharp of mind. At an early age she started working for Hinderlighter Tool Co. as a secretary, and she held that job throughout most of my childhood, the only one of the sisters to become a working girl. In her middle twenties she married Ray, a quiet bookkeeper, atypically diffident as Southwestern men went. Marie's marriage remains, fifty years later, solid and happy.

Tubby was softer of face, freckled, plain, with a tendency to melancholy. She died at an early age of complications when giving birth to her second child. Bonita was the pretty one with her tumble of auburn hair, bounding with vitality and imagination and full of fun. Young enough to seem an older sister to me, she married an oilman, became an alcoholic, then became addicted to pills, and died young.

✦   ✦   ✦

Across the street from our twin houses the vast vacant field was a Never-Never Land in my earliest days. Sometimes a carnival was set up in that field, and in the evenings we could hear the music from the merry-go-round and see the turning colored lights of the ferris wheel from our front porch. Mother, Daddy, and Mammaw (his mother) would take me there in the evening after dinner. I remember riding the little cars that go round and round in a circle. Daddy, a slim, clean-cut man in his late twenties, was exuberant about introducing me to new experiences. He took me on his lap as he sat on a horse that went up and down on the merry-go-round.

But the biggest and most exciting ride was the ferris wheel. The excitement started before our ride began. Mother said we were spending too much money, so she stayed behind, but Daddy bought a ten-cent ticket for himself and a nickel one for me, and we stood in line in the dusty field watching the great wheel of light spinning, reaching way up into the night sky above our heads. A truck engine roared loudly turning a wide wheel, the size of a wagon wheel, with a wide belt that turned a wheel that made the ferris wheel turn. The operator was a young man in dungarees who managed a long brake lever, standing so near the spinning ferris wheel that the descending seats, with their string of light bulbs, grazed his hair. He pretended not to notice and never looked back.

When he finally pulled back on his brake and brought the wheel to rest with one swinging seat over the landing platform, he stepped up quickly and swung up the wooden bar that lay across the passengers' laps, then reached for a lady's elbow to help her step off onto the platform. When a seat was empty, he ushered in two or three of those waiting in line, then snapped down the bar when they were seated. At last our turn came, and Daddy led me up the steps to the platform, picked me up with hands under my arms and swung me onto the seat. It was like Mammaw's porch swing except for the bar across our waists. The seat swung a little as we went up, and I could see Mother below waving and getting smaller and smaller. Then we were moving backwards and over the top and then forward coming down with the warm air making a breeze on our cheeks and the little people on the ground getting bigger. I felt secure, exhilarated, astonished, way up there in the dark. I had not often been outdoors in the nighttime. From the top we could see a dome of light in the hazy distance. Daddy said that's downtown.

✦　　✦　　✦

One fall day I saw smoke from the far side of the empty field and walked to it, a long way, so far that, looking back across the waving tall Johnson grass, I could not see our house, but I heard strange music from a clump of trees—an accordion and a violin— and I wanted to see where it was coming from. Beyond the fringe of trees was a flat, open glade in which hobbled horses grazed around three bright red and orange wagons. They were wagons to live in, with little peaked roofs and smokepipes and calico curtains in the windows.

Gypsies had set up a camp. I knew they were gypsies because I had seen pictures of gypsies in a book. The gypsies wore kerchiefs on their heads, just like in the book. One man stood by a crack-ling fire playing a violin, while another, seated on a keg, played an accordion, slapping his boot on the ground in time with the mu-sic. Funny-looking yellow cigarettes dangled from the corners of their mouths. A pot of something was cooking on the campfire. Grimy babies were toddling nude around the fire. A little boy and girl, older than I, she in a long flowery skirt with a sash, he in what looked like canvas pants, were scuffling in the dust under one of the wagons, but the grown-ups ignored them. They all looked merry. A gypsy woman dipped soup from the pot into a bowl and offered it to me, smiling crookedly, urging me to come closer. I said, "No, thank you, ma'am." I felt brave having let my-self be lured to the edge, but it was time to back away.

I walked home through the high grass thinking that was fun. That was a wonder. That was something to tell Mother about.

✦ ✦ ✦

Mother made a lemon meringue pie and left it cooling on the tiled kitchen counter. Sun streamed into the tiny kitchen. This was before appliances. No toaster, no mixer. A gas stove on tall curved metal legs, four burners, an oven with a thermometer on the front. A wooden icebox that used huge cakes of ice for cool-ing. You chipped off chunks with an ice pick to cool a glass of water or lemonade. Mother washed clothes in the sink with a scrub board. When there were a lot of clothes she used the bath-tub in the winter, a galvanized tub on a box in the backyard in warm weather, and hung the clothes on lines in the backyard.

I knew I shouldn't, but I dipped a finger into the meringue and tasted its light lemon flavor, its airy, sugary texture, the delicate gumminess of brown crust. Later, Mother saw the evidence—a scooped-out spot on the pie. "What did you do, Juddy?" she asked. I was silent, thinking.

"Unless you tell me what you did, I will lock you in the pantry," she said.

I did not tell her.

She locked me in the kitchen pantry for a long time. I sat in the dark that smelled like dirt because of the stored potatoes. Mixed with potato smell were the smell of onions in their bin and the rich aroma of apples. Carrots had the sharp smell of their green tops. On shelves above me in the dark were, I knew, canisters for flour, sugar, and coffee, rows of canned vegetables, boxes of dry food, including the cylindrical box with the happy face of the long-haired Quaker man on the oats, the slim box of Cream-of-Wheat, the chocolate-smelling jar of Ovaltine.

I sat on the floor trying to think how to tell her what I had done, but language failed me. At last she opened the door and asked, "Are you ready to tell me?" I blinked up at the looming form silhouetted in sudden sun.

"Do you call it *wrinkles?*" I asked. I couldn't think of the right word. Mother broke into tears, hugging me to her and telling me she was sorry. I would never thereafter forget the word *meringue,* though I was surely in college before I saw it in writing or knew how it was spelled.

I don't remember being frightened, don't remember crying about it, don't remember even wanting to get out of the closet. I was not learning that the world is mean and painful but that it was arbitrary. There was nothing much one could do about it. The important thing was not to panic, not to let your feelings make you miserable.

Mother didn't believe in spanking. I don't think she believed in punishment beyond denial of favors. I remember her locking me in a closet one other time, when I was about seven. I had talked too much in school and been given a paddling. The teacher was worried about what Mother might think, apparently, so she called home and talked to her about it. When I got home Mother wanted to know what happened in school. I could think of nothing special. I had forgotten the paddling, which hadn't hurt, and kids were getting paddled all the time. Mother locked me in the closet until I was ready to tell her what had happened. I remember sitting there in the dark among the hanging coats wondering what on earth she wanted me to say, just as I tried to remember the word *meringue.* When she finally let me out, and explained what my punishment was all about, I told her quite sincerely that I had forgotten all about *that.* No more closetings.

I guessed Mother was doing what mothers are supposed to do, that the teacher was doing her job by paddling me, and that *my* job was to keep from getting hurt.

✦　✦　✦

Great-grandfather Bartholomew was in the yard sitting on a straight-back chair, his hands resting on a cane, a flat black hat on his head, its brim shadowing his eyes. His long thinning triangle of white beard almost touched the ground.

Aunt Marie had taken me to Glencoe to meet him and Great-aunt Nina, his daughter and Mammaw's sister. I was impressed by this visit back into another century. The farmhouse where he and Nina lived had an outhouse; they used kerosene lamps inside, and the water came from a well, its pump over the kitchen sink. I was told that Great-grandfather Bartholomew blazed the Indian Trail, the last stages of the Trail of Tears over which the Five Civilized Tribes traveled when they were relocated from the Southeast to Oklahoma. It is now a highway across northern Oklahoma. I was impressed that Mammaw, who seemed aged to me but was only in her early fifties, had, as a girl, come to Oklahoma from Missouri in a covered wagon. They told me that in those days she could throw tin cans into the air and hit them with a rifle, like Annie Oakley.

I was living on the frontier. None of the civilization I grew up in had been there when my young parents were born—the prosperous, gaudy oil cities, the lights, the highways and speeding cars, the telephones, the radio, the planes passing in the air. It is jolting to reflect that thirty-seven years before 1927, when I was born, Tulsa was a capital of the Creek Nation, and Oklahoma City was nothing but a railroad station. Oklahoma was not a state, but Indian Territory.

✦　✦　✦

I started kindergarten when I was four. Mother had started first grade in the country school near Haskell when she was four because her sister Peggy, who was seven, was not to walk the couple of miles to school alone. Apparently that made Mother a great believer in getting kids through school early.

Anyway, I flunked kindergarten and had to go a second semester. I remember the exact moment when I flunked. I was taken into a room apart and tested orally. "How many fingers do you have on each hand?" the lady asked me. "Five," I answered. That was wrong, she explained. "You have four fingers and one thumb on each hand." I overheard the conversation she had with mother about the test. She said something about "immature," a new word to me, but it stuck in my mind. I thought the test was unfair. Might as well say we have three fingers on each hand, and one thumb and one pinky. Pinkies and thumbs were just names for special fingers. They were trying to trick me. They just didn't want me to graduate from kindergarten.

But what did I care? The other kids were all bigger than I was, anyway, and they weren't much fun to play with. I was a loner—living in a world bubbling with colors of imagination. It hadn't much to do with what adults thought. It hadn't much to do with other children. It hadn't much to do with bleak and boring Tulsa, which was fiercely cold in winter, blistering in summer, a dreary commercial city on the far horizon of our little middle-class neighborhood. Inside me, I knew, was *fun!*

✦   ✦   ✦

Bonita went through magazines and clipped coupons and sent for free things. She also played paper dolls with me. We sat on her bed in the room she shared with Tubby. In summer we sat on the front porch steps, and Tubby sat on the swing and teased us about playing with paper dolls.

We cut out the dolls from the Sunday newspaper, and their dresses, with little flaps on them that you have to cut around carefully, and put different dresses on the dolls that were wearing only underwear. Better yet were books of paper dolls you bought, for they were thin cardboard, and you could punch out their clothes. We had several shoeboxes of paper dolls. When they were dressed up we made them talk to one another, mostly about what they thought they would like to wear next.

Bonita also showed me how to make flowers grow on a piece of coal by pouring vinegar on it and sprinkling it with soda. My aunts were fabulous creatures who drew me into their secret and intimate lives as they did their dolls.

The snow was over my head. I walked where it had been shoveled. Bonita pulled me on a sled, and we lay on the sled—with me on her back—to slide down hills. She taught me to make angels by lying in the snow and waving my arms and legs. It was quiet and cold down there in the snow, looking up past the ice walls to the blue sky, snow packed against my ears.

✦   ✦   ✦

I see myself sitting on the rug in Mammaw's house watching the sunbeams. They are really dust, I have been told, but I do not understand why they float and slowly rotate in the still air. On this day I am alone with Mammaw. She is vacuuming. There is a radio shaped like a Tudor arch, pointed at the top, on the endtable beside the wine-colored couch. The man on the radio says, "Hoover is defeated" just as Mammaw switches off the Hoover. I watch in wonder as the taut bag subsides. How did the man on the radio know?

That was just days before my little brother was born November 7, 1932. John Stewart Jerome was called Stewky as a baby, Stew as he grew older. Why Mother named him for her father, John Stewart, is a puzzle. She didn't think much of her father. In an autobiographical sketch she wrote for one of my daughters in 1984 she said:

> Papa, he actually didn't make much impression on me. He and his brother were merchants in Missouri before Peggy and I were born. Why they moved to Oklahoma I never knew, but he was out of place. . . . Anyway, after the family moved to Oklahoma Papa farmed (dirt farmed). Mama had ambition for Peg and me to get an education, so she moved us to town. I don't remember Papa doing much of anything—he drank some—came back, but was never in charge again. He was kind and sweet and funny.

Where did Mother dig up *my* name? From the funny papers. Judson was the name of a chauffeur working for Jiggs and Maggie, a popular cartoon strip in the newspapers.

✦   ✦   ✦

13

At Mammaw's there was a knock at the screened door in the kitchen. I went to the door. A man in old clothing asked for the lady of the house. He wore tattered overalls and shirt and high-top shoes like the gardener on the cover of my copy of James Whitcomb Riley's *The Raggedy Man*. When Mammaw came he offered to do chores for a meal. She gave him a bucket of water, rags, and some newspapers and asked him to wash the windows. I went from window to window watching the man with a bristly chin reach for the windows, soap them down, squirt them with the garden hose, then rub them dry with crumpled paper. At the same time Mammaw washed them from the inside.

Hoboes, bindle stiffs, were common in those days, and Mammaw must have had one of their secret signs in her yard indicating that this house was good for a meal, as she always found something for them to do "for their dignity," she explained, and always gave them a steaming plate of food.

✦　✦　✦

Leslie and Thelma Robinet were visiting us on the Fourth of July. Daddy and Leslie had been drinking all afternoon. They had given me a little iron cannon that shot a red rubber ball when a firecracker went off in the hole at the rear. But I was afraid of lighting firecrackers, so the men took over the job of playing with it. After each shot I ran to find the ball in a neighbor's yard. Once Leslie shoved the ball tight into the mouth of the cannon, stuck another firecracker into the hole at the back, and lit it. This time the cannon exploded, flying in pieces, and Leslie yelled in pain. A piece of iron had hit his eye. I watched Daddy lead him down the drive to our little green Buick coupe, his arm around Leslie's shoulders. They drove off to the hospital, Mother and Thelma in the rumble seat. It was just my toy these grown men were playing with. I didn't like the loud bang when I was close to it. I didn't like to light firecrackers, just sparklers. And look at what happened. Big drunk men and toys are dangerous together. I preferred playing with toys by myself, especially under the bushes around the front porch.

The incident was quickly swept under the rug. You are supposed to accept such happenings, I was learning. You react only in practical ways and do not discuss it.

That night we sat on the porch and watched the men shoot rockets and fire pinwheels on the trees. Leslie had a bandage covering his eye, but no one mentioned the accident. They persuaded me to light a fountain, and I did, and ran away in horror as it spewed its colored sparks behind me on the lawn. I swung sparklers through the air, and, when they were about used up, threw them like rockets into the air making long silver arcs in the black night. After the fireworks Sammy Chalmers and I ran around the yard catching fireflies. We put them in a bottle that pulsed with their light. We were taught to punch holes in the lid so they could breathe. I remember watching the fireflies closely, trying to see them breathing.

✦ ✦ ✦

Sammy was there that evening, so that means that the field across the street where the carnival used to come was by then full of houses, because that's where Sammy lived. His father owned the Chalmers Electric Co., and though I didn't know what that was, I had the idea that Mr. Chalmers was very rich and very important. But the Chalmers didn't have a fancy house. It was just one of many brick row houses, each with a front yard and backyard, all barren of gardens and trees because they were so new. It was more fun on our side of the street where there were trees to climb and alleys full of strange dogs, cats, and fascinating trash piles.

Sammy and I were chums whenever our family lived in Tulsa, but the next few years were to see us moving to Oklahoma City and back several times.

✦ ✦ ✦

I was standing with Mother, her sister Aunt Orpha, Daddy, Leslie, and Thelma in a slaughterhouse in Omaha. A long line of cows passed us, led by a goat. When it reached the men at the end, they let the goat step aside, but they put the first cow, then

15

the next, and the next on a wheel that carried them way up in the air dripping blood. The whole wheel, two stories high like an indoor ferris wheel, was full of dripping cows. The goat was called a Judas goat. Judas, the adults explained, was the man who kissed Jesus to show the soldiers which one he was among the disciples. That Judas was a villain, but this Judas was a special goat that wouldn't get killed because it carried out the will of men by leading the innocent—dozens, hundreds of beasts—to slaughter.

✦　✦　✦

I am selling *Liberty* magazines. I have a little canvas bag to carry them in, and I go house to house around the block. The magazines cost a nickel each. If I sell enough of them, I will win a bicycle as a prize. I don't sell enough. I go for blocks knocking on doors of the houses of strangers, but not many of them want to buy *Liberty* magazine to help me earn a bicycle.

When a friend my age heard about this, she exclaimed, "Oh, did *you* sell *Liberty* magazines, too?" When *she* was five, she got up early one morning in Queens and took her brother's magazine bag and, on her own, spent a day trying to help him earn his bicycle. She sold two. Was every five-year-old in America going door-to-door with canvas bags of magazines in 1932? Was this the New Deal? Was this our reaction to 13.7 million unemployed? Was this society's response to *Tobacco Road, Young Lonigan, Death in the Afternoon, Brave New World*—all published that year? Shirley Temple first appeared on film. Hart Crane leaped to his death from an ocean liner in the Caribbean. Johnny Weissmuller swung through the trees as Tarzan. And we sold *Liberty*.

✦　✦　✦

Mammaw and Bampaw lived in a little house down the block and around the corner. It had a real barn where we kept my horse, Brownie, given me the Christmas I was five. I came into our boxy little living room that Christmas morning to find a decorated tree that had not been there the night before. It stood in a corner, the lighted angel on its crown touching the ceiling, a spangle of many-colored lights reflected by mirror-bright ornamental globes, the tree lathed in tinsel and red paper rope. Its base was piled with presents. But most astoundingly, there was a horse, a real horse, sticking his head into the room through an open French window beside the tree.

The horse was, my father told me, *mine*. It was an outrageous gift, characteristic of my father's erratic whimsy, his bursts of ill-considered generosity, his extravagant demands on life. I shrank from his dazzling enthusiasms. I was in awe of the new horse, but uneasy about it. I did not let on—beyond the show of excitement and the thank-yous that were expected of me.

I never did learn to manage that horse. It just wandered the streets with me, and I was content to let it mosey along and graze at will. One day Brownie and I wandered a few miles from home. A man came out from a filling station, took the bridle in his hand, and asked me what I was doing, riding down a busy thoroughfare. When he found out my name and where I lived on Indianapolis Street, he called Mother to come get me. The man helped me down from the saddle, tied the horse to a gas pump (you really had to pump with a handle in those days), and gave me a Dr. Pepper. I waited in the shade while Mother walked the distance to find the station. She thanked the man, took my hand, and we walked home, leading Brownie. Shortly after that the horse was sold. I was never afraid of Brownie, but I had no regrets when he was sold.

My brief experience with Brownie accustomed me to dealing comfortably with large animals, especially horses. I have been a rider, as I have been a swimmer, as long as I can remember.

✦   ✦   ✦

Where the Christmas tree stood that morning was regularly an overstuffed easy chair. I sometimes found coins down behind its seat cushion. I could keep them. I could buy candy or an ice cream cone with them at the corner store.

The coins slipped out of Daddy's pocket when he sat there, but

Mother, at least once, used those crevices for a hiding place. I found that out when I was curled in that chair, Daddy was standing by the door yelling at Mother, and she was standing near me, in the archway to the dining room, yelling at him. He couldn't find the car keys, and Mother said he was too drunk to be driving anyway. He came toward her looking angry and grabbed her wrist. I cringed. Mother was crying, her face knotted and red. She reached past me deep into the crevice beside the pillow of the chair and her hand came up with the car keys. She threw them across the room, shouting, "Go *kill* yourself, if that's what you want!" The keys crashed into the screen door, bounced back, and slid across the polished wood floor to the rug. Daddy let go of Mother and staggered over to pick them up, then slammed out the door.

Mother sank to the chair arm, sobbing, her hands over her face. We could hear the car starting outside. From the chair I could see the green coupe back into the street, then take off, tires screeching.

I figured Mother wouldn't hide things in the chair again because Daddy would know where to look.

2

How Bad Is Fun

At what age does one begin to *think?* The toddler careens like a pool ball diverted by this collision and that, sinking into a pocket of oblivion each night. Such glancing blows begin to establish character, but at some point we become interactive with experience. We piece it together, interpret it, and try to read the signals, to predict. Learn and unlearn; learn and relearn. The screen of one's mind, like the computer screen now before my face, is again and again wiped clean, its contents often, perhaps most often, not being retained. Yet from time to time some instinct makes us punch the STORE button. And those moments, chosen on some principle we can never fully understand, shape experiences that are to come.

For the most part, when we are children, decisions are made in headquarters, and we implement them as mindlessly as troops ordered here and there. I must have gotten used to that early, to arbitrary shifts, to new environments, new casts of characters, new strains on family coherency. For example, I don't know how many times we moved back and forth from Tulsa to Oklahoma City or why. Dad's business, that was why. I went to fifteen different elementary schools in those two cities and in Houston. Except for the bungalow in Tulsa paired with the one where Glen and Agnes, then Mammaw and Bampaw lived, our homes were always rented houses. Dad did not believe in owning property, he said. Own nothing but a car. That strange economic theory had something to do with writing off business expenses, I believe, but, deliberately or not, it served the purpose of keeping all assets liquid. When my father died there was nothing in the bank—and, of course, no property but a car. There was never, ever, solid ground underfoot. You learned to keep your balance stepping from floating log to floating log.

✦　　✦　　✦

On Mother's birthday Daddy brings her a jigsaw puzzle of heavy wooden pieces made from a photograph of her face. I put it together on the floor, and the soft, beautiful face of my mother surrounded by her bobbed dark hair smiles up at me. I take her apart and put her back together.

On another birthday Dad gave her a recording he made of himself singing "I Love You Truly" to her in his fine tenor voice. Someone at the recording studio was softly playing a piano in the background. We played this record over and over on our wind-up Victrola with a picture of a sad dog on it.

My earliest memories of them are of a storybook couple. Aunt Marie, eighty as I write, remembers them that way, too. Ralph, my father, was her favorite brother (and closest to her in age). "And Gwen!" Marie gushes. "Gwen was just *perfect*." Pretty, bright, loving. Both of my parents liked the outdoors, and there were camping and fishing trips often, even when I was a baby. Dad was doing well, in a middling way, in the oil business. At least he was supporting the family in those Depression years. And he had an artistic flair, too. I remember him bending over the dining room table tying flies from little bits of fur and feathers and horsehair and cork that he bound with black thread to a fishhook, winding the thread in a perfect, tight coil to make an insect body, lacquering, trimming with tiny scissors, tiny pliers. When he finished, he sewed the fly to a little printed card:

Ralph's
Hand Tied Flies
308 Ritz Building
Phone 47778

I have one here on my desk. He took these cards to sporting-good stores around Tulsa where they were sold. Miniatures requiring a steady hand. Perfectionism. Close observation. Grace and beauty.

✦   ✦   ✦

I wake up hearing noises and voices in the house in the middle of the night. Dad and Leslie have come in from a fishing trip. Their tackle boxes, rods and reels are in the living room. Dad is sitting at the dining room table where Leslie and Mother are trying to get him to eat some Cream-of-Wheat. They say he needs some food in his stomach. Dad curses them, his words slurring. Leslie shoves a spoonful of cereal into his mouth when he opens it to talk, and Dad spits it out like a baby, making a raspberry sound with his lips. "Go to bed, Juddy," Mother says plaintively.

✦   ✦   ✦

Daddy walked hand-in-hand with me down a busy street. He was taking me to get a haircut. Mother had always cut my hair before, but now Daddy thought I should go to a barber. He knew the barber by his first name. The barber lifted me to the chair and pumped the handle, making the chair rise. He put a cloth around my neck that covered my lap and legs. I cried. "This won't hurt," the barber kept saying. "Just look at that diamond pattern on the foot rest." I screamed. Finally my father gave up and let me down. He led me back into the street, and I was still sobbing. Daddy pulled me along by the hand rapidly down the sidewalk. "Don't be such a baby," he said angrily. His love for me verged on the sentimental, yet his anger could flare unexpectedly and make me feel unworthy to inhabit his world.

I wasn't really frightened that time. I knew very well that it wouldn't hurt to have my hair cut. I was being bullheaded, asserting myself, trying to manage events—and the tactic backfired. I was not being manly. By such incidents I learned not to try to manage events. And not to show my feelings.

That fit with the two most important lessons I learned in my Southwestern upbringing: "Just don't whine," and "Don't be squeamish." Both boys and girls were taught those lessons. They were derived from frontier experience, where one had to be tough and get on with the job, whatever it might be.

❖　　❖　　❖

Abhorrent Acts

If you
will be more proper than real, that is your
death. I think life will do anything for a living.

John Ciardi

The driver flinched at the whirring wings of a grasshopper
and nearly ran his truck into a ditch
when Tom, hitchhiking home from prison, squashed
the insect between his forefinger and thumb.
In Oklahoma we learned not to be
squeamish. The bankers die; the Joads live on.

My mother grabbed her fryers by the neck
and whirled them till their bodies flew off flapping.
One does what must be done. My father, fishing,
snagged the barb of a fly in the lobe of his ear.
I paddled the canoe to a mountain shack. He asked
the woman there to cut it out with a razor.

I watched her do it. Finding, once, a litter
of aborted kittens—a wet mass of five—
I shoveled them onto the compost, but still they breathed.
No recourse but a boot heel. What would *you* do?

They mewed like needles. Necessity has no
scruples, nor does it wait its timely turn.

Who will be spared nursing the smelly ill,
trafficking bare in vomit, pus, and blood?
Whose diapers were changed will someday change
     more diapers.
If you eat meat should you then cringe at slaughter,
the carcass draining, the hacksaws cutting bone?
Transcend repugnance if you would survive.

I hope that those who have known flamed flesh are less
inclined to firebomb, those who hunt in need
will not do so in sport, and those who furrow
their loves in sweat will not hunger for sleaze.
Submersion whets a taste for air, not liquid.
But I most fear the fastidious who might

faint when my wound needs cauterizing, look
away, not say. Oh Rose o'Sharon, when
flood swirls outside the boxcar, your baby dead,
and I, a starving stranger in life's eclipse,
am cradled in your arms, have nerve to lower
your chaste and swollen breast to whiskered lips!

◆　　◆　　◆

   That's the tougher side of a Southwestern heritage. But the
tender side is its hypocrisy. You learn early to deal with a double
standard in regard to values relating, especially, to sex:

Oklahoma City, 1933: the Whore

The halls were long with many doors, each one
a home: some family or grownup person
we didn't know and hardly ever saw.
I wandered on my own down all those halls

(they let me work the elevator),
and down to the lobby where mailboxes were,

and strangers stopped and turned their combinations
and pulled out papers. I watched. It must have been

there that I met her. Why we got acquainted
I don't remember. She was blonde, a woman
like those in Mother's magazines, the kind
who sat before a mirror on her dresser

brushing her long hair in a bathrobe you
could see through. Teenage aunts in Tulsa took me
to see King Kong. It made me sick for days.
But in the movie was a woman who

was wearing clothes that floated. A giant monkey
had lifted her up high, and I saw body
beneath her filmy gown. I never learned
the name of the lady in the lobby. I

just called her "Miss." I don't remember why,
but she took me to her apartment on
the third floor. (Ours was on the fifth.) She had
a rug made from the skin of a polar bear,

its head still on it. I would lie for hours
staring at brown glass eyes, that waxy snarl,
until I scared myself. I liked to scare
myself, just like my aunts went to King Kong.

While I lay there on the carpet staring at
the face of the bear, the woman went into
her bedroom and came back in floating clothes.
She sat above me in an easy chair

and crossed her legs—long legs, silk hose—and we
would talk—day after day. At "home" there was
my baby brother, radio and wind-
up record player, Mother—all confusion.

I hated most when Daddy came home. He
would swing me to the ceiling, crush me to

his mustached face, his whiskey breath, and then
set me back down and argue with my mother.

I looked at books. I may have even read them.
Our dinner times were worst, the three of us
around the little table off the kitchen.
Dad wanted me to eat. I didn't want

to eat, especially when he told me
the chicken was dead. He laughed. He said we ate
nothing but dead things—dead asparagus,
dead meat, and dead potatoes. He said milk

came from the titties of a cow and squeezed
Mother's to show how farmers got it. I
picked at my food and asked to be excused.
But afternoons I waited in the lobby

for Miss to come, her high heels clicking, her
red smile above me like a breaking cloud,
and hand in hand we'd ride up to her floor.
The lock would clunk. Inside was perfumed silence.

And I'd be on my bare knees on the bear,
running my fingers through its silky fur,
hugging that mean old head before I lay
down on the carpet, there to sink into

the mystery of horror, staring deep
into the dark red throat past gleaming teeth,
marveling at black leather lips against
the snowy muzzle hair, and then at last,

when I was brave and hypnotized, I would
allow myself to look into his eyes.
I shiver still remembering their depth.
I knew the bear was dead, his eyes were glass,

and yet if I looked long and long I saw
down there in deep recesses of the light

25

a kind of glow of life. I knew that bear
was in there somewhere, not in his cuddly fur,

not in his phony mouth, but in his eyes
(marbles, Miss said, that's all they are) I knew
a ghost of bear was waiting—not to leap
out growling to hurt me, but to draw me in.

I teetered on the edge in thrilling fear.
Then we would talk. Sometimes I leaned against
her legs to snuggle, feeling the flesh of calf
rubbing the silk. Her voice was soft and tender.

And I remember what we talked about:
the Trinity. I knew a little about
God. Mammaw said you couldn't see Him, but
He always watched us, always was around.

And that seemed spooky enough, but Miss said He
was three—not people, not things—three beings.
She said that He (not really a He) was three-
in-one. Like oil? I asked. Maybe a little like

three kinds of oil all mixed together, except
each one stayed one. I knew that Jesus loved
me, but the song did not explain that Jesus
was really part of God. His love was God's

love all around me like the air, except
it didn't blow and move like air. It was
like light inside the light, even at night.
Like silence, silence behind the noise. Yes, God

is silence. Think of times when there is lots
of noise (I thought of my brother crying, parents
yelling), and you want only silence. Silence is there.
You couldn't stand it if you didn't know

that somewhere there is silence, there is God.
Which part? I asked. All three—and each distinct.
God and Jesus and what? I asked. The Spirit,
the Holy Ghost. I thought of what I'd seen

down in the bear's eyes. What's the Holy Ghost?
It is what holds the other two together—
Father and Son and Holy Ghost make God.
Father? I thought of flying toward the ceiling.

Is God a Father? In a way He is.
Jesus, you know, was here on earth as a man.
A man must have a father and a mother.
Mary, his mother, could not have a baby

unless a father planted seed in her.
His seed? We say his seed to understand it,
but really it's not a seed at all. His spirit
goes into hers just like seed into soil.

A baby is made of him and her together,
father and mother and child—God, Holy Ghost,
and Jesus. Think of carrots. A little seed
takes something from the dirt and water and sun

and turns all big and hard and orange in
the dark under the ground. . . . And so we talked
hour upon hour, day upon day, that spring,
and all the world seemed beautiful and spooky.

One dinner, though, this all came to an end.
They asked me where I'd been. In 307
I said, and Mother gasped. My daddy laughed
and winked his wicked wink. They wanted to know

what I was doing in 307 with
that woman? I told them about the rug.
Well, not about it. I just said she had
a rug made from a polar bear. That didn't

seem reason enough for me to go there twice.
(I didn't tell them I had been there often.)
What did you do? they asked. What did she do?
She changed her clothes while I played with the bear.

What kind of clothes? I told about her clothes,
the bathrobe you could see through—and her hose,

about the fluffy slippers she called mules.
And did she touch you? Sometimes she held my hand.

You mustn't go there ever again, they said.
I stared at the hand that she had touched while Daddy,
his voice the one he used for nasty things,
was joking with Mother, "Well, at least

he didn't have to pay her." Pay for what?
Your "Miss," Mother explained, is the kind of woman
that men pay money to when they go visit.
They sleep with her, as I sleep with your daddy,

and pay her for that. Well, I would, too, I thought.
I'd give her my piggy bank to stay there always.
My parents said she was bad. Up to that point
I never understood the lure of badness.

That ended my theology. I never
did get it straight about the Holy Ghost.
I stayed out of the lobby, like a good boy,
and then, that summer, we moved back to Tulsa.

and I started school. My aunts read me "The Raven,"
and "Little Orphant Annie"—spooky poems.
Then evenings they would sit out on the porch swing
with boys. I heard them giggle, saw hands slide

up thighs. Mammaw said they were bad, and I
began to put it all together then—
the floating clothes, the monkey-squeeze, and Miss—
how bad was fun and spooky was the spirit.

✦   ✦   ✦

In the summer of 1933 we visited Houston. Mother's middle sister, Aunt Orpha, lived there with her husband, Uncle Louie, and
Aunt Orpha's daughter, Maxine (Uncle Louie was her stepfather).
Daddy stayed in Oklahoma. Mother took Stew and me down
by train—quite an undertaking, it now seems to me. I wonder

whether she was already considering alternatives, should her marriage break up. I was impressed by the big two-story house my aunt and uncle owned, their black uniformed maid. No one on the Jerome side of the family had a maid.

My cousin Maxine was nearly six feet tall and very beautiful with black curls down past her shoulders. She had been to college in Ohio for a year, the first person on either side of the family to go to college (and the last until I did so), but she didn't go back after her first year. Rather, she worked as a fashion model, both in California and Houston. Orpha and Louie had large framed photos of her on the walls.

Much of what I remember about that visit concerns Galveston island, fifty miles away. We left baby Stew with the maid—and we were gone at least overnight. I remember the drive over the causeway that links the island to the mainland. All along the causeway were bushes with pink flowers—oleanders. They were poisonous to eat, I was warned, but I didn't see why people would eat bushes, anyway. At the end of the causeway was a drawbridge that was open to let a sailboat pass when we arrived. In Galveston we stayed in a big cabin on the beach. The cabin seemed to me to be full of tall people in bathing suits drinking beer.

In the evening we went to an amusement park where there was what was reputed to be the fastest merry-go-round in the world. I rode with Maxine on a wooden horse that surged up and down as it went round and round so fast that the faces of the people watching blurred. I wanted to wave when I passed my family, but I was afraid to take a hand off the silver pole. A metal arm stuck out in one spot, projecting a brass ring. Whoever caught it won a free ride, but I was too short and too afraid to reach for it.

Further along the long curved scooped-out sea wall was a fun house, a roller coaster, and many other rides that whirled you round. I went on many of these, even the roller coaster, with the adults, and I was only a little bit afraid. But when we started back to the cabin I was dizzy. Maxine lifted me and carried me against her breast, my face against her neck under her long hair.

At the beach a tall young man named Jimmy started talking to Maxine. I watched them playing with a beach ball. Maxine was running with it; Jimmy tackled her and they rolled together on the sand. Then she tackled Jimmy, and they did that some more. He chased her out into the water and tackled her again. They disappeared under the water and stayed down a long time. They were having fun. They were being bad.

Jimmy, then, came back to the cabin with us, and we went from there on a crabbing excursion. On the end of a pier in a salt lagoon the adults tied a piece of meat on a heavy cord and dropped it into the water. Whenever a crab grabbed the meat with its claws, they pulled it up and dropped it into a gunny sack where the crabs all clattered together. You have to kill them before dropping them in the pot to cook. You drive a nail through a certain spot on the back of each one's shell. This requires picking the crab up, holding it with fingers on each side of its shell while it waves its claws around trying to grab you. Don't be squeamish.

Jimmy, a sailor, arranged for us to visit his docked ship. He carried me up and down ladders and into metal rooms with round windows. We saw the engine room with its large turning wheels and giant levers pumping in a constant roar. Jimmy explained that they had to keep the engines working even though the ship was at anchor to make the electricity work. On deck were giant guns and canvas-covered lifeboats. Jimmy had the tailor on the ship take my measurements and cut down a sailor suit for me—a white blouse with a long square collar, trousers with thirteen buttons in a square pattern, a white canvas hat, and, best of all, a black silk scarf three feet square. I soon outgrew the suit and hat, but that scarf was to figure in my imaginative life for years to come.

Also at the dock was a passenger liner that took people on day cruises—out fifty miles and back. Outside the three-mile limit people could drink (illegal on shore because of Prohibition) and gamble. I played the slot machines, and sometimes coins came slithering into a glass-covered box. I asked Uncle Louie for a dollar to play the horses. These were wooden horses about a foot high that a man raced by throwing dice and moving each the appropriate number of spaces with a long shuffleboard wand. I brought six dollars back to Uncle Louie.

✦   ✦   ✦

Mother, Maxine, and I were lying on a beach blanket. I reached over and slid my hand over Mother's bare thigh. Maxine cocked her head in a funny way, questioning. "I let him practice on me," Mother said. I knew what she meant, and knew that she was kidding, but I took my hand away, embarrassed.

✦   ✦   ✦

These were tricky waters. Adults were immense creatures who seemed most intent on doing the things that children weren't allowed to do. Yet one was supposed to grow up and become one of them. You had to learn how secretly to observe and say nothing, and each year to stretch into a somewhat larger skin by imperceptible increments, acquired as carrots grow, inch by silent inch in the dark soil.

Mostly you are bundled up and carried about and snuggled and amused and fed, until you wiggle restlessly and begin to assert that worm of will that gnaws within. You *do* something, and the creatures around you do things in response. (Or don't—and that, in itself, is a telling response.) As I approached school age I am sure I was increasingly doing things to get responses—some responses I liked, and some I did not like. Sorting that out was not always simple. Take the case of poetry.

I knew many poems by heart. I don't remember my parents ever reading to me, but my teenage aunts read to me a lot, and I begged for the same poems to be read again and again, especially scary ones. When I walked out of the house, all dressed up, to go to the first day of first grade, some big kids stopped me. They had heard I could recite poems and demanded that I recite something on the spot. I refused. I can see myself standing there in short pants on the sidewalk in front of our house, surrounded by three or four towering boys and girls.

"If you don't recite something," one guy said, "I'll squash these tomatoes in your hair." He had taken some cherry tomatoes out of his lunchpail. I refused again, and he squashed, and I had to change shirts before going to school.

Kids are not like aunts. They would not think me cute and adorable if I recited "Little Boy Blue" there on the sidewalk for them. They would make fun of me. And if I didn't present the self they could make fun of, they would persecute me. I needed to strengthen my façade. I couldn't really *be* like them, but maybe I could learn to *act* like them. I had to learn the role of a real boy. Eugene Field, the same poet who wrote of the death of "Little Boy Blue," a child too delicate to live in this world, also provided a formula for becoming the kind of boy I saw around me in the neighborhood. I knew Field's "Jest 'fore Christmas" by heart. Here's the first stanza:

> Father calls me William, Sister calls me Will,
> Mother calls me Willie, but the fellers call me Bill!
> Mighty glad I ain't a girl—ruther be a boy,
> Without them sashes, curls, and things that's worn by
>   Fauntleroy!
> Love to chawnk green apples an' go swimmin' in the lake—
> Hate to take the castor-ile they give for belly-ache!
> 'Most all the time, the whole year round, there ain't no flies
>   on me,
> But jest 'fore Christmas I'm as good as I kin be!

This Bill knew how to pretend he was good so he could get presents. I could identify with that. The trick would be to let the "fellers" know that the beaming child who recited poems was not the real me. I was, like them, an outlaw at heart.

Both my father and grandfather wrote poems. Among the books that remained from Bampaw's more prosperous days was a soft leather-covered pamphlet, *Grains of Sand,* poems to his mother, to his puppy, his brothers, and others reflecting upon life, religion (of which he was rather scornful), and his times. Here is the last of three verses of "Memories of Tulsa":

Give me the painted up false and untrue,
    Tulsa, Oh Tulsa, my heart calls for you,
You with your bright lights and places of sin,
    Rags of gay colors and chickens stuck in,
Gray haired old Ladies with skirts knee high,
    Gaited up faster than an eagle can fly,
Faster and faster in all that you do,
    Tulsa, Oh Tulsa, I'm thinking of you.

My father wrote humorous, dialect poems (reminiscent of James Whitcomb Riley) that were published in the Tulsa and Oklahoma City newspapers. Poetry meant being cuddled on the couch while your aunts scared you. Poetry meant writing you could learn by heart—and get up in front of people and recite. It could also, I was discovering, get you into trouble. But I knew early that writing poetry is something a man could do.

3

Games Children Play

The world began to enlarge when I started school, but school seems to have had very little to do with its enlargement. I am always amazed when I meet people who can name every one of their teachers. I remember none, remember almost nothing of schoolrooms, schoolyards, schoolbooks. I think I sensed quickly that teachers were my natural enemies. Requirements were to be gotten round. School days were to be endured. Life was outside, on the street, in yards, mostly backyards, and alleys. Life was play. Life was mostly after school—and during summers—when we ran in the world without disguise.

✦   ✦   ✦

Sammy showed up one day with a bike. He had already learned how to ride it and wanted to take me for a ride. He showed me how to sit on the bar from the seat to the handlebars. Sammy was a good bit bigger than I was, though we were about the same age. All my friends were bigger than I was. That is why adults kept trying to make me eat more.

When I was seated on the bar Sammy climbed onto the seat

and shoved us off. He went very fast, it seemed to me, about fifty feet, when my heels swung into the spokes. The bike flipped end-over-end and I was thrown against the curb. He hadn't warned me to hold my feet out where they wouldn't hit the wheel.

I screamed at the pain in my right arm, but what I remember is my surprise, how I lay there against the curb, and how Aunt Marie, who was twenty-four by then, carried me to the house and laid me on the divan. Someone drove me to the hospital, probably a neighbor, as Dad would have had our car with him, and I don't remember there being one in Mammaw's household. I remember the warmth of the drying cast and its heaviness.

I am lying on the couch at Mammaw's, my cast in my lap, my legs (in short pants) stretched before me across the pillows. I am thinking about bicycles. You have to learn to ride those things. They are scarier than horses, but, after all, I am six. I should learn. Sammy and I could have fun if I had a bike and could ride it.

✦ ✦ ✦

It was decided that I should have tap-dancing lessons. Each week Mother took me downtown to Brown Duncan Department Store where I joined other little boys and girls in patent leather shoes with metal taps on their toes. After some weeks of this we put on a show for the parents on the stage at the store where they held fashion shows. I was a mustached pirate, a bandanna on my head, a sash around my waist, deliberately tattered short pants, and my shiny tap shoes. Shuffle, ball, *chain.* Shuffle, ball, *chain.* That ended my tap dancing. I didn't care much for going to lessons or for dancing, but it was exciting to put on a show.

✦ ✦ ✦

On a hot summer day we kids would pull up pieces of gummy tar from the street and chew it. It had a sharp, oily taste. The iceman stopped his wagon and put a feed bag over his horse's nose. We would beg him for ice, so he would chip off a small chunk for each of us. Then he reached into the dark depths of his wagon with his ice tongs and slid a big cake to the edge. He hauled it up with his tongs, swung it onto the heavy leather apron he wore on his shoulder, carried it to our kitchen, and put it into the icebox. Then he did the same for Mammaw.

Other horse-drawn carts passed often with fruits and vegetables, the peddlers singing out what they had fresh, women coming from houses drying hands on their aprons to buy. A rag-and-bottle man came by to collect things people wanted to throw away. The newsboy passed and tossed a paper to the porch. Sammy, Linda, Mary Fae, and I patrolled the neighborhood to observe these events.

Bampaw made us rubber guns from wood and clothespins. You stretched a band of cut-up inner-tube from the nose of the pistol back to the clothespin and snapped it in place, then fired it by releasing the clothespin. We were cowboys and Indians. We were good guys and bad guys. We were soldiers. Snap. Ouch. You're dead. You twisted on your feet and slumped to the ground gargling horribly then jumped up and cried out, "New man!"

Now tag. You're it. You have to hold the place you are tagged till you get the next guy. Statues. You spin a guy around, holding hands, then let go, and he or she has to freeze and stay in that position till everyone has had a turn. Crack the whip. Hide-and-seek. Punch-the-icebox. Especially when you slap out the screen door after the evening meal for and into the bushes and up the trees, the world seems an endless game. I wondered whether I would ever have knees and elbows that weren't skinned up (and often purpled with gentian violet for impetigo)—especially after I got roller skates.

If you twist the swing round and round as tight as you can twist it and then let go and make yourself spin as it unwinds until at the end it begins winding up the other way and then unwinds again, you get dizzy. You can get dizzy just spinning on your bare feet on the grass, faster and faster, and if you pull your arms into your side you will go faster still and finally can't stand up, and you fall down on the grass and lie there and the world keeps spinning, and if you close your eyes it spins faster, or if you are really dizzy and you try to walk you will stagger, and everyone will laugh at you, and with fever, and in dreams you can spin that way. Dizzy is fun. Maybe that's why people get drunk.

✦ ✦ ✦

King of the Mountain

At last to stand on the grassy knoll above
the sprawling mass, the shouts and sweat, the crush,
to have bubbled to the top of the sticky broth,

to endure that midst of elbows, scrambling drove,
to tug at garments, fling anonymous flesh,
then momentarily float there, free as froth—

unnecessary, light, luxurious,
salty and cool in the tongues of evening air,
while parents in their dim surrounding houses
digest their dinners, placid, unaware

that a featherweight, by accident or stealth,
defying muscle and justice, now from limbo,
is silhouetted, catching a casual breath,
surveying his dominion, arms akimbo.

✦ ✦ ✦

The Oklahoma City oil pool, which had opened in 1928, was booming, and Dad spent most weekdays in the capital, but Mother, Stew, and I stayed in Tulsa. When Dad came home on Fridays he always brought surprises for me and Stew—a Parcheesi game, an ocarina, a kite. One Friday I heard the green Buick coupe pull in the drive, left my Tinkertoy construction, and ran out to meet him. He swung me up to him and kissed me, whiskey on his breath—as usual. "What did you bring me?" I asked. Suddenly he was angry and abruptly put me down and bawled me out. He shook me by the shoulders until Mother intervened by calling out "Ralph!" from the porch. I looked back at her. She was standing with her arms outstretched as though for a hug. Dad lifted his lean chin and turned on her yelling, "The only reason he's glad to see

38

me is that he thinks I have a gift for him!" It sounded as though he thought that were *her* fault. He jerked open the lid of the rumble seat, pulled out his suitcase, and stormed into the house. Mother was angry at him for drinking so much. They argued all evening.

Not until the next morning did he take out of his suitcase what he had brought for me—a cowboy hat, gun, and holster, and, best of all, a waxed rope lariat. He said he would teach me to lasso things and to do tricks like Will Rogers. By evening I knew how to hold the loop to throw it, could lasso a post, and could make the loop spin in a flat plane at my feet.

✦ ✦ ✦

You never knew. One moment he would be a terror, the next a loving, generous, even prodigal father—or person. On one of his excursions near Oklahoma City to buy mineral rights from farmers Dad met a poor little black boy he liked and took him into town to buy toys for him. When Mother found out, she was angry. "You didn't have to buy out the whole damned toy store for that pickaninny," she said.

Pickaninny. I remembered the word but never used it. I didn't know any black children, but I figured I wouldn't call them that if I did.

✦ ✦ ✦

We have set up Bethlehem. The manger is a little room constructed in the living room. It is walled with sofa pillows and has a sheet over it for a roof. I am wrapped in a sheet as the Virgin Mary. Stew, who can walk now, but is still pretty much of a baby, is Jesus. He is naked in a big cardboard box lined with still another sheet. I want Mother to be the Wise Men, but, when she finds out what we are playing, she says that is not a good game. You're not supposed to play stories from the Bible.

✦ ✦ ✦

Dad had his arm around me in the seat of a much bigger roller coaster than the one I rode in Galveston. I was screaming. "Stop

39

this thing!" I yelled. "It goes too damn fast!" Dad laughed and, when we finally got out, told Mother what I said. It was funny to say *damn*. I remembered how everyone laughed when I said at the dinner table that I wouldn't eat okra because it was no damn good. They made me swallow a bite anyway, just to try it. I vomited on the tablecloth. So they stopped making me eat okra. *Damn* was an important word.

◆　　◆　　◆

That roller coaster was at an amusement park on the outskirts of Oklahoma City, a thrilling place. I especially liked the fun house where you walked through a long turning metal barrel taller than a man and on through a passage where one side of the floor moved forward while the other moved backward and into a scary room where everything seemed to be at a tilt though the floor was really flat and places where wind went up under your shorts and mirrors made you look wavy and you could ride on little braided rugs down a long metal slide with swells and curves in it and, at last, into a little room where you sat on a bench made of wooden rollers, and the bench suddenly flattened out and you flew down a long chute all of rollers through a canvas flap and into the sunlight outside.

Along the highway in that part of town were many diversions, but the one where we spent most time was a golf range. Dad wanted to learn to play golf because important businessmen played golf. Golf was a game for rich people. Aunt Audrey, my mother's oldest sister, belonged to the country club in Muskogee and played golf in tournaments all over the country.

Dad bought himself a canvas golf bag with leather trim and a set of woods and irons and signed up for lessons with a pro. The pro taught him how to hold the club with his left thumb held by the fingers of his right hand and to swing with a smooth follow-through, keeping his eye on the ball. When Dad hit a slice he cursed. Golf was no fun for him. But I listened to the instructions and practiced with a short driver they had for children. I had a small bucket full of balls and smacked them one after the other out over the floodlit fields. It was fun. I wasn't yet in business.

They had short putters for children, too, and alongside Dad on the putting range I learned how to swing evenly and just hard enough to make the ball roll over the fine bent grass to the lip of the cup and drop in with a sound like *clock.* I don't know whether Dad ever played an actual game of golf or not.

✦　✦　✦

Oklahoma remained a dry state after Prohibition, so liquor came from a black bootlegger who delivered flat bottles in brown paper bags to the house. But in Missouri liquor was sold legally, and they had slot machines. Once we stayed at a Missouri tourist court (what we would now call a motel) that had a long low lodge made out of logs with a porch running around all four sides. While Dad and Mother lingered over drinks after dinner, I asked for a nickel to play the slot machine, was given one, and, when I pulled the lever, three bars rolled up: a jackpot! Coins tumbled out of the machine for a long time, spilling into a great big pile on the floor. I took a small tablecloth from a nearby table and piled the nickels into it, then carried the bundle around the corner of the porch to where Mother and Dad were sitting. They shrieked with surprise, then Dad carried the bundle of coins to the slot machine area. He played until he lost all the nickels—long after I was asleep in the cot they brought in for me. I woke to hear Mother's angry whispers in their bed across the room. "You should have given at least some of them to Juddy," she said. It never occurred to me that the money might be regarded as mine.

I hoped he had fun.

✦　✦　✦

I am lying on a hard white table covered with paper in an office in a hospital. The doctor is going to take out my tonsils. He thinks I might eat and grow more if I don't have tonsils. "You won't feel a thing," he tells me. He lowers a cone with gauze in it over my face while a nurse holds my shoulders down. I see Mother standing at the foot of the table. She is holding my legs. The cone seems to be full of stinging gnats spinning around. The smell is sharp, like the smell of ammonia.

When I woke I was in a hospital bed. They asked me whether I wanted some ice cream. I could have all the ice cream I wanted, they said. I didn't want any. The adults were disappointed. I think they expected my appetite to improve instantly.

✦ ✦ ✦

Daddy was drunk at the dinner table. He and Mother were arguing, so I asked to be excused and went outside. In a few minutes I came crying back into the house.

"There's a butterfly out there!" I wailed.

Daddy's exasperation at my mother now turned on me—or maybe on both of us.

"Is he afraid of *butterflies?*" he exclaimed in his angry, slurred voice.

Maybe his implication was that she wasn't bringing me up right, that somehow my fear was her fault; but all I heard was teasing, meanness. My father thought I was a sissy. I was momentarily hurt. But the hurt quickly gave way to new information.

"Butterflies can't hurt you," Mother said soothingly. "They don't bite."

Within moments I again escaped the unpleasant scene indoors and was in the yard playing with butterflies, armed with fresh knowledge. I chased them, trying to catch them, but I couldn't.

Survival tactics. Get out. Avoid. Suppress. But extract what joy you can: butterflies can be fun. Each instant of that experience is still vivid for me. I can see the swing-up table in the breakfast nook where we were eating, the debris of fried chicken, mashed potatoes, spinach. My milk glass still full nearly to the brim. (I was anaemic, so, on doctor's orders, I was given goat's milk, which we fetched each week in a milk can from a farm in the country.) My parents were flinging angry words at one another, and I had no interest in food. I knew that when sparks were flying they might come my way. What an immense liberation to learn that I could safely play with butterflies!

✦   ✦   ✦

I was fascinated early by aircraft. When I was quite young Dad took me to an airfield where a barnstormer sold rides for a few dollars each. I remember his climbing into the front cockpit, and the pilot helping me up onto the wing. Wearing short pants, I threw my bare leg over the edge and climbed into Dad's lap. The pilot provided us with helmets with goggles just like his with a strap to go under your chin. A fellow up front grabbed the propeller and called out, "Contact?" The pilot, in the cockpit behind us, called back, "Contact!" and the man hauled down hard on the propeller. There was a loud roar and much wind in our faces, and we rolled faster and faster down the runway then lifted off up above the fields and circled over highways with little bugs of cars on them and houses and tiny farmers throwing corn to little specks of chickens. Daddy held me tight around the waist as I leaned over to look and shout back to him what I saw. A train passed below, looking like a toy.

At home I had a book on flying and studied the diagrams of wings with air flowing over them until I understood about lift. The propeller pulls the plane forward like a screw in the air, and that makes air flow fast over the wing. The wing's foil (its curving top-side) makes a kind of hole in the air by forcing it up, away from the wing, and pressure from below pushes the plane upward and makes it fly, as though it were sucked up by a vacuum. Diagrams showed how the controls work. When you push the stick to the left, the rudder swings left, the left aileron dips and the right aileron rises, making the plane bank. The plane could not turn without banking. Dad explained how highways were banked at the turns—and why. Otherwise centrifugal force might make the cars roll over. *Centrifugal force!*

I used a piece of broom handle for a stick and drew a dashboard of dials and taught myself to fly, step-by-step. I had my own pilot's helmet with goggles and chin strap for this game. I would sit on the couch with my dashboard and fly to Tulsa. "Contact?" I would shout, and Stew would answer, "Contact!" and pull down on an imaginary propeller, make motor noises, then he would climb into the forward cockpit. That was for passengers. In my imagination I took Bonita for a ride. Then I took Marie. (Aunt Tubby had married and moved to Kansas.) My aunts had to take turns sitting in the front cockpit. I wished we would move back to Tulsa and that we lived near Bonita and Aunt Marie and Mammaw.

One day Mother took me out to the airport to see Amelia Earhart. An autogiro was parked out on the runway, and a woman with short red hair waved at the crowd, then took off, the propeller on top of the plane sucking it straight up into the air. Much later, when I was ten, I started a science fiction novel based on the notion that Amelia Earhart and Patrick Noonan, whose plane was lost over the Pacific that year (1937), had found their way to an uninhabited Pacific isle where explorers in a distant future found a race of weird people, deformed because of inbreeding, speaking a degenerate form of English. (I think I abandoned my novel when I got to wondering how, after Adam and Eve, we came out so normal in physique and able to speak such good English.)

During a state fair an airliner took passengers for thirty-minute flights over the city. Planes like this, my parents told me, flew from one city to another, much faster than trains could go. We had to fasten seat belts. Mother held Stew on her lap. We roared up into the night sky and saw the twinkling and streaming lights like scattered jewels below us.

✦ ✦ ✦

I had a Tommy gun. When you cranked it, it made a noise like bullets and sparks flew out of its barrel. At night, especially, it was fun to hide behind the pillars and the railing on the front porch and shoot at people walking past. I was Pretty Boy Floyd or Machine Gun Kelly or Baby-Face Nelson. Or I would be Clyde Barrow if Stew would be Bonnie Nelson. This was a lot more fun than being a cowboy or a soldier.

Outlaws were heroes—in the tradition of Jesse James and Billy the Kid. There was glee and admiration around the house whenever the headlines said another bank had been robbed. The law was the enemy. Cheating the government out of taxes was a favorite indoor sport (especially after income tax quadrupled—from 1 percent to 4 percent—in 1932). In the early thirties, especially in my family, it was assumed that the government was bad. The New Deal. The government interfered with business. "A Chinaman," my father would say, "lands on the docks in San Francisco, and they want to know his name. He draws a picture of a drowning man. They don't get it. He draws a picture of burnt toast. They still don't get it. The Chinaman scrawls the letters 'FDR'—and they all know immediately what his name is: In Too Long." That was the kind of humor common in our household.

◆　　◆　　◆

I also had a collection of marbles, and several of them, Dad said, were real aggies. That meant they were made out of semiprecious stone: agate. Some were marble-sized shiny steel ball bearings. But I was not very good at marbles; my hands were too small. I was better at property. You play property by drawing a square in the dirt with a pocketknife and taking turns throwing the knife to stick in it. When your knife sticks, you make a line extending the straight cut of the blade to the edge of the square. Then you get to pick the larger area as your property. The other guy then has to throw his knife so it sticks in your property. If his knife sticks, he makes a line to the edge of the square or to the line you have already drawn, so his property gets bigger. The idea is to capture all his property. But as it gets smaller and smaller it is harder to hit, and your property gets easier and easier for him to hit. I could beat other fellows at property, I thought, because I was shorter and therefore closer to the ground.

Other boys and girls and I played cars a lot, especially under the shrubs where the earth was soft and moist and shady, and sometimes we entered the dungeon of the crawl space beneath the floor:

45

A Sense of Sin

Under the house was inside of the world—
that tangle of pipe and wire where Nature worked
her juices of supply, evacuation—

the strands and arteries, the acrid groin.
Such play was serious: We wormed under,
earthbound. Above, the toilet flushed like thunder.

No dirt was dirtier: Nails, splinters, bottles
threatened, and spiders laced the ways of hell.
Ah, we were seekers. Sissies stayed behind,

never to breathe dark air, the chill within.
A sense of sin required us so to suffer
what sin itself impelled us to discover.

We built highways and garages and tunnels and made burring
noises as we pushed around the little metal cars and trucks. My
favorites were the racers made of heavy metal. You could push
these on the sidewalk and let go, and they rolled fast until they hit
the grass and crashed.

If no one was around to play with, you could play cars all by
yourself. No one wins at cars. Stew wasn't very good at cars. He
kept getting mad and crying and fighting with me. He couldn't see
very well when he was crying, and my arms were longer than his,
so I could put a hand on his chest and hold him off while his arms
swung round and round like windmills trying to hit me. I remember thinking (and may even have discussed this with Mother) that
eventually his arms would get longer, and we would have to find a
different way of settling our differences, because I sure didn't want
to fight.

✦   ✦   ✦

Dad showed me how to fly kites in the vacant lot. Sometimes
we bought kites made of tissue paper, but when they got torn, we
made new ones out of newspaper or heavy brown wrapping paper

46

using the old sticks. Stew held the kite up over his head, and I ran backwards watching it bob to left and right as it pulled the kite with its long tail of scraps of cloth into the air. Box kites were even better because they didn't need tails. Usually kites would come down over telephone lines or trees and you had to break the string to get them back. When they landed in trees they got torn.

In the winter I made model airplanes out of kits that cost a dime and had strips and blocks of balsa wood and rolls of tissue paper. To finish them you have to buy lacquer and paint them so the paper shrinks and gets tight and hard over the plane like the tight painted canvas on real planes. Then you can wind up their propellers that are hooked to a rubber band inside. If you put these on a smooth straight surface like the street they will taxi and take off by themselves, but usually I flew them in a vacant lot where I launched them by holding them high and letting go. Most of the time they crashed, and I had to repair them. It was more fun making them than flying them.

Model ships were more complicated, with all their ribs and planks and rigging, and they were no fun to play with after you built them. They were just to look at.

✦   ✦   ✦

The schoolground was a place of terror for me. I hated recess and tried to sneak out books so I could find shade and read while the others played games. A boy tripped me when I was walking by the high chain fence to go home after school. "You son-of-a-bitch!" I said. He grabbed me and demanded I take it back. "Do you know what 'son-of-a-bitch' means?" He asked. I didn't. "It means you called my mother a female dog. Take it back, or I'll beat you up." I didn't, so he did. We wrestled in the dirt and he pinned me down and made me say *Uncle*. When you said that they had to let you up.

✦   ✦   ✦

I imagined that all adults were against children. All over town there were billboards showing a policeman carrying a dead little girl away from an auto accident. Across the top it said, "Don't Kill a Child," but the "Don't" looked as though it had been painted by hand in red, while the rest of the words are printed in black. I told myself there was this secret organization of children. The adults put up these signs saying "Kill a Child." Then, at night, members of the secret organization went around painting "Don't" on them. I knew this was not true; I just made it up. But it could be, I thought.

The difference between the real and imaginary seemed to me a boundary as easily crossed as Alice's looking-glass. The two realms could easily coexist, and it was arbitrary whether one inhabited the one or the other. Children of alcoholics, I read, have unusually ready access to the right side of their brains as they are impelled to live so much of their lives in the world of their imaginations. Lucky us! Thanks, Dad, for a major tool of my trade.

✦   ✦   ✦

Dad refused to give Mother any spending money. In desperate need of a pair of shoes, she borrowed five dollars from me, my total savings. Dad came in from the office soused. He saw the new shoes and demanded that Mother tell him where she got the money. She confessed. He turned on me and told me never to lend my mother money again. He paid me Mother's debt, then dragged me by the scruff of the neck into the bathroom, pulling his belt out of his trousers as he walked. I did not understand why I was being punished. He had never told me not to lend Mother money before. I didn't see why it was bad for me to do it. Inside the bathroom, Dad shut the door. I was cowering by the tub. The little gas stove with clay inserts to hold the heat was attached to an outlet with a rubber tube. It hummed and glowed angrily.

Dad gave me one of his broad, mischievous winks and leaned to whisper with his bourbon breath that spanking would hurt him worse than it would hurt me. So we were going to trick Mother. He would slap his leg with his belt, and I was to cry out in pretended pain. I shook my head. I wouldn't do it. It wasn't fair—to Mother or to me. He insisted, grabbed me roughly, shook me.

48

"Now, you *holler*," he whispered fiercely. He whacked the belt against his leg, shook me. "*Holler!*" I let out a weak whimper. "*Louder!*" I yelped a little. "*Louder!*" He whacked his leg again, and I yelled.

We went back to the living room, where Mother had collapsed weeping in an easy chair, her dark hair wild around her lovely face. I snuggled into her lap. I put my palm up to cover my lips and whispered into her ear, "He didn't hit me."

"Don't *tell* her, goddammit!" yelled Dad.

I guess I spoiled Dad's fun. Fun ricocheted. One person's fun was another person's torture. I couldn't figure it out. Both of these people loved me, and I loved them, and yet people kept getting hurt. Even in the warm den of the home you have to be careful. Maybe especially there.

✦   ✦   ✦

Dad had just bought an outrageous number of expensive fire-works and had them in a large brown paper bag on the floor be-tween his knees. Mother was driving down the country road, as Dad was in no condition. He lit a firecracker and threw it out of the window over the top of the car so that it exploded right near Mother's open window. She, of course, screamed, panicked, and almost lost control of the car. "Don't *do* that," she said angrily when she had recovered. "You could get us all killed." Dad thought this was fun. He threw another. "Ralph!" she screamed. "That went off right in my ear. It could make me deaf!"

"Well, stop the damn car!" said Dad. She pulled over to the side of the road. Dad got out, staggered to a full drainage ditch near the road and dumped the entire bag of fireworks into the water. We had no fireworks that Fourth.

Stew and I were in the back seat at the time. I was smirking. Oh, I was shocked, upset by the incipient violence, wary of what might happen next. But my feelings had nothing to do with the loss of the fireworks. Dad bought such a big bag of fireworks be-cause *he* liked fireworks. The things scared me—rockets, pin-wheels, fountains, and worst of all, those that made noise. Spark-

49

lers did just fine, thank you. Then he decided to punish Mother for *his* being so nasty. And he punished her by spoiling the fireworks he bought with his own money. He shot himself in the foot. He was not only dangerous but foolish.

Mother could be just as silly. I remember watching her smashing dishes and glasses in the sink while Dad still sulked on the back porch, swiftly puffing a cigarette, its coal swinging crimson among the circling yellow fireflies. She had caught him necking with another woman at a party in the backyard that evening. But why break dishes? We would just have to buy more. She was always saying we didn't have enough money. She might at least break them over his head, if she wanted to break them. But, then, he would probably beat her up. He might anyway. Parents sure gave a fellow a lot to think about.

✦ ✦ ✦

Dad was driving too fast down a muddy road in the rain heading for a big bridge over a river. Mother was in front, Stew and I in back. Suddenly Dad slammed on the brakes and skidded to a stop inches from the brink of a cliff. Mother screamed. There was no bridge. The river was flooding and had taken it out. Dad told us he knew all along that the bridge was gone. He did this to scare Mother. It was one of his jokes.

Laughing at her fright, he started to back up and found that we were stuck. To get out he had to rock the car back and forth by swiftly going into first, then into reverse. As the car went forward there was danger that it might go over the edge. Mother insisted on our all getting out while Dad maneuvered the car. A cold wind whipped us as we stood on the cliff above the blackly roaring river far below. We stood there cringing at each forward lunge until finally the car broke free and rolled backward. Dad was laughing harshly, contemptuous of Mother's fear. He was superior because he was a man, but Mother, now, insisted on driving.

✦ ✦ ✦

50

Dad had to check court records in various small towns, so we were out on the road for a couple of weeks, staying in a different hotel or tourist court each night. Each day we parked for hours beside a county seat. Usually these had wide lawns and trees around them where Stew and I could run while Mother sat on a bench or in the car and read. This trip ended in horror.

Mother is driving down a narrow, muddy county road, Dad passed out on the seat beside her. Stew and I are in the back seat, Stew asleep. It is dark and rainy out. Suddenly Dad jerks up, gagging, trembling with spasms. "A heart attack!" Mother whispers to me. She stops in the middle of the little back road to tend him. After a few moments his trembling stops and he slumps over, unconscious but alive. When Mother starts the car she finds it is stuck. She tries to rock it as Dad had done by the bridge, but the wheels spin and dig until the underside of the car is resting in the mud. Mother tells me to find a farmer with a tractor or a team to pull us out. I set off down the muddy road in the rainy night, my shoes squishing and nearly pulling off, my clothes drenched, my wet hair slapping my face.

So what does an eight-year-old boy *feel* about such an experience? I can remember. It was an adventure. I had a responsibility. Did I mind the mud and rain? No. It was better being out there than in the claustrophobic interior of the car with my mother's tension and tears, with the mysterious figure of my father, his face a paralyzed grimace. I remember the burly, grizzled farmer standing in his doorway holding up a kerosene lamp to look down at me standing shivering on the porch below his belt. He was impressed by this little city boy appearing in the stormy night. I was brave. And I got to ride a *tractor!* I had never ridden a tractor before. I snuggled against his broad chest, the arms of his rubber raincoat rustling as they enfolded me and reached the wheel. I remember his tall grey rubber boots, the rain in our faces as the tractor lurched and squished down the rutted lane, the beam of its single headlight bobbing on the roadside trees. All this was a lot more fun than getting back into the car.

Dad was dimly conscious, groaning. He had vomited on the seat and Mother's skirt, and the odor of vomit filled the car. She wet a towel in a muddy pool in a rut to clean this up. The farmer maneuvered his tractor around the car to get behind us, slopped through the mud to attach a chain to the rear of the car, then drug us backwards a few hundred yards to a hard road.

✦ ✦ ✦

Nobody in our family ever went to church, but a lady down the block in Oklahoma City thought I should go to Sunday School. I was to walk down to her home and go with her family in their car. I didn't like her little girl, but it wasn't too bad just riding in the car with her. Our class met in a small room in the church basement. The teacher was an artist, and, once, before we arrived, he had drawn a picture on the blackboard to illustrate our lesson. It was the Great Wall of China, stretching way off in the distance. Through a gate in the wall a lot of Chinese people were marching four abreast, right toward us. The line of people extended as far as you could see, the people getting littler and littler. The teacher explained that every fourth person born in the world is Chinese. He said there were too many people in the world, and most of them weren't Christians.

I studied the picture. I saw how he made things look far away by making them smaller and smaller. The people in the back of the line must have been easy to draw because they were just dots. The line of people got narrower and narrower until it was just a line getting thinner and thinner.

I figured I'd try drawing something like that when I got home.

✦ ✦ ✦

I couldn't get to sleep because of my excitement about Christmas. It seemed to be late in the night when I heard Mother come into my room, open my closet door, and take down packages she had stored there. I already knew there was no Santa Claus, that the men in the department stores and those jingling bells for the Salvation Army were all fakes, but never before had I understood

52

the mechanics of how the tree got put up and the packages appeared under it. I am learning secrets, I thought. I will have to tell Stew about this in the morning. Next Christmas we will know where to look.

I stayed in bed, but I could hear my parents whispering and laughing in the living room. I heard the tinkle of ice in glasses. Then, long after, I heard strange sounds coming down the hall: an electric train, the chatter of tiny wheels, the toot of the train's whistle. I knew that Dad and Mother had gotten a train for us, and now they were playing with it. I thought I was surely too excited to sleep—but the next thing I knew it was morning. I hurried down the hall, and there it was—a track circling the tree and packages, and already running around and around the tree was a shiny red oblong locomotive, designed after the new diesels, with its trail of varied cars, one of them carrying a load of logs.

I named the engine "the Dopey Express." This was the Christmas of 1935, and *Snow White and the Seven Dwarfs* did not appear until 1937, so I must have given it that name after we moved to Houston. I would still be playing with that train in my teens in Houston.

✦   ✦   ✦

My parents bought a pure-bred black cocker spaniel with a white blaze under his chin. They told me that he was very expensive but that he was *my* dog—mine and Stew's. I named him Tarbaby. Some weeks later I was playing golf in the yard with one of Dad's putters and a crocheted golf ball intended for indoor practice. Tarbaby grabbed the ball and ran off with it. I chased him around the yard yelling at him, but I couldn't catch him. So I swung the putter at him and just missed his head. The blade of the putter sank deep into the ground. I realized then that I might have killed Tarbaby. He was just having fun.

Another day I told Stew that I was going to teach him Burn 'em Up. That was a game I had heard about in which big boys and men threw a baseball very fast and hard at one another. I had a glove for Stew but no baseball, so I used a wooden croquet ball. I stood

Stew near the house and told him to catch the ball when I threw it from about fifteen feet away. He just stood there and never lifted the enormous glove on his right hand (he is left-handed). The ball hit him squarely between the eyes and flattened him. Mother came running out to see why he was howling. Frightened and helpless, I told her that I only wanted to teach him Burn 'em Up. That was a game. She carried him screaming into the house and put packs of ice cubes on his head. The bump swelled up nearly as big as the croquet ball. I realized I could have killed him, too.

For years afterward I woke up and sat bolt upright in the night with memories of what I nearly did to Tarbaby and to Stew. Memories of these incidents today still make my stomach sink. Tough exterior, tender interior. Live with it.

✦   ✦   ✦

More and more I was aware of colliding egos. Childhood had been a long cuddle until I went to school. It was a world of aunts, mostly of my young Jerome aunts, though all six of my aunts were, as I think back on it now, like the women in Mastroianni's dream in Fellini's film 8½. In that dream he is a grown martinet in bowler and spats, carrying a shiny walking-stick. Old nuns in an orphanage cuddle him, bathe him, swaddle him, tuck him into bed, and sing him lullabies. The yearnings that have fired much of my writing, my political and philosophical concerns, my long excursion into communal living and ventures into group marriage, I recognize with some embarrassment, can in part be explained as the dream of regaining a lost paradise where I grew up as a cute, bright child among women who loved me dearly. Childhood was not paradisiacal for me, but their love and attention were solace for the terror and pain that living in a world of real men entailed.

Aunts taught me the difference between good boys and real men. A good boy is one who does what his aunts and mother teach him to do. He is polite, sensitive, mannered, intellectual, pure, gentle. A boy learned, for instance, to address all women, including his mother, as Ma'am. "Would you like some ice cream?" "Sure!" "Is that what you say?" "Please." "Please, what?" "Please, ma'am." "Here is your ice cream." But whom did these women choose to marry? Real men. A real man is one who, when the family is together, joins his counterparts in the kitchen to stand by the refrigerator, rattles a highball glass, and talks business. Or Republican politics. Some real men—though not, as I remember, those in my family—talked sports, cars, livestock. I thought that something must be wrong with me, because I preferred the company of women, who talked about food and furniture and kids and relatives, who told family stories, who giggled a lot and played cards, who teased and cuddled and joked. Did these jolly, funny, adoring, powerful women secretly want good boys to turn into real men?

I was baffled. Of all the men I encountered as a child, my father was both the most attractive as a model and the most monstrous. He played his part among the male crowd in the kitchen and was likely to be the one to go too far, to drink too much, to be too vulgar, to be more cynical, corrosive, materialistic, and self-seeking than my uncles and their friends and associates. Frequently he would respond to something someone said, especially something my mother said, with a wet raspberry, tongue hanging between his lips, thumb to nose and fingers wagging. The other men were never that coarse. But I was aware, even at an early age, of a sensitive, sentimental, rather artistic man within. I can now imagine his struggle with the overt values of his own father, and of Bampaw's with *his* father. I imagine generations of soft boys being hardened into manhood, learning systematically to suppress whatever might be tender and vulnerable in themselves.

In childhood I protected my own tender and vulnerable self by thinking that my *real* father would never be cruel, gross, lecherous, sarcastic, sneaky, tyrannical. He was more likely than any of the other men I knew to take the time to love a sunset, a dish of ice cream, a song on the radio, a good book, a tussle in a hammock, a ride in a barnstormer's plane. Loving him was an addiction. His utter repulsiveness, the fear and trembling and disgust that he roused in me, seemed to come packaged with the only available example of a man capable of finding joy and affirmation in his life.

4

Alcoholic

Sometimes I hold a cigarette in a way that evokes my father. I grasp it not at the tips of my fingers but back close to my knuckle, letting most of it project, just a bit available to my lips, so that as I draw I can clasp my whole chin with my open palm, caress my jaw as I pull the cigarette away from my mouth. It is my father's face I feel beneath my hand. His cigarette (in his last years, Wings) seemed always to have gotten battered in the pack, so that the white tendril hung wilted and exposed. He smoked like making love, with an amorous suction combined with a sensual, lingering tug of the cheek flesh. I now suspect that the habit came from the drunk's need to test his skin sensations, as one touches himself, particularly around the lips, for that tingling, swollen feeling that tells him how far gone he is. Dad claimed he used cigarettes to give himself time to think. While he took a good long draw of smoke and leisurely exhaled it, he could, he said, generally think up an answer. It was a time out   such as, he said, others take by polishing their glasses.

The thirties were his time of life. He was twenty-five and I was three when they began, and his life was substantially over when they ended, though he lived seven years into the forties. Searching for an early image of him, I see the two of us parked all night in a grassy field a couple of hundred yards from an oil derrick, lights strung up it as on the tower of a ferris wheel. We watched the tall pipes swing as the crew pulled the long lengths of pipe called drill stem to change a bit, then lowered it again, length after length, and finally we would hear the tension-building growl of drilling, water and mud churning into the slush pit, brine and oil in the acrid air. On chilly nights Dad would periodically idle the motor, letting the car heater rasp out its hot breath, and I would doze to the noise of the resplendent rig and, in the car, like a hearth, the soft light of the radio dial, the bubbling melancholy of Bing Crosby: "Come to Me, My Melancholy Baby," "Stormy Weather," "Tea for Two," "The Lady in Red," "Smoke Gets in Your Eyes," "Sonny Boy," "Peg-o-My-Heart," "Mighty Lak a Rose."

We were waiting for the moment the teeth would cut the critical cap of limestone and the well would come in. Usually Dad had no more financial interest in the well than a few acres of royalty on a neighboring lease. He just liked gushers, those wild earthy orgasms, and had infinite patience as he waited in hope of seeing another. I believe I liked to be with him, though all such memory is tinged with sweet terror.

I catch glimpses of him still in old movies—in the gestures, tones, expressions of Jack Oakie and Leslie Howard, of Clark Gable and Jimmy Stewart. I see his business associates, as in bad dreams, like James Cagney, E. G. Robinson, Wallace Beery (who seemed most appropriately named). Fred Astaire seems to me most fully to evoke my young father, though there was little physical resemblance, and Dad had nothing of Astaire's sophistication. Perhaps I associate them only because I remember that *Top Hat* was one of the few films he could sit through. He had a few favorites he would see over and over. Unless the film were one of these, he was likely to stalk up the dark aisle after fifteen minutes and wait for Mother and me (and Stew mostly sleeping in Mother's arms) to see it through. We would find him smoking and pacing in the lobby, usually with liquor on his breath. He was excited to hear that a film had been made of one of his favorite books: *She*, by Sir Rider Haggard (1935), but he was outraged by the liberties taken with the story and stormed out within minutes of the beginning. I enjoyed it and wished he had stayed to see the beautiful woman wrinkle and take on the appearance of her eight hundred years and die right before our very eyes.

"Dancing Cheek to Cheek" was one of those songs that kept recurring to Dad's lips. He was sentimental in Astaire's gay, dry way—and, like Astaire, capable of swift, cutting brittleness. He was a thin man with no hips, long-jawed, nervous, with cynical, watering, hurt eyes, full of heavy, exaggerated winks (you betcha!). Crooning, always crooning—as he shaved, as he drove, as he bent over maps on his high drafting table, or as, foot on the marble sill, elbow on his long knee, he gazed thoughtfully out of his office window down at the traffic of Oklahoma City, drew deeply on his cigarette, then, with a sharp flip, sent the butt sailing out into the summer air, watched it fall to the alley, hawked, cutting off his song, spit, watched the spittle arc down the shaft of grey air, then went back to work, cocking an eye, winking his slow, mocking wink at me when I asked a question. He had style. Fred Astaire with maybe a little of Bob Burns and his bazooka.

But—as I find myself crooning more often these days—that was long ago and far away, and hazy as "Stardust." Back before television. I think of my father learning to laugh with Will Rogers and Marie Dressler. He liked the humor of F. P. Adams, O. O. MacIntyre, Don Marquis. I think of my own values forming to the harder, emptier voices of Fred Allen, Jack Benny, Charlie McCarthy (those long, rich Sunday evenings with the radio). I think of Mark Twain as a giant on the earth. The past seems so much more humane, so much more melancholy and sentimental, like a song of the period, "Deep Purple."

And "Tiger Rag." Drive-in restaurants and miniature golf were innovations in those years, and by the building shaped like a giant Hires root beer mug we sat at the long picnic tables eating watermelon and spitting seeds and drinking root beer from frosted mugs—huge nickel ones for adults and small penny ones for me. Then back into the car in time for Burns and Allen, driving high on a bridge over the dried red mud flats of the Canadian River, which had been reduced to a trickle by the drought, and the no-man's-land of the riverbed was now all a sprawling Hooverville of tin and scrapwood huts inhabited by people who would soon be streaming by our house near the capitol in jalopies piled with mattresses, children, chickens, and pots and pans, heading west along Route 66 toward California in swirls of dust. During dust storms we stayed inside all day with windows tightly closed. Yet dust would gather inside them, an inch deep on the sills. (An *inch* deep? protests my realistic brother. The language was my mother's, who swore we ate a pound of dirt a day, two pounds during dust storms. In the Southwest we tended to round things off on an upward scale.)

From time to time we drove out past the last lights and under the stars, bugs spatting the windshield (Dad said they made lipstick out of those), nerves rubbing like straining hawsers as we swung out and in like a tail behind the tall, red-lit swaying rump of a truck, then whined around it, the two-lane highway now stretching empty and black ahead off toward Tulsa, Dad's cigarette coal sparking on the easy breeze, his sandy tenor rising to compete with the radio's version of "Dinah."

I remember thinking that Mother looked like Claudette Colbert and Dad looked like Ronald Colman—such is the idealization of youth. He was chronically constipated. Perhaps that was from the paregoric—an aroma I still remember, as it filled the bathroom during his benders. Why was he taking paregoric? Was he addicted to *that,* too?

✦ ✦ ✦

I piece those years together as former lovers search backwards for the good times, the bad times, the old feelings, trying to remember what it was they had and where it all went wrong, just when the quality of my relationship with him turned from bitter-sweet to sour. The good times are hardest to remember. Dad loved still rivers at dawn, the mist lifting and the bass hitting in the deep holes under the trees, and as we drifted up in our old green canvas canoe he would whip his long rod back and forth, the line lengthening in somnolent arcs in the sweet, fishy air until he dropped the fly in under the branches, just over a projecting stump, made it skate right and left with little jerks of his wrist fifty feet away! (*Fifty* feet? Well, a long way). Then he would whip it up to sail in long arcs again, the ratchet of the reel drilling like a little cricket in the great humid silence of the Oklahoma woods.

On Mountain Fork

discipline:
> the whispering S of line
above the canoe, the weightless fly thrown through
a gap in the branches, spitting to rest
on the still pool where the bass lay,
> > > > > wrist true
> in the toss and flick of the skipping lure.

love:
> silence and singing reel, the whip
of rod, chill smell of fish in the morning air,
green river easing heavily under, drip
of dew in brown light.
> > > > At the stern I learned
> to steer us—wavering paddle like a fin.

art:
> tyrannous glances, passionate strategy,
the hush of nature, humanity slipping in,
arc of the line, ineffectual gift
of a hand-tied bug, then snag in the gill, the snap
and steady pull.
> > > > His life was squalid, his

temper mean, his affection like a trap.
I paddled on aching knees and took the hook.
My father shaped the heart beneath my skin
with love's precision:
                    the gift of grief, the art
of casting clean, the zeal, the discipline.

Or, driving through a highway cut in the Arbuckle Mountains, Dad would impulsively stop the car to study the twisting formations of old rock and would excitedly explain to me how the angled projections of rock in the field indicated a prehistoric arch. He would show me the parallel structure in the cliff sliced by the highway, and, a few miles down the road, he would find the corresponding rocks projecting back in the other direction, creating for me a vision of that ancient mountain washed away. I would be able to see the prehistoric ocean covering Oklahoma, the life swimming in it, now all skeletons in limestone from the crushing weight, packing down, the bulging up of some hot subterranean force, the cooling peaks, the centuries of weathering that left those tiled tombstones that obstructed the plow. He was reputed to have been the best surface geologist in Oklahoma City—all his knowledge gleaned from reading at night and from roving the land with love.

And he was an expert draftsman. His lettering on lease plats was so perfect it looked like italic print. He would sell photo-reduced copies of these plats for ten dollars each. His printing on the copies was extremely tiny but still readable. A friend would bring one in when a lease ownership changed hands. Could Ralph correct it? Sure. He would erase the old name, touch a drop of India ink to his finely honed pen, then, with a magnifying glass, lean over his drafting table to letter on the eraser-roughened paper, paper avid to suck a blot from his pen. Sometimes he felt his hand was too shaky for the job, so he would go downstairs to the bar for "just one beer," the 3.2 sold in Oklahoma, to steady him. Unfortunately, he was the type of alcoholic who should stay off alcohol altogether. As soon as he drank even a little he was on a course of a bender that would end a week or so later in sick oblivion.

Roving the land looking for money, he thrilled with the romance of the old earth contorting and subsiding. He knew that that subterranean dome, parallel to the surface rock structure, trapped gasses from life decaying in the buried sea, and that if a deal could be made, the dome could be punctured by a long drill stem and rotating diamond teeth, so from the black belly under the red earth of Oklahoma would erupt the slick, stinking stream of rotten life, fountaining up through the derrick, sending the roughnecks diving for shelter, ripping all before it, scattering the boards of the derrick platforms a hundred feet into the air, clouding the sky with a gold gassy sheen and splashing black money, money, money all over the wasted Oklahoma fields.

He never accumulated any of that money, but we lived comfortably enough in what seem to have been a dozen different rented houses. They were always tacky little houses, and our furniture was shabby. I have no idea what our income level was, but in whatever talk of money I heard, there was never enough—though our situation was nothing like the deep poverty of millions in those years. The country was storing its grapes of wrath, but the oil business was booming, a pool discovered right inside Oklahoma City and derricks going up in back yards, even, in 1939, on the Capitol lawn. That year *The Grapes of Wrath* was published.

In a second-rate office building Dad had a suite of several rooms—a rambling, long place with bare wooden floors and a private toilet in which was a cupboard with a bottle and glasses. He was heady with success. The oil business was lubricated by alcohol. Here was Dad, drink in hand, a giant to me, though he was a young man in his late twenties, five-foot-nine. He was drawing geological formations on the white enameled kitchen tabletop, or passing the bottle with a lease owner out in the field, under the thundering rig. When he became too difficult to handle at home, Mother would bundle up Stew and me and strike off for the Kiamichi Mountains in southeastern Oklahoma.

I would wake to black night in the moving car and catch the thrilling scent of pine, hear the rustle of water. We ground around the twisting gravel roads, canoe tied on the roof with ropes to front and back bumpers, Mother driving our sedan, Stew and I in the back seat, Dad passed out up front, his grizzled head on Mother's lap, his bare feet sticking rudely out the window. The Kiamichis are in southeastern Oklahoma on the Arkansas border, and Arkansas was wet. If you've got to have it you might as well avoid bootleg prices.

✦   ✦   ✦

Trips to the Arkansas border brought the Ward family into our lives: Coleman Ward (who wrote a column for a Cherokee newspaper under the pen name of Grey Fox), his wife Little Willie, and their four sons who had been nicknamed for what Coleman regarded as the races of mankind: Injun (the eldest), White Man (who was rarely there: he worked at a refinery in a distant town), Nig, and Hossfly (a carefree joker who, at 22, was still in high school when we met the Wards). The three Ward sons at home were all lean and bronze of skin. White Man, who was there one summer while we were also, was plump and white and clumsy and whiny. Did their names determine their destinies?

Coleman customarily wore a turkey feather twisted into his white hair and dangling along his jaw. Little Willie was a stringy, tall woman with loose, long greying hair and a raucous laugh. Their patch of mountain land along Mountain Fork River was granted them in compensation for seizure of Cherokee land for statehood. The Wards had built a log filling station and a row of log tourist camp houses as a business venture on the dirt road between Bethel and Smithville where two or three cars went past— mostly local traffic—on a summer's day. The filling station was no longer in operation, but it still had its empty pumps by the road. Pumps were pumps in those days. That is, one had to saw the handle up and down to make the gasoline or kerosene flow. They still used the kerosene pump for fuel for their stoves and lamps.

This was the first of many trips when we stayed in the Wards' tourist cabins. I think we were about their only customers except in deer season, and they adopted us as part of the family. A couple of years after our first visit, Injun named his first son in part for me: Judson Tecumseh Ward. They called him Teacup. I remember Teacup in a later year chasing the wild turkeys around the dusty, barren yard that the cabins surrounded. I don't know that he had ever worn shoes. One went to sleep in those cabins listening to the low gobbling and noisy slippage of claws of the wild turkeys perching on the tin roofs.

I followed the horse-drawn plow to dig out the potatoes turned up in its wake. And I followed Coleman everywhere, admiring the sure and silent steps of his tennis shoes through heavy bracken. Indians, I had been told, could steal through the woods without breaking a twig. I watched his feet to verify this knowledge. On fishing expeditions, he used a short rod and plugs, not flies, and fished the little streams high in the hills, not the river. At the end of the day he would have a string of perch for the table. My father, who scoffed at plugs and used a long fly rod, if he was lucky, would have a bass (he threw back the small fish).

Their pigs ran wild—and were practically indistinguishable from the truly wild razorbacks. It was, they explained, too expensive to pen and feed them all year, so they let them run and shot them as they needed them for food. But they did have a kind of corral and some feeding troughs for them a couple of miles into the woods from the cabins, and one of our daily chores was to ride out there on horseback to spill a few dried ears of corn into the troughs—so the hogs would keep coming back to the same spot and thus be easier to hunt.

One memorable day I did this chore alone. I must have been seven or eight, a wisp of a boy pasted to the bare back of a chestnut gelding. About halfway to the corral was a spring where we regularly stopped to water the horses. (It was at that spring that I learned, by vivid example, that you can lead a horse to water, but you can't make him drink.) I remember pounding my bare heels into the ribs of that horse to get him to go that far at a lazy walk. He wouldn't drink, but he didn't want to go on for the next leg. I didn't dare get off him to lead him on down the trail because I knew I couldn't get back on him again except at the hog pen a mile ahead. Eventually I persuaded him to move, reached the pen, dumped some corn in the troughs, climbed the rail fence to mount the horse, and *whoosh,* we were off. Reluctant as the horse was to go out, he was in a great hurry to get back to the barn.

I somehow stayed glued to his back at a full gallop the whole distance home, hooves pounding dust clouds as we careened along the twisting, hilly trail, me pulling fruitlessly on the reins and then dropping them to cling to the horse's neck to keep from falling. When we arrived the horse was white with lather—something I never saw before or since. I remember Little Willie's response when we came pounding into the yard and the horse stopped. Mother was there.

"What you been doing to that horse, Juddy?" she asked in alarm. She ran her hand through the thick white foam. "Why, he's been *lopin'* that horse, Gwen! You shouldn't lope a horse so fast, Juddy!"

That was naughty of me. There was no way I could explain that I had nothing to do with all that galloping whatsoever, that I was lucky to have remained mounted. Her rebuke was somewhat touched with round-eyed wonder, but no one complimented me for not having broken my neck. They didn't send me alone to feed the hogs again for fear I might lope the horse and somehow injure him. Okay, I shouldn't lope horses so hard. I should try harder to rein them in. But I also felt a secret pleasure. The ride was thrilling. It was *fun.*

✦   ✦   ✦

I learned to noodle—that is, reach under rocks and grapple for fish barehanded, which was illegal, as it was considered unfair to the fish, but Injun was the game warden for the county, so friends and family were safe, and he himself participated. I thought noodling was rather unfair to people, as you never knew what you might grab:

Noodling

Where Mountain Fork is wide as an avenue
above the falls I stood all stick-white-legged
in the green stream on slick stones, watching true
noodlers, who wade in shoes, whose hands are ragged
nets in the water reaching under rocky
cavities, catching the quick tense fish
(or sometimes snake or turtle), men soft-talking
above the water, cursing their silent wish.
I bent my own bone back just like the men
and felt my tight hand quake beneath the stream,
an eerie hesitation, grabbed, and then
cold muscle whipped my palm. Now nights I dream
of sinking fingers into unseen gills
in the green deeps of distant burnished hills.

Sometimes a long chain of us would wade in the sloughs (sections
of old river channel that had become long ponds) and stir up the
bottom with sticks, causing the fish to surface for air. We clubbed
them and put them in gunny sacks (another illegal way to fish).
I went on deer hunts (out of season, of course) but never shot
anything.

Deer Hunt

Because the warden is a cousin, my
mountain friends hunt in summer, when the deer
cherish each rattler-ridden spring, and I
have waited hours by a pool in fear
that manhood would require I shoot, or that
the steady drip of the hill would dull my ear
to a snake whispering near the log I sat
upon, and listened to the yelping cheer
of dogs and men resounding ridge to ridge.

I flinched at every lonely rifle crack,
my knuckles whitening where I gripped the edge

of age and clung, like retching, sinking back,
and then gripped once again the monstrous gun,
since I, to be a man, had taken one.

✦   ✦   ✦

There was a pantry in Coleman and Willie's kitchen lined with
quart jars of shredded or ground venison, used as a staple all year
round. Coleman never used a rifle for squirrel, turkeys, or other
small game. He carved what he called an "Indian club" out of
hickory—a large oval knob at the end of a two-foot stick—and
hurled it unerringly at them in the trees.

I wasn't really interested in the hunting or fishing that Coleman
pursued for survival, but I was fascinated by his Indian ways. One
day before we left for a day's fishing trip in the woods he said,
"Wait, I have to pack lunch." He put a piece of waxed paper on
the table and shook some salt into it, then folded it and put it into
his shirt pocket. "Let's go," he said. When the sun was straight
overhead he said it was time for lunch and squatted on a rock beside a stream. With a few quick scoops he swept twenty or thirty
minnows onto the rock where they flopped out their lives. We
waited until they had died and cooked a while in the sun, salted
them, and gulped them down, then lay on our bellies and drank.
Lunch.

Memory of Grey Fox

Coleman, the old goat, could knock a squirrel
out of a tree with a rock and catch more perch
on a plug than you could seine. I see him lurch-
ing through the brush with a seventy-year-old hurl
of his body like a hobbled rabbit, white
head bobbing with its tilted turkey feather
(he was a clown), his tattered sneakers right-
stepping by twigs, silent to earth, his leather
hands fending branches, leaving not a trace.
His was a race of berry-eaters, thorn-
endurers, pinchers-of-women, gaunt of face,

68

who drank belly-down from springs, whose sons were born
like water from the teeming, hanging hill
stretched naked where the heavens chose to spill.

But our casual approach to sustenance eventually kicked back on me. Nig, Dad, and I were on horseback, miles from the camp, and I was very thirsty. We came upon an abandoned homesite, and Nig said there had to be a well around somewhere. At last we found it—a hole about eight inches in diameter covered with thick green scum. Dad said the water should be good, nonetheless, and scooped off the scum. I bellied down and drank.

And when we returned to Oklahoma City I came down with typhoid fever. For weeks I lay in bed delirious with soaring temperature—every other day. It drove my father to drink. (The typhoid recurred several times during my childhood; I would develop a high fever and aching joints on alternate days for no apparent reason.)

✦ ✦ ✦

Home was hell in general. I would often wake to my parents' shouting in angry quarrels. From time to time Mother had a black eye or bore bruises. She tried to persuade Dad to go to a new organization—founded in 1935 in Akron, Ohio—Alcoholics Anonymous, but he would have nothing to do with it. A declared agnostic, he scorned what he regarded as the claptrap of religion. So far as I know, Mother never talked to others about Dad's drinking. I remember once Mammaw visited from Tulsa. Mother had a black eye. "You won't believe this," she said to Mammaw, "but I ran into a door," and she laughed. I had never heard what was apparently a common explanation for black eyes from marital fights.

✦ ✦ ✦

It is odd how one memory opens up others. My first encounter with death comes to mind as a pebble hits a pool and the circles widen to include details that occurred before and after, details not otherwise memorable. Of all my childhood days in classrooms I remember clearly only a few moments of only this one.

I was eight at the time, in art class in school in Oklahoma City, and I had been trying to draw round os on little squares of paper. We had been instructed to make a big one (about three inches in diameter) with a smaller one, parallel, inside it, and I was having little success. Suddenly the teacher was leaning over me at my desk, getting my attention, and when I looked back I saw my mother in a suit and hat and hose, wearing lipstick, at the class-room door. The teacher said I was to go with her. Mother took my hand and led me out, down the hall, and to the car. She explained that Bampaw had died in Tulsa, and we had to go there.

She was driving down the highway when I realized that I still had the long yellow, newly sharpened pencil in my hand. It be-longed to the school. Mother told me I could return it when we came back from Tulsa.

I read the Burma Shave signs aloud as she drove. Each sign had one line of verse on it: "When passing school zones / Take it slow. / Let our little / Shavers grow / Burma Shave." This trip I saw a new one: "If you don't know / Whose signs these are / You can't have traveled / Very far." And no Burma Shave sign at the end.

We walked into the living room of my grandparents' house. It was full of the family. Bonita and Aunt Marie met us at the door. Curly-headed Uncle Jerry was there with his wife Ruby. His name was Claire, but they called him Jerry for Jerome. I didn't much care for Jerry and Ruby. They had loud, harsh voices and were always making jokes that didn't seem funny to me.

Glen and Agnes had driven in from the oil fields. They were quieter folk, very serious and dignified, both apparently somewhat uneasy around children. Agnes wore her shiny black hair snitched back tightly into a bun, and Glen was tall, sharp-faced and nearly bald. My grandparents had three sons, my father the youngest, and three daughters younger than he.

Everyone was there except for my father. Where, I wondered, is Daddy? They were standing around the divan, somber, but showing no emotion. I took my clues from them—and squelched all reaction.

On the divan was stretched a long, sheet-covered body. Aunt Ruby immediately peeled back the sheet and said in her hard twangy voice, "Well, there he is." He apparently died in his sleep. I noticed that in addition to the sheet there was a quilt under him and a pillow under his head. He must have slept there. He was on his back, his still face toward the ceiling, his eyes closed.

Later we stood at the burning barrel in the backyard. For some reason the women thought that his pajamas and the bedding should be burned. "That's what you do when a person dies," they explained. I watched them feed those items one-by-one into a roaring paper fire. "Ruby was so *crude* to pull the sheet back that way," Aunt Marie said to Mother. Aunt Marie was married now, to Uncle Ray, but he worked as a bookkeeper in Stillwater and came home only on weekends, so Aunt Marie still lived with Mammaw.

No one talked about Bampaw, so I didn't either, but I loved him and was sorry he was gone.

✦ ✦ ✦

My grandfather's last days were full of disappointment. The Keno Oil Company had failed. According to his obituary in the *Tulsa World*:

> In 1927 [the year of my birth] he retired from the firm, his capital depleted. Those who knew him said he was unable to keep money because of generosity with friends.
>
> A few years later Jerome attempted to win his way back, associating with his old friend, Jim Cree, in the drilling of several wells in east Texas. Although the wells were all dry holes, Jerome still had visions of making a comeback.

I learned later that during his last days, he, like my father, was scrabbling a living from brokering. He was notorious throughout his marriage for being a womanizer, and at the time of his death had separated from my grandmother Carrie and was living with another woman. When he visited the house to pick up something, Carrie consigned him to the sofa. He apparently died in his sleep of a heart attack at age fifty-four. His death was a relief to the family. Marie tells me that there was great tension between Ralph and his father during Frank's last years. I knew none of this, of course, at the time.

❖   ❖   ❖

At school they told me I was to skip to the fourth grade. They thought I could do the work, but I couldn't. In the fourth grade they were doing long division and decimals, and the kids were even bigger than the ones in the third grade who were all bigger than I was. But I didn't say anything. I still remember the agony of sitting there staring uncomprehendingly at the numbers on the board with dots in them. Mother helped me at night with long division and decimals.

❖   ❖   ❖

Dad decided that part of my instruction in manhood should be to see Sally Rand. She was a burlesque queen, famous for her fan dance, who was making a national tour about 1935 and was booked for one of Oklahoma's palatial downtown movie theaters. I loved shows of all kinds, and this one especially appealed to me. I loved best the comedians with their raucous, grating voices, their slap-sticks, (literally long paddles with many leaves that made a loud crack when they hit a person's rump), their pinching and goosing of girls who appeared in their skits. And their songs—comic poems with tricky evasions of the censors:

> Oh, Casey played ball in the pasture
> And very long flies could he hit,
> But when Casey ran round the bases,
> He found that cows made them of ———
>   Sweet violets!
>   Sweeter than all the roses!

72

Covered all over from head to toe,
Covered all over with dew.

But the men in the audience most appreciated the stripteases. Dad whispered to me explanations of bumps and grinds as, trombones blaring, the bass drum booming, various ladies shed layers of filmy garments until they were down to tiny bras and G-strings.

But Sally Rand, the climax of the show, was another sort of dancer entirely. The music was softer, all strings and flutes, as she rustled onstage with her body shielded by enormous fans of ostrich plumes in each hand. She had long blonde curls above the fans, and high heels below them, but little in between as we gradually learned when she swept the fans in more and more revealing patterns, exposing long slim legs, a trim belly, curvaceous shoulders and swelling breasts. Actually, you saw more of the stripteasers than of Sally Rand, but there was an elegance about her performance that made her soar like a swan in flight above the swampy show that preceded her.

✦　✦　✦

We are on an outing from Oklahoma City. Winter. We are going to gather persimmons, holly, and mistletoe for Christmas. There are six adults on this trip—and five children, including Stew and me. Among the adults are Aunt Peggy and her husband at the time. The adults build a bonfire and begin drinking and eating. Stew is with Mother. We older kids wander the woods. We find a stream that is frozen, so we run and slide on it. One of the boys begins imitating a drunk on the ice, staggering, slipping around, falling, and we all giggle. One of the girls begins dancing out there, and I join her, imitating the ball room dancing I have seen in the movies.

As we are drifting back through the woods toward the bonfire we come upon a man and woman deep in the woods kissing. They are Dad and Aunt Peggy. We giggle, turn, and return to our frozen stream.

✦　✦　✦

Dad taught me how to give him a massage. He showed me how to use my fingers and palms to dig into and around muscles, how to brush my palms together swiftly, pounding their edges on his back. For what seemed like hours he would stretch nude on his bed, and I worked over his warm flesh, finding knots and working them out, up and down his back, around his neck, down his thighs and calves.

After one fishing trip he was badly sunburned. He asked me to peel his bare back. Skin came off in a great grey sheets—some of them bigger than the palm of my hand.

✦ ✦ ✦

I remember being out in the country near Oklahoma City. We had gone to an acreage my parents were considering buying and met a dowser there. Even at that age, seven or eight, I suspected that this magic stuff was a lot of hokum. I think Mother and Dad did, too, but the wisdom of the region was that you should not buy property until a dowser had located a well-site. With his yoke of peach wood the old man paced up and down the brown winter field for some time, but he could find no sign of water. Mother and Dad decided not to buy the property. Their caution, surmounting their skepticism, impressed me. A half-century later, I would still engage a dowser before buying property requiring a well—and would still not buy without a signal that water was to be found.

After that we drove to an enormous estate. This family had a private polo field. We climbed the low bleachers and looked over the grassy expanse where the game was played, and we went through their stables and tack shop. Polo mallets, I discovered, are like croquet mallets but longer and skinnier, and a polo ball is like a croquet ball only lighter. Polo ponies wear funny little saddles with no horns. The saddles look like postage stamps on the horses.

The first thing we saw when we entered the front hall was an enormous Christmas tree in the stairwell at the far side of the house. The tip of it was hidden until you went close. The tree was three stories high, and a stairway wound in a curve around it on each side. Around the tree were many expensive toys—large stuffed animals, a very large rocking horse carved from wood. . . . Their children were not at home. I thought I would be afraid to play with such rich kids.

✦ ✦ ✦

Stew and I are in the backyard of my Aunt Tubby and Uncle Dale's house in a little town in Kansas. A train track runs right by the yard, and there is a high water tank for the trains. We play in the yard and wave at the engineers on trains as they go brawling past or stop to let the long pipe down to fill their empty tanks. We put pennies on the track and let trains run over them. They come out flat and oval with smeary Indians on them. We do the same with buffalo nickels and liberty dimes, but, when Mother finds out, she says that is wasting money.

Now we are going into nearby Hayes so my parents and Dale can visit Tubby in the hospital. The streets are straight, quiet, tree-lined, and shady. Because my brother and I cannot go up to Tubby's room, we wait outside and play on the hospital grounds. I was nine and Stew was three. This was May, just before my parents' divorce.

✦ ✦ ✦

I remember Dad's anger as he drove too fast on the dirt road. We had to get a fishing license for Mother. A game warden had caught her pulling a trout out of the glacial lake high in the Rockies behind us. We pulled up at the little bait store where he and Leslie had bought *their* licenses before we went up to our campsite.

"So go on!" he snarled at her. "Go get it!"

Mother got out of the car and went up the wooden steps into the store. Stew and I cringed in the back seat.

This was New Mexico. The man leaning against the post on the porch of the store looked like people I had seen in pictures of Old Mexico. I whispered to Stew that I bet he spoke Spanish.

When Mother came back to the car her face was grim, and she didn't say anything, just got in and faced forward.

"Did you get it?" Dad asked.

75

"I got it."

"I thought you said you weren't going to fish on this trip."

"I changed my mind."

The game warden had said she wouldn't have to pay a fine if she bought a license down at the little town forty miles away on the flatland. Now we were roaring along the dirt road leaving a swirl of dust behind us, tension thick in the air inside the car, heading for the long winding climb on a narrow road up into the blue mountains.

That evening Dad took me with Leslie and himself in the canoe. The lake was a round circle with water that looked black but was very clear. The men said the lake had no bottom. Dad cast a fly out on the lake and then handed me his rod, saying it was time I caught my first fish. I looked up at the high pines and snow-capped peaks all around us, then back where the fly skipped as I made little jerks on the rod, imitating Dad. Suddenly there was a splash and the line started pulling straight down. I was startled, and I let go of the rod. We watched helplessly as the rod—and Dad's brand-new reel—circled down in the dark, icy, clear water. He cursed at me. I should have held tighter. Did I have any idea how much a rod and reel cost?

That called for a drink. Dad pulled a flat bottle from his fishing vest, took a swig, and passed the bottle to Leslie.

We camped out there for two weeks, sleeping the chill nights on thick straw we bought from a nearby rancher. Mostly Stew and I wandered deep woods and climbed the mountain with Mother and Thelma while the men fished.

When we came down from the mountains, Dad, his chin grizzled with two-weeks' growth, driving along a narrow dirt road in a cloud of dust back down on flatland, stopped the car alongside a teenage boy who was walking along barefooted, a bamboo fishing pole over his shoulder. It was the first person outside our party we had seen since the day of Mother's fine. Dad leaned out of the window and asked the boy, "What's happened in the war?"

The boy looked puzzled. "What war?" he asked.

Dad drove on in disgust. Again and again he said sarcastically,

"*Whut* war? *Whut* war?" In the back seat I didn't ask the question I most needed to ask: What war? I was probably sitting there thinking, that dumb kid doesn't even know what war's going on, though I myself didn't know.

◆　◆　◆

It could only have been one of two wars, and it surprises me even now that Dad was that interested in either. That dates our trip sometime between the period of the conquest of Ethiopia by Italy, October 1935 to May 1936 (unlikely because the trip was surely in the summer), or after July 17, 1936, when the Spanish Civil War began. The summer of 1936—our last summer as a family.

How little I was aware of the world! I suppose I picked up a little from newsreels. I remember the stentorian voice of the narrator in frequent shorts called *The March of Time*. (We were seeing such films as *It Happened One Night, Captain January, Treasure Island, Mutiny on the Bounty, David Copperfield, The Last of the Mohicans*.) I wish I still had the set of soldiers Mr. Welford, a business associate of Dad's, gave me: a boxed set of cast-iron toy soldiers, arrayed like chessmen. The good guys were black men, in turbans and short white swaddling, carrying swords: Ethiopians. The bad guys were white, in belted uniforms, carrying rifles: Italians. They were having a war in Africa, Dad explained. The Italians were Fascists. The League of Nations condemned them for invading Ethiopia. I didn't know what all that meant. I probably lost the soldiers in the trenches I dug for them in the backyard.

Much must have been left behind when we moved away. There is a snapshot of Stew and me sitting on a pedestal of our porch rail at our last house in Oklahoma. I have my arm around Stew, and we are holding hands, my head leaning to touch his. His face is angelic beneath his dark curls. We are both smiling. It looks as though Stew is wearing a one-piece suit with short pants; I am in what seem to be wool shorts and a white shirt. Both of us are wearing leather oxfords. Stew is three. I am nine.

This photo often comes to mind as I recall that busy year. I have blanked out all the final unpleasantness that must have occurred as the marriage came to an end. I think we fled. I don't remember being told of our plans. I have no memory—after that last fishing trip—of seeing my father again at all until months later, in Texas. Mother took us to Mammaw and Marie's, but I remember little of our stay there. Bonita was married, and I must have visited her home and met her new husband. My memories resume in Dallas, on our way to Houston. I try to imagine that journey—the beatific nine-year-old in the photo with a trace of deviltry in his grin.

5

I Swear to God

Sexplay, I should explain, was no new thing for me. We started early, back in Tulsa. Sammy, Linda, Mary Fae, and I had a treehouse behind the garage. Big boys built the treehouse, but when they got older they abandoned it, so it became *our* clubhouse. We said we wouldn't let anyone else in it. There wasn't anybody else who *wanted* to go in it, but we had this rule. Up there behind the rough plank walls and curtains, on the crude wooden floor spread with blankets, we played doctor. We took turns nursing and doctoring each other. The parts that need the most attention were under our pants and panties. We made medicine out of sheepsour (the dictionary says *sheep sorrel,* but we called it sheepsour), nasturtium leaves, and wild onions. We mixed these with water and drank the water, or we just chewed them up.

Sometimes we played doctor in the loft of the garage. Bampaw had his workshop out there in half of what was built as a two-car garage. He made beautiful furniture and wooden toys. I often watched him, and he showed me how to use his tools. I helped him sand and varnish the smooth, blond wood. On the other side, where my parents sometimes parked our green Buick coupe, there was a ladder up to the dark loft. The four of us kids had furnished the loft with blankets and pillows, but our parents would not let us spend the night up there. We would be scared, they told us.

But to climb up the ladder behind Linda or Mary Fae, to see under skirts darkening as they neared the loft, and to be up there on our blankets in the dusk . . . and then to reach and slide a hand up a smooth thigh and feel myself get all pointy in my pants. . . .

Eroticism suffuses my memory of childhood. Though the surface culture was sexually repressive, children had a lot more freedom in those days than they do now. They were out-of-sight and out-of-mind for most adults most of the time. In the interstices of society the healthy filaments of life stretch and grow. Mr. Welford, who gave me the set of Ethiopian and Italian cast-iron soldiers, sometimes brought his daughter Daisy to visit. Daisy and I would steal off to the bedroom or garage together for private play. Mr. Welford drove a Cord convertible whose headlights cranked in and out, hiding under a lid that made them disappear into the fenders. We also toyed with one another in the back seat of the Cord while my father and Mr. Welford rode up front driving around in the dark with the top down. Somehow sexplay was much more romantic with blonde Daisy in her father's fancy white convertible than it had been in our clubhouse in Tulsa.

But it was Polly Popper who taught me what such things mean.

✦ ✦ ✦

The years right after we moved to Houston seem to be, on reflection, the most crowded in my life. They make me realize how much more happens in the lives of children than adults are likely to be aware of. Since I began writing this book I have begun seeing children in a new light. *They will remember,* I think, speculating about their secret lives. So much of life is new in our early years. It is our later years when we are no longer so impressionable, when fewer things happen for the first time, that events even out. I could probably tell you less about what happened in any adult year of my life than I can about my years of childhood.

80

Houston was an alien world to an Oklahoma boy. I remember the car moving down the strangely humid, warm, and silent residential streets lined with those ever-amazing bearded oaks. Aunt Orpha, Uncle Louie, and Maxine lived in a brick house two stories high on Shakespeare Street at the corner of Rice Road. Though it was quite an ordinary, rather small house, it seemed like a castle to me—the first time I ever lived in a house larger than a bungalow.

Two blocks away was a new low, long school. I was a grade ahead of others my age, so my social relations with classmates who towered over me were a bit strained. But I remember liking the school very much. In our class was a boy who wrote and drew everything upside down and backwards—and he drew very well. I remember a very convincing locomotive he created on the blackboard, its smoke streaming toward the floor. I don't know that anyone ever asked him *why* he drew and wrote that way. I simply accepted it as an example of the amazing variety of human behavior. Another boy drank ink from the inkwells.

I drew fairly well also, right-side-up, and won a scholarship to the Art Museum with a crayoned head of a horse on poster paper. The scholarship meant I was to take a bus downtown on Saturday mornings for art lessons and meet with strangers in a stately mansion on a wide green lawn. The teacher often took us outside into the formal garden so we could sketch the walkways and shrubbery.

Mother found work as a secretary for an oil company—her first job since I was born—and went off dressed up spiffy every morning on the bus. Maxine was working, too, so Orpha must have tended Stew during school days. All these adults dressing up and going off to work. All this independence. No bad scenes with Dad. I thought Houston was swell.

✦   ✦   ✦

Especially because of Polly Popper. Polly, a high-school senior who lived just across the street, was in full bloom at seventeen. She seemed a towering woman with rusty flowing hair and freckled face, her breasts like clouds. I puppy-like imbibed her smiles and laughter. Polly and another girl, Sue (from my class at school), and I started a rental library. In the garage out back of Polly's house, we built some shelves, borrowed some books from parents. After school we'd gather there each afternoon, we three.

I doubt we ever rented a book, but we stayed open. I was sappy in love with Sue, her dusky skin and honey hair, long lashes batting, her seldom smile. She was eleven, beginning to mature, two years older than I was. She liked the boys a grade above us who spent their afternoons at softball, boys who thought no more of girls than I of softball, but I was beneath Sue's serious regard.

Since no customers came to our library, we spent hours slouched together on the sofa and easy chairs we had scrounged for furniture—bare legs, shy looks, and idleness, all sprawled. And so we started playing Post Office. Spin-the-bottle was no fun because three people do not make a circle. Mostly the bottle pointed right between us. But we could take turns at sending letters to one another, say how many stamps each required, each stamp a kiss, and since I was the only boy, on every turn I either sent or received. Sue would say, for instance, "I send a letter with three stamps to Juddy." Then we'd squat behind the couch—down out-of-sight—and I'd get three pecks on the cheek. Sue would invariably kiss my cheek. I think she once touched lips with me—after some weeks of this—but I could tell the kiss was for a child.

Polly, though, kissed my lips—and used more postage. Those large, damp lips I still can taste and feel. She hugged me to her as if she were a man, and I her little maiden. Once she pressed me down on the rug (we'd also scrounged a rug) and lay right on me while she kissed. I felt the crush of breasts, her bra beneath her blouse. I saw Sue peeking at us, giggling, and I tickled Polly's ribs to get her off.

In Houston's fall we all grew hot and lazy. Then we just sat on the couch, me in the middle, girls taking turns at kissing—with no more talk of stamps. Then Sue lost interest. She'd leave early or not show up at all, leaving the business to Polly and me. With Sue gone, games with Polly grew intense. The neighborhood had many houses under construction where the two of us would climb in rooms upstairs—their walls bare studs—and then we'd find the

82

crawl space under the house and sit face to face in the dark on the ground. We played Post Office—just us two—because kissing was not so naughty if it were a kind of game. We just took turns, one kissing, the other being kissed. We did not French kiss. I didn't learn to French kiss until I was in the army. No, Polly and I just kissed. She never seemed to want to quit. If I got bored, she begged.

One day, back in our library, I felt fingers slip under my short pants. Clear up. Manicured fingers, long and cool. I let her. She let me put my small hands down her blouse. Later she sat on the couch and spread her knees and told me to go down and look. She had pushed her panties down around her ankles. My head under her tent of skirt in darkness, I could not see much but caught the strange sharp scent. "Feel it," she said. I felt the curls. Oh, I knew about dry hairless slits, but this was something else again, so I explored, and she explored, and then, her parents gone, we stole up to her bedroom and closed the door to keep the dog out. Polly had a bulldog that mounted our legs whenever he was near us. What is he doing? I'd ask—although I knew. Polly just laughed. He sniffed her crotch. I guessed her dog had been her playmate until I replaced him in her lonely hours. But now we didn't want the dog to join us.

Polly undressed us both and let me suck those melons. She liked to suck my little dingus, which stood like a finger—maybe an inch-and-a-half long. At last she said she wanted me to *do* it.

"You're sure," she asked, "that you can't get me pregnant?"

Was the doll real? Not yet. Not quite. I had explained that I had never spurted, and unless I spurted she would not get pregnant. How I knew that, I'm not sure; nonetheless I knew. Maybe from aunt-talk. I was bookish, but I don't think I found out in a book.

"Well, then," she said, spreading her legs, "go on."

I didn't mind, though sucking was more fun. And so I gave her her sex education.

At high school she had boy friends, but she never let them do what she liked to do with me. She might get pregnant. She at least might get a reputation. How I hated those faceless young brutes she told me all about. Once she put on her cheerleader dress for me, her tall hat with its pom-pom, slippery boots, silver baton, and talked about her heroes—the football players who took her out on dates.

What did they do? I asked. Maybe they'd go to a theater. (There were no drive-in movies then.) Maybe they'd hold hands; maybe he'd brush a hand against her thigh or breast. She'd whisper no. Then, after the movie, they'd stop at a drive-in restaurant, have a malted, talk. They teased and joked and flirted. Then the guy would make a pass. She let him kiss her, that was all. No hands below her shoulder level. Their arms would be around each other when the carhop (in her sequined little skirt) would come to take the tray. The rule was Polly had to be home by eleven weekend nights. No date on any night before a schoolday. I was her boyfriend weekdays four to six.

I guess that if they knew about us those other guys gladly would have traded places, but I was jealous. I was just her doll. A lively doll, however. She may have been disappointed later when she learned that real men come to a conclusion. A doll can last forever. She would scream again and again and cry for more. And then we'd hear her parents driving in and quickly get our clothes on. They had no idea why their Polly spent so much time with a nine-year-old like me, but they thought it was for the good. Why, who but I had ever gotten her involved with books? They looked upon me as her business partner.

◆　◆　◆

Uncle Louie didn't take too well to the Jerome invasion of his home, especially when our cocker, Tarbaby, tore up his poinsettias, so we moved into a garage apartment which we shared with another working woman, Lois. Rosie, our maid, came every weekday to be with Stew while I was at school. Both Mother and Lois were dating. That meant someone had to be found for nights with Stew and me. This was before the world knew babysitters. That term came to our language when the war disrupted households. Mothers rarely left the home for jobs. A 1948 movie, *Sitting Pretty*, with Clifton Webb, made fun of this new situation where one hired a stranger for a task that aunts, grandmothers, cousins, neighbors did for free. Mother remembered there was a high-school girl who lived across the street from Orpha.

Polly? I asked. Why, sure. I think she'd do it. Thus, on evenings both of them had dates I'd go the couple of miles to our former neighborhood to get Polly. Why did I have to go get her? It may be that we had no telephone. At any rate, I have a distinct image of riding double on a bike with her. She brought books along, supposedly to study. I rode between her arms, her red hair blowing around my face, her breasts against my back.

When Mother left, we'd hurry Stew to bed and play our games. Night after night we did this before my father came to visit. After we moved to Texas I came to know better the side of Dad my mother once had loved. He wrote long letters to me—always neatly typed on office stationery. These were full of sane and loving talk, father to son, about things no one else told me about. He made me think. He made me find the words to say what I was thinking, what I felt. I told him I had started Sunday School. Dad sent me a Bible with my name embossed in gold on its limp cover. A Scofield Reference Bible. I still use it. Here, look how he inscribed it, "Jud," he wrote, "I am proud of you today—and every day." Pentameter. Iambic after its initial anapest. Then, "Dad." No mush. He told me I should read it, know its stories, study its history, and read the footnotes. It was from Dad I learned things of the mind. Sober, he seemed the gentlest man alive. Now at safe distance words on pages brought us thinking heart to thinking heart.

He had been writing Mother, too, for he showed up in Houston seeking another chance. He came one evening, sober, calm and kind, wearing a coat and tie. I entertained the two of them with marionettes, recited some poems I had learned, and showed him the portrait of Edward VIII I had copied from the photo on the front page of a Sunday supplement. He told us that he had spent some time in a sanitarium where he learned much about himself. He said for too long he had worn his heart on his sleeve. I studied his sleeve. But now, he told us, he was stronger, better able to face the world. Never would he touch alcohol again. And then we boys were sent to the bedroom so they could talk. I could hear the mumble of their long and earnest conversation. I believed his promises and thought we'd be a family again. But Mother said she could not take the risk of trusting him. And so they parted, but he planned to come the next day, pick up Stew, and take him to the zoo, then bring him home before my school was out. He had a long drive back to Oklahoma. We kissed goodbye. I went to bed.

But when I came from school I found a worried Rosie. No Stew. Mother had gone from work out on a date, not knowing he was missing. Lois stayed with me. The evening darkened. I was sick with worry.

Suddenly I knew what to do. I sat at Mother's desk and wrote a promise to God that if He would bring back my brother, never again would I do what I had been doing with Polly Popper. Now— where should I put the note where no one else could find it? I struck a match. God had received the message, I figured, and so I burned it in an ashtray.

I thought I should save the ashes—in some special place. Well, where, for such a religious kind of thing, but in my Bible? I pulled it out of its box case and opened it in the middle, after Malachi. There is a page of history, "From Malachi to Matthew," then "The New Testament." Between the Old Testament and the New seemed just right.

I dropped the ashes in and closed the book. Just then the door-bell rang. It was a taxi driver, Stew in tow, who told Lois that Ralph Jerome was in his cab, passed out—dead drunk. God sure works quick, I thought.

Mother came home just then, and surly Dad was staggering up the stairs to our garage apartment planning to spend the night. My mother called the cops and had him taken off to jail. And I was stuck with my sacred promise.

I told all this to Polly when she next came to sit with us. "Oh, no!" she said. "How *could* you?" What were we to *do?*

I said I'm sorry, but I promised God. We talked it over. Polly seemed to think that if I just lay still I wouldn't be actually doing anything bad at all. I wasn't sure her logic was quite sound, but after all, she was a grown-up, sort of, and good boys do what grown-ups ask them to.

I think that was the last time we played games.

✦ ✦ ✦

Aunt Peggy, a soft beautiful woman of thirty-three with long hair and rounded features, was bathing me. I was ten years old, having been left to spend the summer at the new home she and Uncle Douglas bought near Dallas. I had been bathing alone for a long time, but I figured maybe she didn't understand about children, not having had any. Peggy, just having gotten out of the tub herself, was nude as I was. She washed me especially carefully between my legs. After bathing me all over with the washrag, she helped me out of the tub, picked up a towel, and dried me just as carefully and thoroughly.

Then she carried me, both of us nude, into the bedroom. I knew I was small for my age, but nobody carried me anymore. She nestled with me on an easy chair, hugging me to her breasts. I sat up and caressed these. They were even bigger than Polly's. "Do you want to suck them?" she asked in a throaty voice.

Why, yes ma'am, thank you, ma'am. . . .

Peggy was well on her way to alcoholism. She was probably tight at the time of that incident. Drink gave her a dreamy, sweet smile and kind of lazy amiability. Once I came upon her in this state when Jim, her black yardman (who rarely entered the house during the day, though he did serve dinner in a starched white coat each evening), was in the kitchen. Jim was to play the role in my head of Nigger Jim in *Huckleberry Finn* when I later read that book—a huge and powerful man of great simple kindliness. At the moment I entered the kitchen Peggy was saying in a loud whisper, "Douglas would *kill* you." But she didn't say it in such a way as to reject utterly whatever suggestion Jim had presumably made. Aunt Peggy certainly charged my imagination.

✦ ✦ ✦

Molly kept pulling her skirt up over her face. She was only four and didn't know any better. The other fellows were teasing her, and I told her she shouldn't do that.

"Why not?" she asked, pouting.

"It isn't nice."

"Why not?"

"Well, if you want to show yourself, why don't you take your panties off?"

She took her panties off.

We went on playing and ignored Molly.

At dinner there was the call of a woman's voice from below the stairs of our garage apartment. Mother went out on the porch to see who it was. Soon she put her head in the door and said, "Juddy, come out here."

I went out onto the porch and looked down. A lady I didn't know was standing down there with an angry look on her face. "Did you tell Molly to take her panties off?" she asked me.

I was embarrassed. "I was trying to get her to stop pulling her skirt up," I said.

"*Did* you tell her to take her panties off?" Mother asked me.

"I asked her why she didn't if she wanted to keep on pulling her skirt up. . . ."

I felt the lameness of my explanation as I gave it. On Mother's instructions I told the lady that I was sorry and that I wouldn't ever do that again. Sex is risky.

✦ ✦ ✦

During the winter I started going to the ice rink. Remembering the semi-tropical climate of Houston, it seems impossible that I could have learned to ice skate there, but I did. Deep in the black section of the city there was a little ice rink. I went by bus, then walked a few blocks to the rink and rented a pair of skates. I taught myself to skate. I felt so independent in a dangerous world.

And there I saw Sue again—as in a vision. She was wearing a violet velvet skating costume, its short skirt lined with fur, fur trim around her coat's high collar, hat and muff of fur. She skated daintily around the rink, a flower followed by a line of bees—the big boys in their hockey skates, who jostled around in horseplay, laughed and teased her, yet they followed. When she clumped across the floor to buy herself hot chocolate, still they followed. I skated near—on splayed and aching ankles. I waved, and she waved back. We did not speak to one another.

✦   ✦   ✦

Love and sex. These ran parallel courses in my life. Much later, in graduate school, studying the tradition of courtly love, I came to understand what had hit me during my crush on Sue. Another, much more severe attack, would come on one day in high school. I was struck by the arrow of Eros. In courtly love the lady is always in the tower, proud and useless, the hero always below, dedicating himself and his deeds to her in hope of favors—like a handkerchief he can wear on his helmet. Love itself is worshipped as a god, and an exacting and irrational code governs the rites of its celebration or worship. This love is invariably pre- or extramarital. Males avoid it like a disease, and when we fall into it, our friends tease us. We suffer paralysis, fever, and chill. It has very little to do with affection or lust or even sex. In fact, it has little to do with the lady in the tower, who may be Rosaline or Juliet indifferently. It is an obsession, something like what a pupa must go through in metamorphosis, which transforms the worm into a silly bright creature capable of giddy flight. All this is in the courtship phase, and usually it comes to nothing. There is little or no physical contact between the lovers. Should they actually find themselves in one another's arms, they are likely to seek sexual release, like the lancing of a boil. That cures the disease.

Imagine how confusing I found courtly love to be when it happened to me at Austin High, and I looked upon a bony beauty with long caramel curls named, I believe, Shirley, and knew I had been smitten. I came down with a fever. I vaguely remember day after day writhing in my bed, slipping in warm and chilly waves from dream to wakefulness and back again. My fantasies were elaborate, usually having to do with a desert island and very little to do with sexual activity, except, perhaps, an occasional ceremonious kiss. This was good boy love.

Surviving the initial coma, the lover moves on to perform his derring-do. The next crisis is that of letting her know that she has been chosen as the beloved. I had only one shirt with which I could wear my single tie. The collar was too tight; the cuffs didn't cover my wrists. It was pale green. I wore this daily (if I could persuade Mother to launder and iron it when she came home from her secretarial job). I went to school in my coat of mail, face red, eyes bulging, armpits cut and wrists exposed, tie awkwardly tied. My idea of announcing my love to Shirley was to sit in class dressed in this manner, fingering my tie and combing my hair frequently. She did not seem to catch on. While I had no difficulty talking to other girls, I could not bring myself to say a word to her, and, in fact, I would gaze abstractedly in the other direction if she seemed to notice me.

These obstacles required the dangerous next step of the intermediary. To tell a male friend was unthinkable, embarrassing, and too great a risk, for he might prove a John Alden. Neither of us had a wily servant. I got on well enough with a fat little girl who was clearly out of it and who could in a friendly manner indicate my interest to Shirley. When I knew that the message had been delivered the affair took on a whole new excitement. I began wearing a sweater with a clover flower or other decoration and a tie clasp. (I do remember clover blossoms. This must have been in the spring of 1942, when I was fifteen.) Then, when I sat in the classroom ostentatiously looking the other way, gagging on my collar and blinking what I hoped were sensitive lashes, I *knew*, I just *knew* she was looking at me curiously, considering.

It would have been fortunate at this time if I could have gotten in a fight with someone or been spectacular at touch football during gym period (when she, in her bloomers, with brittle brown legs, flew after a soccer ball in a neighboring field), but I did not dare and was unable. I slew dragons in secret, performing a variety of lone feats on a rope swing in the woods along the bayou or stunts on my bicycle on my paper route. I was up at four every morning, took an icy shower for Shirley, engaged in imaginary conversation with her as I rolled and stowed my papers in the canvas bags on my bicycle, and I imagined her following as I rode the dark streets sailing the papers expertly thirty feet to thud to rest by the dark doorways. The kind of girl I want to marry, I told myself, was one who would go around with a fellow on his paper route. Was my heroism making any noticeable difference in the size of my muscles? in my bearing? I wondered, looking away. When we passed in the hall I gave her a casual, almost condescending smile—and imagined I heard her giggling as she and her girl friends walked away behind me.

The first Favor was granted at a party, under the sheltering guise of one of those Post-Office-type kissing games we used to play. This party was held in a house near Shirley's, in a relatively lower-class environment that made life seem a bit racier than it was in Idlewood (a subdivision of Houston where we were living at the time), more full of daring and possibility. After mischievously dodging me most of the evening she finally let herself be tagged (or whatever), and her forfeit was to walk around the block with me. We set out stiffly, Shirley setting a brisk pace. I reached for her hand, and she let me hold it, or, rather, used mine to drag me after as she sailed along. It *was* a rather chilly evening. But at some point I dug in my heels and pulled her around to me, shaking, teeth chattering, embraced her hard frame, stood on my tiptoes, and kissed her cheek. She let me! I released her hand and danced down the sidewalk ahead of her back to the house.

Though we had not yet exchanged any words, the romance had taken a serious turn. She knew through the intermediary that I was her declared lover. Our silent exchanges had confirmed that I was interested in Shirley and that she was at least watching me—with amusement and curiosity. I had touched her, held her hand, and kissed her cheek. Ahead lay all the perils of writing her a note, speaking to her, and kissing her lips. I quaked and despaired and spent another feverish night.

Of those necessary next steps, writing notes seemed least terrifying. I began composing long ones on green-tinted notebook paper (green was becoming my pennon color; I was practicing fancy signatures as an armorial device). I even permitted my fat friend to deliver some of these notes. I don't remember ever getting any reply. But a crisis could not be postponed indefinitely. At the end of the semester came a dance. If I did not ask her, someone else would. And yet I didn't know how to dance very well, and particularly couldn't dance with Shirley (who had several inches on me), and could hardly imagine the succession of horrors involved in (1) asking her, (2) getting an answer, (3) if she accepted, dressing to go, (4) sending or taking flowers, (5) picking her up—on foot? on my bicycle? (6) talking to her through an evening, (7) deciding whether or not to try to kiss her—all this besides the problem of staying up till nearly midnight and still managing my paper route the next morning.

Brash youth that I was, I *did* ask her, though—and in person. It was by her locker in the hall. I just stopped, cocked my head, grinned suavely, and said, "Shirley, would you go to the Junior-Senior Prom with me?" It was crudely, impetuously done. It was treating her just as though she were a person. And this error undoubtedly was the factor that brought the romance to disaster. She said she would let me know. But day after day she did not. I passed her more notes—directly now, without the intermediary, so callous had I become. I grew cocky, reckless (for example, riding with no hands on a busy street pretending to read a book), self-confident in bearing: had I not, after all, asked my girl for a date— indeed, to a dance? And I waited for her reply with a sickening dread. When she received my notes she passed them around, I knew, hearing giggles—and I bore my punishment with desperate dignity.

I can see now that she was waiting for another invitation. Her note finally came one day in solid geometry class, and the folded notebook paper, elaborately blotted with very distinct lipstick impressions of a passionate mouth, was passed back down the row to me, all eyes, like those of courtiers in the presence of the Queen, following its progress until I took it in my trembling hands. It was perfumed, written in purple ink, the is dotted with little os. It said she was very, very (with many underlinings) sorry that she could never, never feel about me the way I seemed to feel about her. Obviously, though it was intended to look casual, the note had been prepared with great pains the night before, perfumed and blotted. My blood rushed from my face, and I folded like a fish de-boned.

A true knight would not have been deterred. This was simply one more terror after the dragons. But it finished me. By the end of the hour I had loosened my tie, rolled back my sleeves, unbuttoned that strangling collar, and wadded that note into a ball. I rolled it round and round in my fingers. They were pink and scented until I washed them in the boys' room. Going down from the third to the second floor, I flipped the ball off my thumb up to an inaccessible, wide, marble window sill, where, so far as I know, it still remains. I whistled off-key and went back to the fellows. From time to time thereafter, in passing, I looked up at that window sill with a self-satisfied smirk. Boy, had I fixed Shirley!

✦ ✦ ✦

But sex was another matter, as I learned from Merwin. Merwin and Betty lived several doors down Sylvan Road from ours in a big and fancy house. Betty taught me to play tennis on their dirt court, and I played with her often. I wanted her to be my girlfriend. She seemed earthier than Shirley and was quite attractive in a fresh freckle-dusted way, but though she was always friendly, I was obviously too small and young for her.

Merwin was even older than Betty, about seventeen, and he rarely played tennis. He was more of an intellectual (though I didn't know that term). The whole family was fascinating. Their father was a ham-radio operator, a retired professor, and now was constantly in touch with other operators the world over. He let me talk on his radio to distant strangers. I don't remember the mother well, but they were all exceedingly gracious to me. I loved going into their vaulted, paneled living room, its walls lined with books.

Reflecting on it now I think that Merwin may have been a homosexual. I don't remember hearing of homosexuals in those days. It seemed quite natural for boys and girls to play with one another sexually when we were young. And, as did the scouts at camp, some of my friends engaged in masturbation in one another's company, circle jerks, though I don't remember their touching one another in the process. Sex was funny, a sport. For example, one moonlit night several of us in our scout patrol, the Trailblazers, were walking along the abandoned interurban tracks (an interurban train once connected Houston and Galveston) after a scout meeting. I told them I could suck myself, and they didn't believe me. So I pulled down my short pants, lay on the ground, swung my legs back over my head, rolling up on my shoulders, and showed them. No erection, but impressive gymnastics!

Merwin's quiet, cultured, somewhat effeminate manner was certainly different from that of other boys I had known. And he did like playing with our penises, an inclination which seemed unusual at our ages. He sucked me and masturbated me, sometimes masturbating himself at the same time. I suppose I sucked and masturbated him, too, though my memory isn't clear on that point. How passive I seem in all these sexual encounters! That may be age hiding the truth from me, but I think it more likely that I *was* passive. I was cute and looked younger than my years, and people seem to have been drawn to making advances. Merwin, of course, could come, and I enviously witnessed his ejaculations.

The sexual aspect of our relationship caused an ambiguity in my feelings about him. On the one hand, he was a model of a kind of manhood I admired. I enjoyed talking with him and his family, but when I went to this home with so many attractions and interesting people, he was obsessive about getting me off to his bedroom. That was fun, but frustrating, too, as I didn't want to be doing that *all* the time. It was something of a relief when Merwin went on to college the year after we moved to Idlewood. After that I saw him only on his visits home, and there was no more sexplay.

But Merwin broke me in as a masturbator. As I grew more mature, masturbation became more pleasurable, even before I began ejaculating.

✦ ✦ ✦

I was fifteen, in our house in Idlewood. From my upstairs window I looked down across our neighbors' drive into the bedroom of the adult daughter of the husband (from a former marriage). I knew just when she would be coming home from work and would change her clothes. She never drew the blind—a great convenience. I still didn't spurt, but I was enjoying myself as I watched my neighbor's daughter standing in her bra and panties fanning herself with a cardboard fan. She spread her legs and fanned between them, holding the crotch of her panties first to one side and then another so she could cool important places.

✦ ✦ ✦

And then, one day, in the little bathroom off Aunt Orpha's kitchen, while the adults were outside having a barbecue, the little pearl emerged that indicated that in one primary regard I was on the verge of manhood. I still had no pubic hair.

It is interesting that I remember that little pearl more as an achievement than as a thrill. A friend contrasted my response to *his* first orgasm. He says that I must have thought, "There, that's how that happens," and he's probably right. But, he says,

> I masturbated because it felt better and better and better and finally oh my god my spine melted and ran out my penis and my eyeballs rolled back in my head and I was slathered in hot honey-butter from knee to armpit and it was the most gorgeous thing that could ever happen and all I wanted was *that*, again and again, over and over, the rest of my life, and I would do anything for it.

Those words bring again to mind what seems to be a core of coldness at the heart of my being, no doubt a result of learning the techniques of damage control early in my emotional life.

✦ ✦ ✦

95

But for those months I was hooked. I masturbated several times a day. I had forgotten all about Polly Popper and her fears of pregnancy. What I feared now was madness. The fellows said that if you overdid it, you might go crazy. I tried to stop—but couldn't. It wasn't even fun—merely obsessive. A kind of ache in my groin would send me to my room, and I lay there pounding, hating myself, and hating that growing organ. My emotional heritage required that I resist self-indulgence, and I knew that, however much sensation, how much pleasure I might be having, I was indulging myself. I prayed.

And I wrote another promise to God, although the other one had slipped my mind. Again I burned the promise in an ashtray and wondered where to put the ashes, again selecting that same page between the Old and New. Of course, I found the old ashes, spilled some in my lap and with them all the shame that I had buried, and with that shame a memory of Polly, an apparition now standing nude before me wailing, "How could you!"

I wondered how I could.

Maybe, I thought, if I didn't put the ashes into the Bible, the promise wouldn't count. Maybe what I should promise was never to make reckless promises again. I stared at ashes and remembered Polly, feeling a stirring I could not suppress. Unbuttoned, I felt a surge of liberation, threw my head back, laughed aloud. Oh, thank you, Polly!

6

Some Southwestern Women

An Australian film of some years ago, *Careful! He Might Be Listening,* depicts the plight of a boy orphan of about six who is caught in a struggle for custody between two aunts of very different social backgrounds. Though Stew and I weren't orphans, and though our aunts were not seeking our custody, we did have the experience of living in one after another strange household where aunts of contrasting dispositions gathered us into their ample care. I recognized in the little boy's eyes the emergence of essential survival tactics under such conditions. He was quietly compliant, yet wary. How long any particular domestic setting would last was unknown. He had to gauge contrasting temperaments and learn to play upon them for the security and affection he needed. And, in the film, it was a brief visit from the alcoholic father who had abandoned him to the care of these aunts that taught the little fellow how to assert himself, how, finally, to determine that the choice of homes was *his* choice. I could have learned a lot from that boy had I known him when I was his age.

After Mother's divorce and our move to Houston, I saw a lot more of my Stewart aunts than of the Jerome sisters. Aunt Peggy, who bathed me in more than water, was the youngest and dearest of my three Stewart aunts—all powerful, colorful women, who seemed to overshadow their men in personality and stability. Audrey, the oldest, was a teenager when the Stewart family moved to Oklahoma. They seem to have settled on land owned by Jack Summers, whom I knew as Big Jack, a frightening, fat blind man with a huge dent in the front part of his bald skull. He presided in awesome silence over their mansion in Muskogee. He had appeared out of Missouri with a mysterious past (it was rumored that he had killed a man). Big Jack had prospered in partnership with a rich rancher named Charles M. Haskell who became Oklahoma's first governor and who, in 1909, was indicted by the federal government for conspiracy to defraud the Creek Nation of its land holdings. Jack got Audrey pregnant when she was fifteen (about the time Mother was born), and they were married.

My grandfather John Stewart was apparently a weak man, but his wife, according to my mother, Gwen, "had spunk and I'm sure never gave Papa a chance to have a say about living." That is from the brief memoir I quoted earlier—a few pages she wrote for one of our daughters in 1984 (the year before she died). She says about her mother:

> We moved a lot. She worked in a dry goods store some. We always kept some boarders. I was her errand "person"—on skates. Haskell had an oil boom so Mama fed the drillers, too, tool dressers, and roughnecks—packed aluminum pails. She canned fruit, baked bread, and all the other ways she knew to keep Peg and me in school. She was a pushover for book salesmen. *The Book of Knowledge* was our world.
>
> Orpha was married and had our dear baby girl. The marriage didn't last too long and Orpha and Maxine came to live with us at a very early age. We moved to Tulsa in 1919 when I was 12 [she was born in February, 1907; Oklahoma became a state that November] and started in high school. Mama rented a big two story house one block from the Y.W.C.A. I had learned to swim in school so the "Y" was my hang-out and hang-up. We had quite a few roomers and boarders there and I guess things weren't bad. I

never felt poor or disadvantaged. Mama made clothes and kept us housed and fed—only I never had enough shoes to suit me. I was a Girl Scout and loved hiking and camping out.

Peggy quit high school and took a business course—so she had clothes and shoes and sometimes I grew green with envy. Mama's efforts got me (her last hope) through with a diploma. I was only 16 and too young to work, so I swam!

She won a number of awards for her swimming. And a treasured family tale is of how she was nearly thrown out of her Senior Life-Saving class for biting the instructor. He was holding her under for her to practice a release, but she couldn't free herself, so she bit his thumb. Not an approved technique, but it worked. She continues her story:

Mama and Papa died in 1925—she of heart disfunction after pneumonia and he of cancer of the stomach. In the meantime I grew up some—never the best—sometimes better. I loved school and had visions of teaching Phys. Ed. Always physical, not much mental. I had the usual amount of highschool dates, dances, etc. After graduation I worked some. Having taken typing in school, I was equipped to hold down copy work, also shorthand, but I was still young.

After Mama and Papa died I guess I needed a home of my own. I had my eye on Ralph. He came from a nice family and they all courted me. So, December 30, 1925, Ralph and I were married. We were poor—together we made $210 [a month]. Orpha told me how not to get pregnant (just take a sodawater douche). Well, it did take four months before the seed caught on.

The first three months (morning sickness) were hard to hide from my employer. Ralph thought we could have this child without anyone catching on that we had been sleeping together. We would see old friends and he would say "don't tell them." [I have no idea why he wanted to keep her pregnancy a secret.] It became quite obvious after five months because I was healthy and happy and no one thought of diet for a prospective mother—I plain bloomed. That was over February 8, 1927, just four minutes before my twentieth birthday. Ralph gave me a new purse with five ten-dollar gold pieces in it. I thought they were new pennies. I never knew where he got the money for such a gift.

In the Stewart family, after Audrey came a brother, Blake, who was gassed in World War I and seemed very quiet and strange thereafter. He worked in the oil fields—a driller—most of his life, though I remember visiting him at an army base in the thirties, where he was earning the famous twenty-one dollars a month regular soldiers were paid until salaries were raised to fifty dollars in World War II. (He may have been in the National Guard, serving summer duty.) I remember him sitting with his chair leaning back against a barracks wall, his wide-brimmed dress uniform hat tipped forward over his face, his heavy boots and puttees.

Audrey's son, Little Jack, went to a prep school in the East decked out in a racoon coat in a luxury convertible—and promptly flunked out. Back in Oklahoma, an alcoholic, he gambled, caroused, ending up time after time in jail, then went off to Hollywood, played bit parts in movies, and dissipated in high style. He owned a three thousand acre ranch between Muskogee and Haskell to which Audrey moved after Big Jack died. She ran the place while Jack played.

✦   ✦   ✦

At the time we moved to Texas, Audrey and Big Jack still lived in Muskogee in a house that was a wonderland to me. It had plate glass windows like sheets of ice blanking the gray stone. Big Jack mostly sat in a den with huge leather chairs, a wolf at his side, isolated in his blindness, never becoming accustomed to walking even around the house. (His police dog, Mickey, was actually—I am told—very gentle: I never got close enough to find out.) Sometimes I would see him feeling his way down the hall in a satin dressing-gown, and I would streak off through the endless corridors that led to rooms that led to rooms that opened embarrassingly into bedrooms, beyond which were bathrooms with enormous fixtures that opened onto sun porches. Panting, I would find the teak-smelling room with the exerciser, rest myself in the wide canvas strap like a swing, turn the switch, and jiggle myself to insensibility.

Their servant, Old Rob, who remembered the Civil War, stepped off the sidewalk when a white person approached, doffed his hat, and bowed his head. The only inhabitant of that house who seemed to know I was there, he would take me through the garden (in which I could easily get lost) and toothlessly tell me stories that were all the more frightening because I could hardly understand his dialect. His wife Lilly, the cook, a skinny little white-headed lady, would sometimes let me into their quarters above the garage where a large, luminous cardboard skeleton hung on the wall at the head of the stairs to their entrance. She churned in the basement, and the *knock, knock, knock* of the stick on the keg would echo through the cool, summer, adult, and darkly shaded house.

I would go to the attic, where there were steamer trunks and souvenirs of Egypt and my aunt's old hats—a yard wide, velvety with great arched ostrich plumes. There was a helmet and dented canteen from the War, a bayonet, a sword—all these memorabilia collected by Uncle Blake. In the attic was also a dressing dummy, standing with dignity with an undefined swelling bust and no head. I dressed it in Audrey's stored and fancy outdated gowns. In the trunks were postcards from the Orient, photos of Audrey—on a camel by the pyramids, by the Eiffel Tower, in an unidentified jungle wearing a pith helmet. Sachet. Strange bottles with aromas intoxicatingly sweet. An endless attic with unlit gables, except for dusty, stained-glass, round windows. There I was safe from my uncle and his dog.

From time to time they hired women to help tend Big Jack, but he molested them, and they all soon quit, and Audrey was too busy to bother with him. She would hop in her Pierce-Arrow limousine and tootle out to the country club with me riding in back, behind the glass panel intended to separate a chauffeur from the passengers. There were pull-down seats and a built-in bar to play with. At the country club I swam while she golfed, or, better, I would sneak around the locker rooms (of either sex: I was young enough to be neutral) and lounges, watching adults in their end-less performances. I remained hushed so as not to spoil the show, the scandalous stories and mannered gestures, the remarkable clothing and mysterious moods. Audrey had won many trophies for golfing all over the country, and she spent most of her summer days at the club. After her game she might putt with me on the club's putting green. Then we would go up to the lounge for a drink. She was a handsome horse of a woman of boisterous humor with bunions like granite and removable teeth, who loved me with hearty indifference. She thought I should get more sun. But she didn't really give a damn. She let me watch and knew she was a show.

For example, we were sitting on the lounge porch one after-noon with a group of women. Someone mentioned false teeth. Aunt Audrey popped both of her plates out of her mouth and held them in her hands. "Here're mine," she said. "Wanna see 'em?" I shrank in embarrassment for being with her.

✦　✦　✦

Audrey's Blaze

Aunt Audrey had it: Oh, I was convinced
nothing would wear like gold, the way she blazed,
a wheel fluttering, strung with electric dance;
but she turned fifty—and was reappraised.
I know. I peeked in the bedroom, saw her peel:

her shinbones stood like poles above her dress,
and how I stared at my first sight of Woman—
bosoms like symbols of all fishiness
swinging upon her ribcage like the lanterns
forsaken on lattice after carnival,

and flesh, in fact, appeared to stream in tatters
of crepe, wind-whipped, and too entwined to fall.
Gay oranges and purples, now rain-spotted;
lime streaked the buttery pennants of her hair,
and chalky pink were now the cheeks that waited

like posters for another day of fair,
that would not come (she knew it), or that *would* come,
blaring and bannering, fun for young and old,
with desperate paint to banish any mood one
might have, reflecting, how has peeled the gold.

✦ ✦ ✦

I am sitting on a Shetland pony by the French window with a little balcony outside Big Jack's study. The cotton suit I am wearing has short pants and sleeves, one-piece but belted. I am grinning at the man who goes house-to-house with this pony to take pictures of children.

✦ ✦ ✦

Orpha, like Audrey, had little physical beauty, though her daughter Maxine was stunning. When we moved to Houston, Maxine had married an army air force captain who was away in training, so she was living with her mother and stepfather Louie. Orpha claimed to have delivered me; at least, she was the nurse on duty when I was born. She was the most expert cook in the family, specializing in such dishes as green beans cooked for hours with bacon, potato salad, fried chicken, biscuits. "Don't we eat *good?*" she would exclaim as we sat down to a family meal. "Now you eat every bean and pea on your plate," she would say to me raucously, knowing the pun embarrassed me. They were always urging me to eat more because I was so tiny, so meals were ordeals. Orpha was the daffy member of the family, and she sometimes said outrageous things that made me doubt her sanity. Louie was a quiet but quick-tempered fellow I steered away from. A short, thin, dark German, he had little use for children and no interest in them. He loosened up only with other men, in the kitchen, drinking highballs. A real man.

✦ ✦ ✦

Peggy and my mother, the younger Stewart sisters, had all the beauty the others lacked. Peggy was married briefly to a high-

103

school sweetheart, then to a rowdy, fast-living oilman, and they were part of Mother and Dad's social life in Oklahoma City. Divorced again, she had just remarried when we set out with Orpha to move from Tulsa to Houston.

Peggy's new husband was an Englishman, an executive of the Sun Oil Company, a wiry, witty, learned gentleman who did not fit Southwestern stereotypes at all. It was night as we drove into Dallas. Three-year-old Stew was sleeping beside me on the back seat. Aunt Peggy and our new Uncle Douglas were staying in a tourist court while looking for a house to buy in Dallas. Orpha looked back over her shoulder, telling me to say "*Comment allez-vous?*" I wished she would keep her mind and eyes on the traffic. Peggy had written that Douglas spoke French, among his other accomplishments.

At their cabin we met a tall, lean man with a little moustache that looked like Charlie Chaplin's. He bent to shake my hand, and I delivered my French greeting in a tiny voice.

"*Oh, parlez vous français?*" he responded, and followed it up with a stream of what was gibberish to me.

✦   ✦   ✦

My memory of festive family gatherings is primarily of these Stewart sisters and their men, whether in Oklahoma or Texas. When I was very young the women taught me to fill in as a fourth for their bridge games (the men didn't play). We bid by Culbertson honor count; Goren's point count was not introduced until 1949. Generally Orpha was my partner, and we generally lost. Maybe folks attributed that to my youth, but I am certain that at least once she bid us to game on a suit of which she was holding only the top three cards. She often did things like that, things I had been taught never to do in bridge. I was also often a fourth for games of mah-jong, played with a beautiful set of ivory tiles that came in a case of inlaid wood.

Most holidays involved a lot of card playing. Or the gang of women would be leaning long hours over jigsaw puzzles spread on a card table. I would sit on the couch, pretending to read, and eavesdrop on the ladies' unselfconscious madness and mystery. The Stewart sisters did not dote on me in the way the Jerome sisters did. I'm sure they loved me just as much, but they had one another, their men, and the world for entertainment, and if I was to participate it had to be on their terms. For example, I don't remember any of them, even Mother, reading to me. Of course I had long been old enough to read for myself by the time we moved to Texas, so there was less need.

✦   ✦   ✦

We are driving from Houston to Dallas. I am nine. Orpha, Louie, and Mother are all in the front seat, Maxine in back with Stew and me. Stew, newly four, starts to say something and I cut him off to finish the idea for him. Then I have a sudden misgiving about what I have done. "I do that too much," I say. "I say things before he can say them so people will think I am smart."

Aunt Orpha turns to speak to me with uncharacteristic softness, affectionately but gravely: "Well, you shouldn't do that, Juddy," she says.

It seems like an important moment—must have been, for so slight an exchange to remain in my mind. On the one hand I must have felt a surge of maturity—to be able to look at myself, judge myself, criticize myself. As I remember it, that was a new experience. On the other hand, there may have been an element in my statement that was fishing for a compliment or reassurance: "You *are* smart. You can't *help* it." And what I got instead was a gentle but thoughtful reproof.

✦   ✦   ✦

Our family and the Sauers (Orpha, Louie, and Maxine) were on our way to the new house Peggy and Douglas had purchased on Willowbrook Road on the outskirts of Dallas the Christmas after our move to Houston. Their place was actually a country estate— a rambling ranch-style house on vast grounds with a large barn and separate house for their black servants, Ruth and Jim. That Christmas still remains the most elegant in my memory—a gigantic tree lushly decorated and piled with presents that we could open only after everyone was up and had a formal breakfast in the long dining room, served by Ruth. For Christmas dinner we gathered there, too, and the table easily seated the eight of us. We left Tarbaby with the Collingwoods (Peggy and Douglas), since we couldn't keep him at our garage apartment. He became the first of a kennel, as Douglas began to take a keen interest in raising cockers.

Stew and I spent several summers with Aunt Peggy, but the first, when I was ten, I was left there without Stew. Here was Uncle Douglas—ramrod straight, thin, and very very British—an executive with the Sun Oil Company who went off to work each morning. Peggy would drive him in to the city and pick him up in the afternoons, and I often accompanied her, awed by the gleaming towers of Dallas, one of which had a giant red Pegasus (for Mobil) turning slowly on top. Uncle Douglas was somewhat cold and distant, but I remember liking him and looking forward to his coming home from work. He was witty, learned, and an ace on the badminton court, a game about which he was very serious. I remember breakfasts at the gleaming long table in their dining room—Douglas and Peggy sitting at either end, me sitting in the middle on one side. We were served, of course, by Ruth, in uniform. Ruth also cooked and cleaned the house. She was a very attractive, well-spoken, dignified young woman who had little time or patience for me, but I was very fond of and looked up to her. The dining room had windows on three sides, and these breakfasts always seemed to me to be full of sunshine and birdsong.

There were three main ways to spend the days. One—the least attractive to me—was with Peggy in the garden. I vividly remember the time I picked okra. Sometimes it seems as though my childhood was a long series of battles over okra. Whenever I said I didn't like it, some aunt would say, "But you haven't tried it the way I fix it," and would make me take at least a bit of gumbo, fried slices, or some other preparation of the hideous stuff. Eventually they all gave up trying. But I didn't know the vegetable was offensive even to pick. It has fine hairs that sting like nettle. After picking a batch I was so miserable I was in tears. Into the tub.

Peggy was usually already woozy from beer by the time she went to bring Douglas home from the office, and though they never fought or argued loudly in my presence, there was tension in the air. Both Peggy and Douglas were inclined to read after dinner, as was I—wonderful adult books from their shelves, such as *Seven Pillars of Wisdom* by T. E. Lawrence. Well, I didn't read that one, but I spent a lot of time studying the pictures. I did read one—on that visit or later—about British General Wolfe at Quebec; it occurred to me for the first time that the British had *their* heroes, too.

At any rate, one way to spend my days during my visits there was with Peggy, and that mostly meant working in the oven heat of the garden. I had better times with Jim. He was usually out around the barn, where there were chickens, guinea hens, Penny, and Ha'penny. Penny was a sheep, grown from a lamb they had treated as a pet, and Ha'penny was her daughter. These sheep were very friendly, coming up readily for petting, and I could ride them at least a few feet before they scrunched down their hindquarters and left me behind in the dust. One learned not to turn one's back to them. They often butted and knocked down those they could catch from the rear.

One of my jobs was to search for hen and guinea eggs—which might be anywhere around the barn or barnlot. The guineas were quite wild. "You can't catch a guinea hen," Jim told me—and, true enough, I couldn't, but I couldn't catch a chicken, either. When Ruth wanted a guinea for the table, Jim would shoot one with a slingshot and a rock (the kind of slingshot with rubber straps fastened to a wooden Y, commonly called *niggershooters* by whites; I remember pondering the paradox: Jim was a *nigger*, but he used a *niggershooter*). I admired his marksmanship. Indeed, I admired everything about Ruth and Jim, especially Jim, who seemed to like to have me tag along as he did chores around the estate. He took me fishing with long poles and worms in a rowboat on a nearby lake. And we would gather blackberries together. We were berrying once in a field (a later summer: Stew was there) when Jim spotted a snake head coming out of a hole in the crotch of a tree at about his eye level. He smashed the head with a rock, and the dead snake began sliding out and down the tree. It was a blacksnake about eight feet long: I remember Jim holding it up by the tail, his arm extended over his head, the snake's head trailing on the ground.

The third way to spend daytime hours was with the Keller kids at a considerably more luxurious estate across and down the road. The Kellers had their own swimming pool and lots of expensive toys, and their property was on the edge of woods that were good for endless exploring. Hunter, the older of the two boys, was my age, and the younger, Smitty, a little older than Stew. He was endearing like Stew, and made me homesick. I remember his coming into the house once while I was having breakfast with Peggy and Douglas. He asked for a glass of water. "Why, Smitty," said Peggy, "just drink from the hose in the yard."

"I'm not 'sposed to drink that water," he said with a pout. "It has third degree in it."

Peggy and Douglas laughed, and Peggy asked Ruth to give him a glass of water. She explained later to me that the "ground water" at the Kellers' came from an untested well, so they were only able to drink the water in the house. But the Collingwoods used the same well for the house and grounds, so it was safe.

Some such incident broke me down, however. Smitty's "third degree" reminded me of Stew in the Kiamichis. One morning Stew asked Mother, while she was dressing him, whether he could go barefooted. "Why, of course you can go barefooted," she said. "You go barefooted every day!" Stew broke into tears and bawled, "But I don't *want* to go barefoot!" He had hot and cold mixed up and would say things like "I'm too cold. Take off this sweater!" The cuteness, the adorableness of such confusion, invariably evoked a sharp pang of love in me.

At any rate Peggy found me crying in bed one evening.

"What's the matter?" she asked.

"I miss Stewky," I said. I was, indeed, homesick. So Peggy called to tell Mother she had better come and fetch me. I had been there ten days.

✦　✦　✦

108

Both Stew and I spent the summer of 1939 (when I was twelve and he was six) in Dallas and on Aunt Audrey's ranch near Haskell, Oklahoma. I suppose now that we were sent to our aunts to get us out of the way while Mother and Ott conducted the last stages of their romance before their wedding in December.

One day Peggy was laughing with Mother about fewmets. Peggy's last husband, Len, had sent her a copy of a new novel, *The Sword in the Stone,* by T. H. White, based on Arthurian legend. In that book an elderly knight tracks dragons by looking for fewmets, or dung; Peggy's ex had looked up *fewmet* in a dictionary and inscribed the book, "I thought of you when I found out that *fewmet* means 'dropping of a deer.'" That was the joke that aroused their laughter—the pun on *dear*—and as I reflect on it now, the whole situation seems surprisingly sophisticated to me. *Fewmet* is not in desk dictionaries (today, and probably not in 1939); my unabridged tells me it is a variation of *fumet,* which means dung in general, and, archaically, dung of a deer. It surprises me that people in and associated with my family were reading a lot of current fiction. Mother subscribed to the Book of the Month Club, at least after she and Ott were married, and there was a constant flow of current books through our home after this date. I read *The Sword in the Stone* while in Dallas, and I remember being delighted, thrilled, and amused by it.

✦　✦　✦

I asked Peggy a lot of questions about the car during the summer of 1939, studying it as I had studied airplanes from a book. I'd watched how adults drove it whenever I had the chance (Mother had no car). I knew all the steps, and I spent a good bit of time out in the car going through the motions of starting it, shifting gears, and turning the wheel.

One afternoon Peggy came out of the house carrying two pillows. She was in one of her dreamy states. "You'd like to drive it, wouldn't you?" she asked.

She put the pillows under me, then got in on the passenger side. I could hardly reach the pedals, but the next thing I knew I was driving. I pushed in the clutch and started the motor, shifted into reverse, eased the clutch out as Peggy instructed, and backed away from the house. Then I shifted into first, second, and third as we went down the long drive and turned into the lane without stopping. Peggy told me when to shift.

We went a few miles. All was going well until she directed me into a neighbor's drive to turn around to go back home. I headed down off the road into their drive all right, but I couldn't remember how to *stop* the car. "The brake! The brake!" Peggy yelled, but it was too late. We plowed at slow speed into one of the huge brick posts that stood on either side of the driveway.

Peggy took over the wheel, but the bumper was wedged in such a way that she couldn't back out. We walked home and called Douglas, who left work early to tend to the car. I remember that after he jumped on the bumper and freed the car he drove it home in silence. Riding beside him, I was impressed at the firmness of step of his heavy boots on the clutch and brake. Again and again I apologized. Finally, looking straight ahead at the road he said, "It's not your fault." This was the last I heard of the matter (and I didn't drive again until I was sixteen). I don't remember, during my childhood, that anyone in my presence ever mentioned Peggy's drinking.

✦   ✦   ✦

Peggy came out all right. After battling her alcohol problem for years, she straightened up in old age and gave it up. Apparently Douglas was generally regarded by the family as an S.O.B., and he may have contributed to Peggy's drinking problem. When Douglas retired they bought a house on a lake near Dallas, and Peggy became enthusiastic about fishing, acquiring a large inboard motorboat and boathouse. The last time I visited there, in the seventies, Douglas was of clear mind, but in a wheelchair. I enjoyed his company—as I always had. Peggy cared for him and spent much of her time out on her boat. Both died soon after that visit—first Peggy, then Douglas, who was about ten years older than she. They were snappish with one another from time to time, but each had a sharp sense of humor, too, and they kept their marriage together for over thirty years.

✦   ✦   ✦

Audrey drove down to Dallas in 1939 to pick up Stew and me and take us back to Oklahoma. She and Little Jack were living at the ranch near Haskell, so we had a whole new range of experiences. The ranch house itself was long, low, and modern—one wing being occupied by Jack's long bedroom, bath, and an attached garage. Jack wasn't using it that summer. He was staying in town with one of his ex-wives, trying to persuade her to marry him again. So Stew and I used his bedroom. I was impressed by the crank telephone in the kitchen. It had a two-digit number. When the ring was something other than long-short, you could pick it up and listen in on the party line. When you placed a call, you cranked a handle, then told the operator what number you wanted. She sometimes said things like, "Beulah's not home, Audrey. She's over at the Bergstroms'. Do you want me to ring her there?"

Audrey and Jack were towering figures. With only a fifteen-year difference in their ages they looked like sister and brother rather than mother and son. Their resemblance grew as they both became white-headed. I based the characters of Harry and Olive in my novel, *The Fell of Dark*, on this pair, making my cousin seem a good bit more heroic and loving than he was in real life. Here is a rendering of Audrey on the ranch front porch from that book. The sheriff, Lew, speaks from my memory of her later years:

> Olive sipped her bourbon-on-the-rocks, ladylike, with her gown pulled up to her knees, her square, heavily bunioned feet propped and crossed like a man's, and yet she seemed strangely romantic and delicate. Seventy years. Not a woman—a *lady*—but tough as a lizard. Lew imagined they might have been in a penthouse, New York, above the neon metropolis, or by the sea, Riviera, or maybe the Bahamas, or Singapore. Lew thought of those places, knowing that Olive had seen them, the old she-goat, grand dame. Lew, as a boy, had seen pictures: huge black hats luxuriant with black ostrich plumes, steamer trucks, ship-

rail smiles. One by the pyramids, with Olive, beplumed, on a camel. An air of old travels stayed with her even back in cattle country. He imagined that, conversely, she had carried the scent of horse foam with her to Paris. And he bet they loved it; she must have gone over big.

I was afraid of Jack, but he was gone most of the time. Here he would come in his two-cockpit open plane, landing with a stream of dust in the pasture in front of the house. Or he would pull up in a Cadillac with a carload of drunken friends. Real men and their women. For a big, tough man, he had a surprisingly high, whiny voice. I remember him yelling at me after I had written my name with my finger on the dust of the trunk of a limousine. The car belonged to the orchestra leader, Sammy Kaye, who was in the house with some members of his orchestra, drinking. "Don't you know that makes permanent scratches in the paint?" he wailed. (I did know. Dad had bawled me out for doing that on our car some years before.) Jack sounded as though he were going to cry.

Behind the house was a large garden, then barn lots, a saddle and tool shed, and a huge barn. They had a couple of Shetland ponies that I could saddle and take Stew, who was six, out on adventures. They were very stubborn ponies, and Stew, especially, had a hard time keeping the one he rode in motion. In the pasture out in front of the ranch house was a hill, rather large for that flat country, with a patch of trees on top. We packed a picnic lunch one day and eventually got the ponies to the top of the hill. After we ate and started back, the ponies knew they were heading for the barn and raced at full tilt, but we managed to stay mounted.

We graduated to horses. I generally rode Lige, his name being the middle syllable of *Elijah*. The hired man would saddle him for me, and I would take off, exploring for miles. I occasionally rode with Jack, too, running fences or herding cattle from one pasture to another. Once Jack was on King, a dangerous stallion, and I was on Lige, riding about a hundred yards apart to the rear and on either side of about twenty steers. Something up front (maybe a snake) spooked a steer in the lead. The herd veered and found a place where the barbed wire was down at the edge of a cornfield. We had to ride through the high corn, stalks falling right and left, hooting and chasing to drive the bumping and jostling herd back to where the fence was broken and they could get out.

When we finally got them running through, heading for open pasture, one of the steers got a foot tangled in the barbed wire curled at the break. I watched from horseback as Jack, cursing, labored with his wire snips to free him, the steer kicking and tossing all the while.

In one pasture a second cousin, Sonny Hanlon (Jack's stepson by a former marriage), and I often played cowboy and Indian. There were groves of trees, a creek, low hills, and an abandoned Holy Roller Church (as we called it)—a little frame building that served any number of purposes for these games. We galloped around with cowboy and Indian yells, chasing one another and waving cap pistols for hours. Once, however, neither Lige nor I saw an upcoming fence, and Lige dove straight into it, throwing me over it. His neck was severely torn—a gash a foot long with blood pouring out of it. I led him back to the barn, and Jack washed him and sewed him up. Lige survived, but I was appalled at what I had done. These experiences made their way into *The Fell of Dark*, combined into one episode in which the horse of the protagonist gets his throat cut when he is tangled in wire during the cattle chase.

Jack's stallion, King, was considered too dangerous for anyone but Jack to ride, and he was kept penned, getting crazier and crazier as he aged because Jack was so seldom there. When the horse died in that pen the hogs got in and ate him. Jack was to marry again before he died in the sixties—by that time a derelict on Muskogee's version of skid row. But he still owned the ranch, and it went to his wife.

Stew and I took a bus from Muskogee to Tulsa to visit Mammaw and Marie, who were living in an apartment by 1939. Aunt Bonita had married and had a son, Pudge, with ears like batwings. Bonita and Marie took us to the zoo one day. As Stew and I walked along looking into the cages, they trailed behind, giggling. Bonita had just read Steinbeck's new novel, *The Grapes of Wrath*, which was considered scandalous in Oklahoma. She was apparently telling Marie some of the racier tidbits. The only thing I overheard clearly was, "And he never buttoned his fly." Not until I read the book some years later did I know she was talking about Granpa.

We spent weeks in Oklahoma that summer, and the question of our seeing Dad was never mentioned. I didn't ask for news of him, and my family didn't offer any.

◆　◆　◆

We were back visiting the Collingwoods most summers. After the war started, a new factor in the lives of Peggy and Douglas was a pair of English cadets Douglas had met and invited often to their home. These handsome young men were in a program to train them as pilots for the RAF, and they added immensely to the weekend badminton games, romps with the dogs, and general fun around Dallas on the weekends, which included weekly atten- dance at operettas in an amphitheater at the grounds built for the Centennial. We saw productions of *The Chocolate Soldier, Naughty Marietta, Babes in Toyland, Rose Marie,* and several by Gilbert and Sullivan. From time to time these would be spiced up with allu- sions to current events, as when a woman explained that she was "Sittin' knittin' for Britain."

These summers—1937 to 1942—comprised my only young ex- posure to rural living—and to a social class a cut above our own. Above all, though, they gave me the impression that women ran the world. When the Stewart sisters gathered, the house filled with laughter and family tales. Audrey was famous for insisting on rearranging the furniture in the houses of her sisters, especially when they all had a little to drink. Orpha had a marvelous sense of humor and was lovably rattlebrained, especially when drinking, which meant at most gatherings. And Peggy, wistful, alluring, lovely Peggy, always my mother's favorite, had eyes that danced with wicked thoughts. I loved them all, but I was at times *in* love with Peggy.

7

Showtime!

In the upstairs hall of Orpha and Louie's house in Houston I watched Stew climb the stairs—wobbly, pudgy, pulling himself up with a hand on the rail. We were nine and three. At the top of the stairs was a full-length mirror. As he approached I jumped forward to make a scary image in the mirror—my hands lifted like claws, my face in a hideous grimace—and I let out a monster roar. I wanted to make an image on the screen as in a horror movie. It was just a show. The monster wasn't real. It was meant as a joke. Stew screamed and fell backwards and tumbled clear down the stairs and cried long and hard. This was not funny.

✦   ✦   ✦

When Uncle Louie insisted that we move out of the Sauer household on Shakespeare Road, Mother, who now had a job as a secretary for an oil company downtown, brought home seventy-five dollars every month. She could afford a garage apartment if we shared it. So we moved to our first of two garage apartments on Buffalo Speedway, our housemate Lois and Rosie (our black maid, hired at a dollar a day) came into our lives, and Mother began taking seriously her role as head of the family. For example, each person was to learn one new word each day and explain it to the others at the dinner table. I was impressed by her rationale. "Families need traditions," she said. "We are going to start a tradition." Since I never remembered this tradition until dinner was on the table, it meant I had to dive at random into the dictionary in my room, learn a word, try to understand its pronunciation and definition, and try to remember all that until my turn came to recite at the table. I don't remember how Stew coped with this problem.

Lois and Mother were different from other women I grew up with. They read books. They had ideas. They talked about the news.

✦　✦　✦

Mother woke me in the night. She wanted me to listen to the radio. We heard a man screaming a strange language. He sounded angry. Now a voice in English was telling us what he was saying as he screamed in the background. I didn't understand the English any better than I did the German, but Mother told me that the man, Hitler, was starting a war in Europe. His army was invading Poland.

She woke me to hear King Edward VIII say that he could not marry the woman he loved, an American who has been divorced, and still be king. He was—a big word!—*abdicating.*

Later I was to copy freehand a portrait of Edward VIII that appeared on the cover of a Sunday supplement in the newspaper. I remember showing that drawing to Dad when he came to try to persuade Mother to return to him. That memory—and that of the boy in New Mexico asking "*Whut* war?"—enable me to frame the tempestuous events of the summer and fall that I was nine.

✦　✦　✦

I remember my young mother as lively, animated, quick-tongued. She was proud of the fact that she had been born in Indian Territory. She was less colorful and vibrant than her sisters, but was distinguished in other ways. They always turned to her as the "bright one." And they always cherished her as the youngest and most beautiful. This must have been a difficult autumn for her, getting a divorce, moving, working full-time, raising two boys, setting up a household, and setting about the business of getting herself a new husband.

I had one picked out for her, but he belonged to Lois. Hubbard (always called by his last name) was, aside from my father and Uncle Douglas, the most important model of manhood for me in my precollege years. A proofreader for *The Houston Press*, Hubbard got to read the funnies weeks ahead of time and so knew (but would never tell) how things were going to work out. Whenever he came to pick up Lois he would take time for a conversation with Stew and me, an adult sort of man-to-man conversation involving books, world affairs, views of life. Quiet, mannerly, well spoken, prematurely grey, he seemed a genuine alternative to the real men around me. Hubbard was the sort of person one wouldn't mind growing up to be.

✦ ✦ ✦

For as long as I can remember, I have been putting on shows. There was very little difference in my mind between play and play-acting. Whether I was performing as the Virgin Mother or the Indian Prince, it was all an act. I was standing on our pirate ship we built between our garage apartment and the adjoining one. It had a cabin below its plank deck and, above, high masts and yardarms to swing from. My sailor's scarf was sometimes a pirate flag, but this time it was a cape because I was the Indian Prince. To be the Indian Prince I needed the cape and my joy buzzer. A joy buzzer was one of those wind-up devices you conceal in your palm. When you shook hands with someone, or touched someone's back, a little tip was released that vibrated and tickled, the motor making a buzzing sound. You ordered joy buzzers for a quarter from ads in comic books.

I had mystified and menaced my buddies around the neighborhood with this device for some weeks, telling them that I was a reincarnated Indian Prince and my touch had magic powers. But now I wanted Herbert to roller-skate with me, and he said he was afraid to skate with an Indian Prince. I tried to convince him I was *not* an Indian Prince. I showed him the joy buzzer and how it worked, but he still would not believe I was not an Indian Prince. I explained that my cape was just an old sailor's scarf. He still was afraid. So I called up to Mother, who was having a party and was a bit tipsy, "Mother, are we Indians?" The answer I wanted was the plain truth—that we were not.

But the answer I got from Mother was "Sure!" and a *woowoowoowoo* as she clapped her fingertips against her lips. Herbert shot down the block like a streak, and I had to tackle him to talk to him again. Drat Mother and her playacting!

✦   ✦   ✦

Home, I learned early, could be made strange if you turned chairs over, blocked doors, draped bedclothes, and moved lamps. I remembered setting up Nazareth in Tulsa, using baby Stew for Jesus. The homes of aunts—especially Audrey's attic in Muskogee—seemed like stages with prop rooms to me. Perhaps what attracted me to poetry in the first place was that it could be memorized and performed. Though I didn't much care for tap-dancing (and lessons), I did love dressing up as a pirate and doing my shuffle, ball, *chain* before the assembled mothers at Brown-Duncan Department Store in Tulsa. "The hills, pardner, the hills!" That line is the refrain of a poem by Berton Braley that I memorized at age ten to recite in a declamation contest sponsored by the American Legion—and won a ten-dollar prize. In our garage-apartment I began putting on marionette shows in a little stage that had actual curtains and a flashlight spot. The marionettes had plaster of paris heads, hands, and feet for me to paint. I wrote the scripts in my head if not on paper.

I suspect that all this showing off was in compensation for my small size and immature appearance. It was my way of pleasing women, of evoking the praise that was taking the place of cuddling. But, as I relate it to clay modeling—at which I became moderately skillful—or to writing, which was to become my major occupation, I recognize also an urge to *do* something with life. Just living was never enough. I still have trouble understanding how most people can live without recording it in some way, making something of events. Life streams past so rapidly that unless you somehow *use* it, it will soon be gone. Using one's life, like eating the leftovers in the fridge, seemed to me to be a matter of simple economy. I don't sense pride or vanity in the impulse. I have never truly been satisfied with my performances in these various arts. But at least, I felt, I have not let life go to waste.

✦ ✦ ✦

Stew was my principal companion. I worshipped him, thinking he was the most beautiful (with his thick brown curls), most brilliant child who ever lived. We put on shows together. For example, in Oklahoma City we had staged the Jerome Brothers' Circus. The audience of family and neighbors was to sit on the back porch while the two of us performed various acrobatic feats and bicycle tricks in the backyard. My specialty was to zoom around to the front of the house, into the street, and up the driveway while Stew put up various ramps and devices for me to ride over or through on my next trip round. It rained on the day of the performance, so only Mother and a friend were there to watch us—from our roofed back porch. My bike slipped from under me during one of my trips around the house. I got a bad cut on the back of my head (which left a permanent scar), and that ended the performance.

Our showmanship got a great boost in 1937 from the Outdoor Panoramic Cavalcade of the History of the State of Texas, a show held over from the Texas Centennial in 1936 in Dallas. After my bout of homesickness at Aunt Peggy's, Mother and Stew came up on the train to fetch me, and they were there for the weekend. Douglas took us to the Pan American Exhibition, which followed the preceding year's Texas Centennial on the same fairgrounds. And we saw the Cavalcade of Texas History. In a huge stadium actors rode horseback, fired rifles at each other as cowboys, Indians, Texans, Mexicans. There were antique cars and trucks, and a real train with a steam locomotive came hooting across the prairie scene past movie set buildings and houses. The next day Douglas bought us first class tickets for the overnight train ride home. That's the only time I have slept in a berth except on a troop train from Salt Lake City to Seattle in 1945.

Back home Stew and I decided to put on our own cavalcade. Our version began, as did the one in Dallas, with the landing of De Soto on the Texas coast. We had found a sheet of corrugated metal that served as one side of the bow of De Soto's ship. I also found a ten-foot carpenter's bench that someone had abandoned. We turned the bench upside down and rigged the metal to its legs, then rested the front edge on a pair of roller-skates. Stew stood in front as De Soto, wearing a black felt cowboy hat with its brim folded in on both sides to make it look like one of those pointed metal hats worn by the Conquistadors, and, out of sight of the audience, I shoved the bow of the ship into view with Stew riding it grandly, his hand shading his eyes as he viewed the Texas shore.

The climax was the fall of the Alamo. For this event the bench was stood on end, and I climbed to the top. Stew was the Mexicans, again in his cowboy hat with brim turned under to represent their helmets. After hooting like an attacking army and making a lot of *kggh, kggh* noises—throat sounds for gunshot—he toppled the bench, and I rode it screaming to the ground. My screams were not all acting. My leg was skewered on a protruding nail. I still have a purple scar to memorialize that battle—my second permanent reminder of the dangers of show business.

Central to all this drama was Jimmy's scarf—the sailor's scarf I had been given in 1931. That scarf became cape, turban, loincloth, and skimpy toga. I learned to snap it like a whip at Stew's bottom, and it would be my muleta if Stew would be the bull. It figured in every production.

✦　✦　✦

A couple of years later we were living on the second floor of a house on Youpon Street. At this house we had access to a basement—where the other guys and I roller-skated, punched a punching bag, and necked with girls—and a garage, where Stew and I set up the Garage Playhouse. Here we had a six-inch platform and curtains (sheets hung from a joist). None of my friends was theatrically inclined, which was just fine, as they provided an audience for the two of us. My favorite of the many plays we performed there was *The Pit and the Pendulum.* I would lie writhing on the floor tied up with ropes while Stew, from offstage, lowered the pendulum. The latter was a curtain rod with threads tied to each end. With the thread at its tip he could make the pendulum swing and with the other end, which was over a rafter, he could lower it until it grazed my ropes. These magically dropped off. Then I got to my knees as the walls (cardboard, shoved by Stew) moved me toward the pit. Suddenly the walls would fly back (usually falling completely), and Stew, cowboy hat turned inside out to look French, would leap in and grab my arm as I toppled fainting into the abyss. He was to explain in a ringing voice (which never quite rang: he was timid) that he was General La Salle, and the French army had entered Toledo, and the Inquisition was over in Ohio.

Stew was not always the stagehand and supporting actor. He played the title role in our production of *Rip Van Winkle.* He would walk on stage, stretch, yawn, and slump to sleep, while, for twenty minutes, I performed twenty years of American history—the Boston Tea Party, Bunker Hill, Benedict Arnold, George Washington, and Nathan Hale, Yorktown, and the Constitutional Convention. Then I would disappear behind a primitive scrim (cheesecloth), and Stew, who had surreptitiously fastened on a cotton beard during his nap, would yawn, stretch, get up, and walk off. Curtain. We simplified stories somewhat because our cast was small and I could never depend on Stew to say lines loud enough to be heard.

✦   ✦   ✦

Mother made me a sailor suit for the British navy because I was one of the chorus in *HMS Pinafore.* The music teacher told me not to sing, but only to mouth the words, since I couldn't carry a tune. But this was a class production, so I was included, and, besides, the more sailors they had, the better.

I liked memorizing the words and dancing in time with the

other boys (some of whom were girls). Many of the songs were funny poems, and I did like funny poetry.

✦ ✦ ✦

I think I liked being on stage, too. I don't know that I ever *saw* a play on a stage—except operettas in the amphitheater in Dallas and Thanksgiving programs at school assemblies when the Pilgrims met the Indians for dinner—until I acted in one in the eighth grade. For many years I kept a long, thin volume entitled *101 Famous Poems*, with an oval picture of each poet at the head of his or her poem. Inside it was inscribed, "For Jud Jerome, the best boy actor in *Danger at the Door*, 1940." That play, a detective story, was our class's entry in a drama competition of some sort, and we won, but I can't imagine how. I was the detective. Somewhere in the first scene, one of the actors gave a line from the second and last scene by accident, and the rest of us simply followed that cue. The ending must have occurred three times. Familiar passages kept recurring like Grape-Nuts burped all day from breakfast. We were hysterical, terrified, dared not look across the lights at our patient schoolmates, and saw no possibility of the thing ever really ending, as each line seemed to bring on an entrance or a response (from Scene I) that swung us always right back into the misty mid-regions of Weir. Somehow we did manage to bring it to a conclusion and the applause was thunderous.

How I studied that anthology! I lost my copy some years ago, but it has been reissued by Contemporary Books, so I was able to review the kind of poetry that influenced me at age thirteen. There's a lot of sentiment and moralism in these poems, but many evoke fond memories: James Whitcomb Riley's "Out to Old Aunt Mary's," Tennyson's "Charge of the Light Brigade," Sam Walter Foss's "The House by the Side of the Road" ("But let me live by the side of the road / And be a friend to man."), Francis William Bourdillon's "The Night Has a Thousand Eyes," grim-looking, young Alan Seeger's "I Have a Rendezvous with Death," Lt. Col. John McCrae's "In Flanders Fields," Whitman's "O Captain! My Captain!," Oliver Wendell Holmes' "The Chambered Nautilus" and "The Deacon's Masterpiece or 'The One-Hoss Shay'," Words-worth's "The Daffodils," Emerson's "The Snowstorm" (a favorite of this Houston boy!), Longfellow's "Hiawatha's Childhood" and "Paul Revere's Ride," Sandburg's "Grass," Joaquin Miller's "Co-lumbus" ("Why, you shall say, at break of day: / 'Sail on! sail on! sail on! sail on!'"), Kipling's "Recessional," Lindsay's "Abraham Lincoln Walks at Midnight" (I memorized this one, and recited it somberly), Eugene Field's "The Duel" ("The gingham dog and the calico cat / Side by side on the table sat;"), Lanier's "Song of the Chattahoochee," Ella Wheeler Wilcox's "Solitude" ("Laugh, and the world laughs with you, / Weep, and you weep alone."), Leigh Hunt's "Abou Ben Adhem," Poe's "The Bells," Henry Holcomb Bennet's "The Flag" ("Hats off! / Along the street there comes / A blare of bugles, a ruffle of drums . . ."), Mary Howitt's "The Spider and the Fly" (sexy, that one: "Up jumped the cunning spider, and fiercely held her fast, / He dragged her up his winding stair, into his dismal den. . . ."), Guest's "Home," and Millay's "Renascence." In a prose supplement there is "The Gettysburg Address" (which I memorized), "The Ten Commandments," "Magna Carta," Patrick Henry's speech ending "give me liberty or give me death!" and "The Declaration of Independence" (of which I memorized the first paragraph). It grieves me to think that chil-dren today probably lack such education as I pursued voluntarily and with gusto.

◆　◆　◆

There was no "legitimate" theater in Houston that I knew of. Occasionally the motion picture theaters would have personal ap-pearances (I remember seeing Zazu Pitts on the street, looking, as an earlier dramatic character described herself, "like an old peeled wall") or special performances by people like yo-yo artists or magi-cians. Thurstone the magician made a great difference in my life because he talked too much. He said, for instance, that when he pointed, an adult looked to see what he pointed at, but a child watched his hand. I thereafter watched his hand, and the illusion of magic was replaced by the much more exciting recognition of skill. I went up on stage with a gang of kids, and all of us put our hands on a birdcage which he held in his hands. There was a presto and violent jerk and the cage had gone. The bird must have been smashed. I learned of the expendability of canaries. Thurstone levitated a girl with a sheet over her, walked her all around the stage floating in mid-air, and then said, "And now I am going to show you something you will remember all the days of your life." He jerked the sheet off, and she was gone. I learned that people will never forget things you tell them they will never forget for the rest of their lives. *Hellzapoppin'* with Olsen and Johnson came to our high school auditorium and tore down some assumptions about the relation between performers and audience. The cast kept drawing people from the crowd into their shenanigans. I loved the elaborate marionette shows presented in some school assemblies or at department stores downtown, and the traveling exhibition of *The Holy Land*—a vast display of little figures representing scenes from the life of Jesus. Lazarus would come out of the cave carrying his bed, then back into it and lie down again, repeating this action endlessly as the crowd filed past. The show went on all by itself. Barnum and Bailey brought their huge tent to town every year. I would go to the fairgrounds early to watch the crew put it up. A gang of roustabouts formed a circle around each stake as they came to it and swung sledge hammers to strike it in turn, a circle of rhythmically rising and falling hammers like a rotating flower. I liked to sneak around the trailers and costume tents and animal tents. How do they put this show on? I wanted to know. How did they get all those clowns into the little car? It could only be from a hole in the floor, yet I hadn't seen them dig one. And though I was thrilled by the performances themselves, what really drew me were the sideshows, the freaks, the boy with a pinhead, the eight-hundred-pound lady ("All this meat and no potatoes," she would say with a wink), the bearded woman, the half-man-half-woman, the African ladies with platter lips, the two-headed pig, the sword-swallower, the fire-eater. Most were fakes, I knew, which did not decrease my admiration. I couldn't learn to be a freak, but I *could* learn how to fake.

124

When I was about thirteen someone gave me a ventriloquist dummy modeled on Charlie McCarthy, so, of course, I took up ventriloquism, studying the art in a book from the library. I read another on magic, learned a few tricks and bought the apparatus for others from a store that specialized in such things. But I preferred performing with the dummy, whom I named Eugene. Mother knitted a little sweater and sewed a wardrobe for him. I wrote and memorized humorous dialogues and practiced a voice quite unlike my normal voice and taught myself how to talk without moving my lips. When the show was ready I performed it for our Boy Scout troop. Word got around, and I was invited to all sorts of places—lodges, clubs, church groups—and put on a half-hour show for five dollars. That was the best money I had ever made, but there weren't enough jobs—and soon all the likely places in our area of town had seen my show.

◆ ◆ ◆

Mother and Ott's room was a sanctum I never entered when they were home except with express permission. It was always the cleanest, neatest room in the house, and the coolest and darkest, for the drapes were always drawn.

Alone, though, I had explored Mother's dresser drawers (all scented with sachet) and come upon her diaphragm. Not knowing what it was, I opened the little folder of instructions in its box, and was shocked to see explicit drawings of how it was to be installed. Gradually I deduced what it was for. I wondered, does she do *that?* With *Ott,* of all people?

One afternoon, though, I was simply lying on their bed reading *Ben Hur.* I was wearing nothing but the sailor scarf as a loin cloth and eating huge purple grapes, immensely enjoying my sojourn in biblical times. Suddenly I was suffused by an inexplicable sense of euphoria. It was a feeling that it is good to be alive in a vibrantly good world. I jumped up, dashed out of the room, slapped out the front screen door, and ran as fast as I could around a couple of blocks, then came back in, sweating now, returned to the bed, picked up the book and read on.

Theatricality was in my blood from an early age, and my experiences with drama continued as long as I lived in the Southwest (and while I served overseas in the army). Teachers in high school often called upon me for readings of speeches from *Macbeth* and *A Midsummer Night's Dream,* and readings of poetry. So, though I did not try out for plays in high school, I thought I had some acting ability. I did try out during my first year at the University of Oklahoma, and I was cast as Jake, the teenage son, in *Papa Is All.* This play, all in Pennsylvania Dutch accent, was a great success, and we were invited to perform it at a number of army and navy bases near Norman (including Gene Autry Field). Packing the cast into a university bus, mounting the set in limited and strange spaces, getting into costume and make-up was a real thrill. The military audiences were great—roaring with laughter at jokes we hadn't even realized were in the script. For example, in the play, a woman is visiting the family. She excuses herself and exits. After some time she comes back onstage with a line about finding something in a Sears catalog. At that the soldiers and sailors would stop the show with laughter. The audience at the University, the director, and the cast hadn't caught on till these men showed us that where she had been was to the outhouse. How we needed the servicemen and they needed us. How they needed illusion, and how much more real was our hour upon the stage than, for example, KP, close-order drill, the facts of life.

Some of the humor was backstage. Melvin Alpern, who played the mean and stingy Papa, had to cross the stage angrily and jerk open the door of his daughter's bedroom. He looks inside, then accuses her of extravagance. "To bed you go mit candles burning?" he thunders.

The prompter sat behind that door. During one performance, when Mel roared that line, the boy sitting there quietly asked, "Who's this guy 'Candles Burning'?" Mel slammed the door on cue and turned before he caught the joke. Then the problem was keeping a straight face, which he barely managed to do. I feared breaking up in each performance at the climax of the play. The title means "Papa is dead," and it's Jake's line. Jake has plenty of motivation for doing his father, the old tyrant, in, and finally gets up his nerve to do so—offstage, on a car trip. He returns to the house and enters, his head hanging in shame. "Papa is all anymore, Mamma," he says.

"You lifted your hand against your father?" is Mamma's line, and then comes the line I dreaded:

"No, Mamma. A monkey wrench only." (Papa, unfortunately, survives that blow.)

Now I was *in* (at least for a while) the real world backstage, seeing how it was done, knowing the clever people, and seeing the props assembled. I learned to paint to look more natural. I saw what it was like to put on the show, to steal a glance at the crowd, to hold a grimace while they laughed, to labor with all sincerity to make them believe my lie. I was not much of an actor, but I began to have a sense of how it felt to walk in another's skin.

The next production of University Theater was *Tomorrow the World*, about an American family that adopts, for the duration of the war, the son of a friend in Germany. The child, about twelve, turns out to be a member of Hitler Youth. I tried out for the adult parts, but the director most seriously considered me for the part of the little boy—which gives you some idea of what I looked like. He finally decided, however, that I looked a bit too old, so they found an eleven-year-old to do the part. The director kept me on, however, as dramatic coach, both for the boy and for some of the adult actors. As a souvenir of that play I know one line of German, which I spring on every German I meet. At one point the boy says to the family's German maid, "*Ich habe sofort bemerckt dass du für das vaterland arbeitest,*" meaning "I have already noticed that you work for the fatherland." It's a conversation-stopper.

✦   ✦   ✦

Before I went to college Dad had sent me a book called *Today in History.* It told about some event or events that had occurred on each day of the year. Why not put that on the radio? I asked myself. So I did some research in the university library and wrote up some five-minute narrations about these events, limiting myself to American history and giving the narrations a strong patriotic flavor. I took these to the director of the campus station, WNAD, and he was enthusiastic about the idea, so they were broadcast each day at noon.

That went on for some months. Although the program was short, it required hours of research in the library, as I tried to find material to make various obscure events seem dramatically significant and intriguing for our times. So I discovered the library. I had been to the public library in Houston often, of course, but never to a library where one could wander through floor after floor of stacks. I had no notion at first of how to go about research, but the demands of my radio program drove me to learn.

Eventually I dropped my daily program and began writing, instead, a weekly quarter-hour dramatic radio show, at first entitled "This Week in History," then, to give me more latitude, "Know Thou this Land," a title suggested by a friend, Bill Talkington, who said it was a partial translation of Goethe's *Kennst du das Land, wo die Zitronen blühn?* It was still patriotic and historical corn, but I had more time for research and could give more attention to problems of presentation. The experience was invaluable. I was writing for a deadline, getting the show into production each week by the skin of several people's teeth. Writing became an extremely unselfconscious process. I was never permitted the paralyzing luxury of thinking, "Now I am Writing—and it must be Immortal." I knew only that I had a couple of hours before dawn, and they were crying for the script.

I acted in those plays, too. We never rehearsed. Productions were casual. The scripts would be dittoed on the morning of the day the show was to appear. As we entered the studio the director would hand us a copy and whisper, "You're Samuel." And moments later we were on the air—all over Oklahoma. It was all this-will-do and who-will-know? and on-with-the-show. Aunt Marie wrote a fan letter from Tulsa, and the station director was very proud of it (so I never told him that Mrs. Huffine was my father's sister).

A frequent actor in my radio scripts (also in the cast of *Papa*—as the policeman) was my greatest buddy during my first year at college. He had a room next to mine in the first dormitory I was assigned to. This was John Chrystal, from Coon Rapids, Iowa, who is now a prominent Iowa banker and farmer and an informal agricultural consultant to the Soviet Union. John often helped me brush up my scripts. For example, he was to play a Frenchman, for whom I had written dialogue in what I conceived to be a French accent—with phrases such as "*zee hour has arreevay!*" John pointed out that the French do not spell their language, "*Wee Wee m'zure.*"

Why my big interest in radio? I am certain that I never thought that I would eventually become a radio or movie writer or write for the stage. (Television was, of course, still in the realm of science fiction. It existed—I had seen a demonstration of it in a school assembly. The 1936 Democratic convention was televised, though not, of course, publicly broadcast. But it was not in homes until after the war, and one did not think of it as a medium for drama.)

The director of the station convinced me that there was an art to writing radio scripts. We had read Archibald MacLeish's *The Fall of the City* in English class. Now he directed me to other radio scripts by MacLeish and by Arch Oboler and Norman Corwin to use as models. I remember one lesson in particular. I tended to clutter my scripts with sound effects. The sound-effect technician had a little booth in a back corner of the studio. He (or sometimes she) would set the needle on records of recorded sounds to bring in "night sounds" (crying insects) or a train whistle or whatever the script called for. He had a door with a knob to open and close for that sound. He had shoes and a sanded board for walking sounds . . . and so on. I thought that part of good scriptwriting was to make full use of the sound technician's range of effects.

But, said this wise director, that's not the point at all. He said you use sound sparingly but significantly. He pointed out a script in one of the collections I had borrowed from the library. It was about Anne Rutledge, written (I believe) by Corwin. At the end of the half-hour script Lincoln has left her to set out on his career as a lawyer. And the closing moments of the play are all sound effects. We hear her weary steps as Anne, left alone, climbs the stairs. We hear her open and close the door to her bedroom. Then we infer her hopeless mood from the sound of the bedsprings as she sits. We are to deduce from that sound that she recognizes that Lincoln will never return.

◆　◆　◆

Drafted in 1945, between VE-Day and VJ-Day, I arrived in November on Okinawa to become part of the Occupation Force. Within days after our arrival the island was hit by Typhoon Mary, in which, I believe, the navy lost more ships than it had at Pearl Harbor. I wrote a musical review in commemoration of that event. Several men in the small phototechnical unit to which I was assigned and a number of Red Cross girls and nurses from nearby barracks had musical instruments and talent.

My loose connecting script was intended to tie their performances together into a kind of story. All I remember from it are excruciating jokes, such as when a man says romantically to a woman, "Let me run my hands through your hair. There were no towels in the washroom," and, on another occasion, "Let me run through your hair—barefooted." (Recently I watched a VCR tape of Fred Astaire and Ginger Rogers in 1935's *Top Hat*—still a first-rate movie. The barefooted joke occurs therein.) I remember writing the script and planning the review with the others involved, but I don't remember the performance itself. Maybe it never happened.

◆　◆　◆

The effect of my love affair with playacting was to infuse my poetry with drama. Verse is the medium—the way the language is arranged—but the product is drama, the interchanges of imaginary personalities in imaginary situations. An individual poem is something someone says on some occasion, like a speech from a play. My experience with the theater has been chiefly mooning around the wings. But from there I learned to love the clean form of a play where the setting and description are clearly distinguished from what people say and do. I liked the passivity of the author—like a kid in a house full of adults—never speaking in his own voice. I like the swiftness of drama, its condensation and economy. And I like the conscious artificiality—for a novel pretends to be history, but a play pretends only to be a performance. Writing in dramatic form makes me feel strongly the obligation to entertain. My bad dreams are of an audience restless in the dark.

My theatrical moments have been those that induced fear or laughter because they gave me some perspective on my experience. I had to go to the spooky home of an aunt to see life. Elegant, bizarre, gaudy, phony, distorted, and spectacular experiences give me a sensation at the base of my spine that lets me know that the world and I are real—then I go back into it and am as absorbed as Lassie (who panted through her—or really *his*—performance without a thought of grooming or artifice). One of my daughters once asked if we were on someone's television set—and while part of me cried, oh God I wish we were (wish that someone were watching), another part recognized that at the moment one asks such a question he is most truly alive, conscious, and human. The beasts know life is not a show, and we, like them, are bound to practical needs and mortality. But what excitement and fulfillment in illusion! Frame it for a moment in an imaginary proscenium arch, and life seems to have some point. The fact that we *can* so frame it may indicate that we may be able to give it meaning.

Another daughter mispronounced the word *clay* as *play*—and had a great sense of its significance. What are people made of? I would ask her. "Play." What are houses, trees, ideas, feelings, foods, and families made of? And she would answer with the single-mindedness of Poe's raven, "Play." She was, of course, right.

We have our moment in the air. Before cracking my head on the board a few times, I used to be a fairly fancy diver, and, having

sprung from the board, knowing that the water was certainly below, I relished the moment of contortion, of performance, and
neat disappearance at the end.

Diver

A parable: You behold
toes tightened like cords'
white on a burlapped board
and see below the chlorine
green dance electric with surface
swords and hear the hush
racketing in a tile tomb
overlit, too white, your thighs
too white, swollen above
your dripping knees (and each
drop hanging by a hair)
as on the balls of feet you rise,
your belly parting from trunks
where the hips hang, hands
lifting unbidden, and under
your arms the cold because
you tilt, drawing a knee
high, chin on chest,
waiting, ribs fanned,
until all stiffness suddenly
is sprung, the burlap lost,
a last touch of toes,
echo of lumber—late,
oh late is release of weight
in the spring, and now this moment
above the water, defining
everything: the right approach,
certain pace, life's
instant contortion, then
water and final grace.

We are called upon to act, not simply to be, but to make a bit of a show, not so much "showing off" as using the instant, achieving an artful goal, defying and then learning to get along with gravity (for the dive would have no meaning if we could suspend ourselves in the air and contort at leisure). It is not the most efficient way to get into the water. It is not—except finally, beautifully, and incredibly—realistic. It is best done nearly naked.

8

One of the Boys

An artist recently described to me an image in one of his paintings: "There is this body—myself—naked in the cup of a wave. I was trying to express the security I felt in the surf; a security I did not feel in my family and social relationships," he said. I knew instantly what he meant. After my initial fear of the ocean (in 1931 in Florida) I learned to love body surfing, though we did not use that term. It was just playing in the waves. But a trip to Galveston meant for me primarily throwing myself with abandon into powerful waves that would tumble and carry me again and again to the sand. For the most part you go limp, surrendering to the violent force encompassing you, yet you are alert and quick to respond to the decisive mini-seconds in which you can exercise control.

I think perhaps the greatest gift my mother gave me was a sense of security in the water. From the age of about eighteen months I knew the water would not hurt me (though the waves might be dangerous). You can always hold your breath. You float. You come up eventually. In salt water you can lie for hours on the water completely at ease with only the faintest sculling of your hands, borne by the sea's kindly swelling and subsiding warm bosom. Mother. Water. The sea.

My trust of the sea was shaken later, sailing in the Virgin Islands, where I learned a healthy fear of those vast depths and unpredictable currents and what they could do to a boat. And once I encountered my limits—this would be 1971—body surfing on Oahu in waves that towered ten or fifteen feet high as they smashed themselves on a steep beach. I had been tossed around for about a half hour by these massive, thundering combers, thrilled by my helplessness in their churning race, the inescapable soft, suffocating depths of their foam, the muscle of their hurling and the crash to bottom sand that knocked out of me the breath I held so long. I decided I was tired and should get back up on the beach for a rest. One last smash, my face crushed into the sand, and I got to my knees, only to be sucked back by the vacuum of another wave gathering its wild mass behind me, sucked back and up and tossed flat again, weak, now, and scared, and in the churning foam that covered my head, I dug my toes in and pulled myself forward desperately and finally collapsed on dry sand. I did not go back in that day, nor have I ever braved waves so immense again, though I have gone with gusto into wild surf in the Virgin Islands and Dominican Republic in more recent years. Submitting myself to surf remains for me a major symbol for survival by relaxing in the sweep of forces one cannot control, yet somehow managing to squirm out alive.

◆　◆　◆

Childhood stays in my memory as a series of summers with mostly blank spaces for school in between. Play was getting rougher as I found myself increasingly outside the succoring limits of home and the arms of women. Because of my small size I worked at earning acceptance by a kind of recklessness in games such as soccer and football, recklessness perhaps encouraged by my habit of denying pain. At school we played touch, and I wasn't much good at that, as I hadn't much skill at throwing or catching the ball, and didn't really understand the game very well. But after school, on vacant lots, we played tackle—teams made up of both boys and girls—and I threw myself into the line with such fearless enthusiasm the boys wanted me on their team for my ability to worm past the opposing linemen and dive into pumping knees. I was no good at baseball and avoided the game. When they made us play softball at school I was always the last to be chosen and always assigned to the outfield. It was boring to stand out in the sun wearing a heavy glove and wait for flies and grounders I could never catch. But I was fervent at shinny. One block of a street in the neighborhood had little traffic. There, with a sawed-off broom, its straw covered with friction tape, and a much-skinned-up volleyball, I skated like a demon. I played water polo with the same determination: I was fast, rough, could stay under for long periods (even swim with the ball under water), and the water compensated for my slight size and weight.

Though I was a very fast swimmer in all strokes, and had passed my Junior Life Saving exam, I was too small for the swimming team in junior high. I was, however, on the diving team for a brief time, but before our first meet I hit my head on the board doing a half-gainer and, another time, came out of a one-and-a-half to collide heads with a surfacing swimmer. I dropped off the team (which required after-school practice—a nuisance at best), relieved to avoid those terrible sessions of towel-snapping and mutual teasing in the shower room. To this day I am ill at ease in locker rooms.

✦　✦　✦

What passes for childhood play is often hard work—and often risky, too. For instance, shoplifting became a temporary diversion among the kids in our neighborhood. We took only small things—mostly candy—from a dime store. Safely outside, we would compare the items we had taken, rather proud of our daring, and our motivation seems to have been more social competition than acquisitiveness. For one thing, I never cared all that much for candy. But this, too, was a sport.

Chinaberry trees are God's gift to Texas children. They are just the right height (about fifteen feet) for climbing and have their limbs arranged (after a leap or shinny to the first branch) for climbing, with bark that doesn't scrape too much and limbs spaced for easy movement up and out and all over. A good chinaberry tree can easily accommodate a half-dozen kids in various perches. One could buy for a penny a three-inch-long Y-shaped heavy wire slingshot with rubber straps and a canvas pad just the size to hold the hard green marble-sized smooth berries that were perfect ammunition, administering a sharp sting but not really injuring your target. A treeful of prepubescent monkeys of both sexes pelleting each other with chinaberries through an afterschool day afternoon is a Brueghel vision of Paradise. Missing the trunk and intervening branches to pop a friend on a thigh is an art like casting dry flies.

✦　✦　✦

The Earp twins were bigger and older and more sophisticated than I was at eleven, and it puzzles me that they put up with my company, but they did. Their last name seemed funny to me because it was the common word for *vomit*. These brothers were always together, and I could never tell one from the other. But in their company my adventures ranged wide as we cruised for miles together on our bicycles.

For one thing, I needed things for my lab, and they helped me get those in exchange for use of the lab. My lab started with a three-lens microscope and one of those boxed chemistry sets given children as educational boys, but I soon grew bored with the experiments in the book and began to yearn for more elaborate equipment. We found this in two places. One was a private laboratory that did some kind of tests commercially. We had seen from the street its elaborate networks of glass chambers and tubing filled with mercury. I had heard about mercury, or quicksilver, had even acquired some from a broken thermometer, and tried to squash it and roll it in my hands. If you rub it on a dime, the dime becomes shiny silver. In your palm it sucks itself up into a ball.

We checked out the alley behind the lab, and, sure enough, there was a lot of broken glass tubing in various sizes and lengths, beakers, both triangle-shaped Erlenmeyer flasks and Florence flasks with ball-shaped bodies. Some of this glassware was in perfect condition, and we could not figure out why it had been discarded. Often there was waste mercury in the tubing, and we collected all we could find. To move mercury from one place to another you suck it up into a pipette and then let it out—but don't suck too hard and get it in your mouth! It's deadly poison. Over time we collected half a beaker of it—several pounds. From the garbage dump of that little lab we went to a much bigger dump—the one for the laboratories of Rice University. There we found more equipment, including a Bunsen burner, rubber tubing to attach it to a gas outlet, and iron trivets to hold glassware over the flame. So we took up glass blowing and bending of tubing, in addition to heating up chemicals. But the real fun was the expeditions themselves. We didn't learn much science. I shudder to think of the dangers in those garbage dumps, not to mention the dangers of conducting our experiments on a card table in a wooden house. I could never have raised a boy like me.

✦ ✦ ✦

Across the street from our house on Youpon was a small private mental sanitarium. We occasionally heard strange cries, screams, and sobbing from inside it. One day a police car pulled up beside its high iron fence—and the Earp twins, who had been in hot pursuit on their bicycles, skidded to a stop nearby. They had seen the whole thing, they told me excitedly, as the police hauled a handcuffed man in a torn shirt out of the car. The man had escaped from the asylum; the police found him a mile or so away, down by the railroad tracks, trying to rape a woman, Well, maybe *persuade* her to have intercourse would be a more accurate way of putting it. The Earp twins happened by just as the police car pulled up beside them. The man had his clothes off and was holding the woman by her arm begging her to cooperate. "Not till Jesus Christ is born again," she kept saying. I was impressed by her rhetoric under duress.

As the Earp twins told this tale to me we became aware of a

crowd of four or five boys and girls from the neighborhood, including Hanko Horn, who had gathered round. Hanko Horn lived next door, the son of our landlord. He walked and looked like a miniature Groucho Marx without mustache, but with heavy glasses. When Hanko was irritated with me, which was often, he would wag his finger at me angrily and yell, "You get off my property!" This could happen in the yard of his home or of the house where we were renting an apartment from his parents.

I began to worry about what Hanko might have picked up and might repeat of the Earp twins' tale, so I walked back toward home with Hanko, being atypically friendly, and took him into the garage for a talk. "Do you know what *fuck* means?" I asked him. He did not. "Well," I said, "it's the most dangerous word in the world. People in a secret society use it as a password, and if anyone who isn't a member of that society says it, the members kill that person. So don't ever, ever say it." Hanko nodded solemnly and the conversation ended.

I had forgotten all about this incident until I next irritated Hanko. He had taken my football from the yard and was hitting it savagely around his own yard with a garden hoe, so I retrieved it from him. He lifted the hoe to hit me, and I took that away from him. (He was bigger than I was, but was famous for being a coward and a weakling.) Instead of telling me to get off his property as usual, he yelled at me, "You old fuck! You *fuck fuck fuck fuck fuck!*"

His mother called him in from the yard. What is worse, my mother happened to be outside watering the lawn when all this occurred. She took me into the house—indeed into the bathroom—and asked me where Hanko had learned that word. Trapped as I was, I told her the whole story. After all, *I* hadn't used the word except to tell Hanko not to say it. And it was obvious that Hanko had no idea what it meant. Nonetheless she washed my mouth out with soap, instructing me never to use the word again. She also was a great believer in cold baths. She told me that if ever my penis stood up by itself I was to get into a cold tub immediately. I nodded in acquiescence, more deeply aware than ever of

140

how the secret world of childhood must be shielded from the intrusion of adults.

◆　　◆　　◆

Memories of school during those years are dim, and these are less of school than of play. While I was still in the last of many elementary schools a gang of about six girls, all larger but probably not older than I was, adopted me as a kind of pet. A temporary building on our school grounds was on stilts, and the space under it was a great place to avoid boys—and both they and I had a primary interest in avoiding boys at recess-time. They would take me under there and smooch. No sexplay, just smooching.

◆　　◆　　◆

I remember showing a poem I had written to one of my teachers. This was after school, and we were alone in the classroom. I don't know why I dared approach this strange adult with so intimate a matter, but I remember my trepidation, standing there in the still schoolroom, motes swirling in the late afternoon sunlight. She read it, told me it was very good, and told me that I mustn't hide my light under a bushel. I knew what a bushel basket was, and supposed that was what she called "a bushel," but I think it was years before I found out what that saying meant or where it came from. The teacher explained that unless I used the gifts God had given me, He might take them away from me. Oh. I was a little shaken by this unexpected twist that took her from poetry to religion.

But most clearly I remember learning to diagram sentences. A teacher showed us how to do it one day, with examples on the board, and it opened up the world of language for me. That evening, at home, I diagrammed the first sentence of the Declaration of Independence, which I happened to have memorized. It is a very long sentence, but not all that difficult to diagram. I had to use a shirt-board from the laundry to get all the spiderweb of connections in their proper relation to one another. The next day I showed it to my teacher. "Why, Juddy!" she exclaimed. "That's very good!"

"But is it *right?*" I asked, truly anxious to know whether I had made any mistakes.

"Oh, Juddy," she said, "I wouldn't have any *idea* about that." It wasn't in the book, like the examples she had put on the board. From that time on school has seemed to me a form of fraud.

◆　◆　◆

Sixth through eighth grades were junior high, where students went from room to room and the teachers stayed put—the opposite from grade school. I had two years of Latin, which I loved. And hated penmanship, the Palmer method, taught by the same fat old woman who taught Latin. She was a compassionate and effective teacher, but children in groups are like dogs in packs: unpredictably mean. We said she had dinosaur eggs in the folds of her neck. We said she knew Latin because she grew up in ancient Rome.

In shop I got Cs on my cedar chest and bootjack. I had a unit of mechanical drawing in a roomful of drafting tables. Some of the fellows in the back of the room used the cover of their wide tables to play with themselves during class. That classroom evokes a rather mysterious memory of Dad, who visited me at that school. He was glad that I was taking mechanical drawing, one of his own major skills. I had a small hard black instrument case that sprang shut and snapped open. It was about 3″ × 6″ in size. The silver instruments nestled in cavities in a blue silky lining: dividers, a pencil, and a pen compass, a penshaft with two points with silver beaks for ink and adjustment screws. Dad and I talked briefly on the schoolyard during my gym class; he was sober, quiet, serious. He must have been in Houston on business. I don't know whether he saw Stew and Mother or not.

◆　◆　◆

I am running along the sidewalk in high-topped black sneakers, knickers, and a jacket. It seems as though I am always either riding my bike fast or running. There isn't time enough in the world.

Across the railroad tracks are the woods. I highstep through the dry thorny vines along the edge and then run again under the pines in the wintry shadows. I am not going anywhere. Just running.

✦   ✦   ✦

As soon as I turned twelve I joined the Boy Scouts and went to Boy Scout camp the following summer. I was outfitted with a new bedroll and mess kit and canteen. The week I spent at a campground outside Houston was a very lonely experience, but one that opened my eyes to a lot of things. I didn't know any of the other boys there and was put by myself on a cot in a tent that would hold four. At meal times we gathered at the mess hall and, waiting to be served, would bang our utensils on the table to the rhythm of an apparently traditional song: "Here we sit like birds in the wilderness, birds in the wilderness, birds in the wilderness. Here we sit like birds in the wilderness, waiting for something to eat."

Days were heavily scheduled with things like crafts and close-order drill and swimming. Evenings we would play rough field games like Capture the Flag. And then the real games began—having to do with sexplay. There I was first exposed to the circle jerk, conducted by the four boys in the tent across from mine, who were, I gathered from what I could overhear, able to ejaculate. In my lonely tent, I was envious. I squirted a water pistol at them in revenge, gasping in imitation of their gasps so they would think it was come.

On the next-to-last day of camp every camper was called to the swimming pool. When we were all inside the chain link fence, it was locked, and the scoutmaster, a wiry, elderly man in full uniform (with shorts) and flat-brimmed hat, gravely told us that something had been stolen. He said the staff knew who was guilty, but they were going to give that scout a chance to escape punishment. "I'll be in my tent with the lantern burning all night," said the scoutmaster. "I want you to come in to confess and return what was stolen. That will show that you have learned your lesson, and there will be no further punishment." We learned later that ten dollars had disappeared from the wallet of one of the staff members. The scoutmaster did, indeed, sit up all night by his lantern, but the only one to come in, according to camp scuttlebutt, was a crying scout with a roll of toilet paper he had taken because he had a cold and had no handkerchiefs. (Had disposable tissues appeared on the market? I think not.)

At the end of the week came Parents' Day, and Mother arrived to pick me up. But first we gathered at the pool to show off our newly learned life saving and other swimming skills. We showed them how we could dump over a canoe, right it, and get back in and paddle to shore with the canoe full of water. If your boat capsizes, we were taught, you never leave it, for it will hold you up until help comes.

✦   ✦   ✦

I think it was while we lived in that apartment on Youpon that I had the parakeets. A man down the street, Mr. Kedgwick, raised parakeets and had enormous cages with hundreds of the birds in them. I was, for some reason, a favorite of this Mr. Kedgwick, a middle-aged, paunchy, cigar-smoking bachelor (or widower). I remember that he took me to a professional wrestling match—the only one I have ever seen. And he gave me parakeets—about six of them at first, and more later, as the first escaped. I never liked parakeets. When I reached into the cage they bit me and escaped. I would spend hours climbing chinaberry trees to try to catch them—and did catch some. But eventually they all got away.

My puzzlement about where we lived is because of the cage. I kept the parakeets in a large cube-shaped cage, well-crafted and covered with window-screening. It had a trap door in front for putting in food and water. The sides, top, and bottom were fastened together with hooks and eyes so it could be disassembled for cleaning. It was surely Ott who built that cage. I can't think of anyone else we knew who would have the skill or tools to do so. Ott was a tall, muscular man with sandy hair receding at the temples on a large, skeletal head with a wide mouth. Of all the men Mother dated, I cared least for him. He and Mother were to be married in December 1939, and he must have been hanging around a lot. I remember he was at the house on Youpon for New Year's Eve, 1938. In Texas people shoot off fireworks at midnight on New Year's Eve, and I remember standing in the yard with Mother and Ott watching distant rockets on every side. I believe it was that winter that it snowed—a rare event in Houston. It was really no more than a shallow dusting, but pipes in Houston were laid close to the surface, so they froze in many places, and school was out for several days.

Now Mother was going to get married. She asked what I thought of that, and I begged her not to do it. Ott had come to Houston from Illinois to work in an oil refinery, had married and had a son, and was divorced. It was obvious that he was a very practical man, handy with tools, thrifty, of moderate habits, and a disciplinarian with his son Bill (then five years old) and with us. Mother may have suspected that I would have objected to any man she might want to marry, and in this she may have been right. At any rate, Ott was having a new house built for us out in Idlewood, a new residential tract. We were moving up in the world. As she explained in the brief autobiography I have quoted earlier, "Jud didn't like that idea much. We didn't have much fun anymore. I know my main reason was security, a home and plenty of grocery money."

✦   ✦   ✦

The next three years provided the most stable home life I had known—or would know again until 1953, when, at 25, I became a professor, and Marty and I established a home of our own. I was to call our house in Idlewood home for longer than I had called any place by that name in my life—and longer than any place I was to live in the future until 1959–69, when Marty and I owned our first home in Yellow Springs, Ohio.

The wedding was in December. I remember Mother looking very glamorous in her suit and hat, and Ott, a tall, brawny man, standing with a wide grin beside her. Stew and I stayed with Aunt Orpha while they honeymooned in Mexico. And then we moved to Idlewood, a rectangle addition, as we called new subdivisions,

145

about twelve blocks long and three blocks wide, our house being on Sylvan Road, the bottommost street in the neighborhood. The house was brick, with five rooms (when the attic was finished and became my room) and kitchen. There was a large yard with steep terraces in front that were hard to mow. At the back of the large lot began deep pine woods that extended for miles along Brays Bayou.

✦   ✦   ✦

After we moved to Idlewood, my best buddies were Edwin and Mike, who introduced me to Boy Scout Troop 50. Troop meetings were on Friday evenings in the room above the Sunday School at Riverside Baptist Church, near Edwin's home, and my circle of friends expanded when I started attending these. Gangs of us would spend long days after school exploring the woods along Brays Bayou. There was a canebrake down there where we could pull up six-foot lengths of dried cane that made great spears for our wars.

Another favorite playground was a cemetery—a hilly, green shaded acreage excellent for hide-and-seek and general rampaging (and, somewhat later, for necking with girls). Across the street from Idlewood was a convent—a large fenced lawn and garden with tall brick buildings in the center. We loved to speed over its walks on our bikes or skates, dodging the nuns and monks who stopped where they were to pray when the bell rang.

Ott had put up a climbing and swinging rope at the back of our lot, and we practiced climbing up some twenty feet hand-over-hand without using our legs. Ott also made a swing set in the yard with heavy cast-iron pipe, holding two swings and a trapeze. I especially liked the trapeze and taught myself all manner of circus tricks. I could hang by my heels, or, hanging by my knees, do flips and twists as I let go to fly to the ground.

At one point we had to move the swing set so Ott could build a screened room for outdoor meals. As I was helping drag the frame across the yard, the whole structure fell on my foot, catching me

146

behind my right heel. We didn't know the foot was broken for three days: I scooted around on my hands and good foot that long. Nobody in our family ever went in much for doctors. Orpha finally insisted that Mother take me to a doctor, and he bawled her out roundly when an x-ray revealed the break. So I was in a cast and off my bike for six weeks.

✦   ✦   ✦

Though he had no verbal or tactile way of expressing affection, Ott worked at being a father to Stew and me. He had a shop in a room attached to the garage where he taught me the fine points of bicycle mechanics—including how to balance wheels with a spoke wrench, how to repair broken chains, and how to take apart and reassemble coaster brakes. As Bampaw had, he liked to have me work alongside him in his well-equipped shop and patiently showed me how to use tools and helped me with my projects.

Why, then, did I regard life with Ott as primarily a torment? I suppose I was lazy about doing my chores, for one thing. The vegetable garden he and mother put in at the back of the lot was a perpetual cause of contention. It was my job to weed it, an irksome task in the Texas sun. (I have never been an enthusiastic gardener.) Another chore was mowing with our rotary pushmower. I figured out that I could stand at the top of the tall terraces and let the mower down on a rope, then pull it back—which helped some. But if Ott talked to me at all it was usually to instruct or reprimand me. I couldn't have conversations with him, as I could with Hubbard, or Uncle Douglas, or Dad. He was fanatically parsimonious, though we never seemed to be in need. I can't remember his ever doing anything for fun—except play croquet occasionally. Nor do I remember his reading anything except technical material and the newspaper. He seldom smiled and seldom seemed to have a good time. He was always in his shop putting together uninteresting mechanical contrivances or at his adding machine or drafting table. Stew endured him many more years than I did, and, I believe, is much more bitter about that marriage than I am. It lasted until Ott died of cancer in the seventies.

Ott seemed to believe that I was drawing childhood out endlessly. Next door lived a little boy about nine and his sister who was about four. I played with these kids and Stew a lot when my scouting friends weren't available, and Ott looked on our childish play with dismay. I have an image in mind of the little boy running around with my sailor scarf around his neck as a cape yelling. "I'm Superman," and after him would come his little sister, wearing a towel pinned around *her* neck, yelling "I'm Hooperwoman!" Ott had a serious talk with me to tell me I should spend more time with boys my own age. Once I was up in my room when Ott brought a friend to meet me. I heard him tell the man at the bottom of the stairs, "He's very bright, but he's not much of a boy." I would never be a real man like Ott.

✦   ✦   ✦

Many of my games were still with Stew, who was seven in the summer of 1940 and my major responsibility until Mother came home from work. I would fix lunch for us—usually pork-and-beans or tomato soup or peanut butter sandwiches. I remember thinking that I could live forever on lettuce and grapefruit, but I didn't try that. Then I would pump Stew on my bike several miles to a public swimming pool. There I would practice my diving. I considered myself fairly expert, except I would no longer do gainers. I hadn't gotten up my nerve to try one since hitting my head on the board. But I did various front and back flips, twists, and combinations of these from the one-meter board and swan dives and jackknives from the three-meter board, and I imagined I was getting a lot of admiration from all those strangers. In the locker room I learned that some of the boys stuffed a sock or two into the crotches of their bathing suits to impress the girls, but I never indulged in that practice myself.

Stew's room was at the rear of the house on the first floor, and mine was in the attic space centered under the roof. I rigged a telegraph line from his room to mine, and we communicated some by

Morse code (I had my merit badge in that code), but we were never very good at it. After sending a message we would stick our heads out the window to yell verification of what we had sent or received. My scout buddies and I also tended to shout for verification when we were standing on hills far apart signaling with flags or, in the dark, telegraphing with flashlights.

I ordered a crystal radio set from a comic book ad, put it together, and got it to work, at least on a few stations, which one tuned in by scratching a fine wire along a coil. It had a cardboard case shaped and printed to resemble the tudor-arch "cathedral" radio sets that were still popular.

✦ ✦ ✦

Imagine, if you will, a Houston without air conditioning, a steamy sink for most of the year. One summer a hurricane swept in through Galveston, and the tall pines in our front yard bent over our house threateningly as we sat inside without electricity, helplessly staring at a wind that seemed to hit us like a solid mass of howling horror. After hours of this there was a sudden hush: the eye of the hurricane. We stepped outside into a strange purply wet and windless world.

After some minutes the storm hit again, from the opposite direction. One of the pines snapped off about twelve feet above the ground and crashed into the street. We never removed the stump. The last time I saw that house—after World War II—the bare pine pole still stood there memorializing the day that fishing boats from Galveston had been carried inland past Texas City.

✦ ✦ ✦

The world continued to expand. Ever since I was ten I had been going downtown alone, but such excursions became regular occurrences after we moved to Idlewood. About ten blocks from our house was a busy thoroughfare where the bus passed every thirty minutes. On Saturdays I might take a quarter and go downtown to a movie. That took a nickel for the bus each way (I could still pass for under twelve), a dime for the movie, and a nickel for a deli-

149

cious chili hot dog covered with chopped onions for lunch, which I ate sitting on a tablet-armed chair, one of a long line along the wall of the narrow cafeteria. If I had an extra nickel I might have a tall coke or glass of *ice*tea (the way we said it) as well. If I didn't have an extra nickel I drank water. At Christmas time I took my total savings, a dollar, downtown and bought presents at Kresses' for Mother, Ott, Stew, Mammaw, Marie, Bonita, and Aunt Orpha, carefully reserving a nickel for the bus ride home.

✦   ✦   ✦

The Houston airport was a long bike ride from Idlewood, but my buddies and I went there often, too. Many private planes were tied down in rows out in the field, and we climbed on the wings—and into those that had no covers on their cockpits. Some had enclosed cabins, sometimes with unlocked doors, and these were likely to have steering wheels instead of sticks. The wheels moved back and forth to make the plane go up and down. I explained to the fellows all about airplanes, on which I considered myself an expert. We liked to watch planes landing and taking off. There were not many commercial planes then. Some corporate cabin planes that would seat four to a dozen passengers were parked there. These were always locked up tight.

✦   ✦   ✦

About the only time in my life I was at a resort for a vacation was during my Idlewood years. We went to New Braunfels, Texas, where there were several inexpensive vacation spots along the beautiful Comal River—the shortest river in the world, and one of the most beautiful, with clear, cold water that wells up from springs right in town, passes through a power station (which warms it some), and, just outside town, empties into the Guadalupe.

We stayed in a cottage at one of the resorts. Some of them specialize in long inner tube floats down the river, but the one where we stayed was distinguished by a quiet, deep stretch of mostly shaded water—almost too cold for swimming for very long. I met a very pretty girl from San Antonio, Sarah, about my age but several inches taller than I was. We decided we were having a summertime romance, though I don't remember that we even kissed.

We danced together, though. Every night a band at the main hall of the resort played rollicking tunes such as "Put Your Little Foot" and "Beer Barrel Polka." These are not, of course, cheek-to-cheek dances, but I had fun dancing with Sarah and with Mother.

And Sarah and I ate prickly pears together. These grew on cacti aross the river—pear-shaped fruit covered with fine spines. I speared them on a knife and, handling them very gingerly, cut them open so we could dig out the sweet fruit inside.

✦   ✦   ✦

A country club dance. Why were we there? Ott and Mother were surely not members of such an establishment, so we must have been guests of one of the executives at the refinery where Ott worked. I was wearing a jacket and tie; Mother was in a long dress such as I remember her wearing at no other time, and Ott was wearing a suit—no doubt the one in which he and Mother were married. I remember the glitter of the long ballroom with tables around the sides where the adults sat and drank between dances.

I was bored. If Stew was along he was surely bored, too, and may have followed me out of the clubhouse and down to the starlit lake where some other children had gathered—children from homes out of our class. There was a diving board. I knew I could show off on a diving board, so I went out on it. A faceless girl hovers in the background of this memory, probably someone whom I didn't even know but for some reason wanted to impress. I began taking approaches—three steps, a leap, a bounce, and landing safely on the quivering board. Higher, higher. I was no doubt spectacular.

And, of course, I fell in. I remember swimming for the ladder in my tie and jacket, my shoes and socks. Bedraggled I sloshed up to the clubhouse and trailed lake water across the floor as I made my way to our party's table. We left early. I sat like a dripping washcloth wadded into the back seat.

✦   ✦   ✦

I spread the afternoon's *Houston Press* on the rug in the living room and, as is my custom, turn immediately to the comics. Mother asks me whether I have seen the front page, and I close the paper to see what she is referring to. It is the biggest headline I have ever seen, in letters four inches high: **ITALY GOES IN.** It is June 10, 1940. I am thirteen.

✦　✦　✦

This was the first time I remember thinking much of anything about the war that had started the previous December. I remembered my father's question to the boy with the fishing pole: *Whut war?* Why was it so important what Italy did? What did it have to do with me?

I saw *The Great Dictator* and knew who Hitler and Mussolini were. I remembered listening to Hitler making speeches on the radio. I would comb my hair down over my forehead and hold the tip of the comb under my nose to imitate Hitler. But I saw little connection between these figures of fun and my own life. Even when President Roosevelt disrupted Sunday afternoon radio to tell us about Pearl Harbor I saw little relevance to me. It first sank in close to Christmas. I had been promised a new bicycle. And then one evening we were riding along in the car, me sitting in the back seat with Stew, Ott driving with Mother beside him, the radio mumbling the news. "I guess that means no bicycle," Ott said. "*What* means no bicycle?" I asked. "There's a steel shortage." The war.

Before long Ott was wearing the steel helmet he used at work at the refinery on the streets of Idlewood. He was an air raid warden. When sirens went off we blacked out all the lights and went to our posts. My job, like that of other members of Troop 50, was to run messages on bicycles. It was fun whizzing down dark streets with no lights. On Saturdays our scout troop would take a large flatbed wagon intended to be pulled by horses and drag it around the neighborhood collecting newspapers, tin foil, grease, and coat hangers to fight the Nazis and the Japs. I accompanied Mother on

152

*In the birdbath,
before age two, one
of my earliest memories.*

*Before age two. The car must
have come before the coupe with
a rumble seat that I remember.*

*I think I'm about
three here, in Tulsa.*

*The photographer brought
around this pony and took
the picture outside Aunt
Audrey's house in
Muskogee.*

My parents just before
they were married in 1926.

In 1936, when Stew
was three, I was nine, and
our family life in Oklahoma
City was nearly at an end.

Dad at about age thirty-five in 1941.

Mother in her best years, about the time of our bicycle trip to Galveston when I was fifteen and Stew was nine.

The Trailblazers about 1941. Edwin
Parkinson and Mike Clevenger are at the far
end. I may be the one with the scout hat.

Stew with Rob outside
Aunt Audrey's house
in Muskogee in 1941.

Dad with me at fifteen, Stew at
nine, in 1942 on our summer visit
with him and Evelyn in Oklahoma City.

Two views of the Stewart sisters, Gwen, Peggy, Orpha, and Audrey, the first in the early twenties (Mother appears to be about fifteen), the second in Houston in front of Orpha's home, about 1935.

Ready to jump off the cliffs, Okinawa, 1946.

Mike Clevenger on our camping trip in Colorado, summer of 1944.

I was a corporal here, in winter garb. This was on Okinawa just after I turned nineteen.

By 1946, I was acting first sergeant of the 10th Photo Technical Unit on Okinawa.

the bus to go to the butcher to spend our allotment of ration stamps. She traded with a Chinese butcher whose shop was in the heart of the Negro section of town near the ice rink. The butcher complained that he was losing customers because so many people couldn't distinguish between the Chinese and the Japanese. The Chinese, he said, were our allies. While Christmas shopping that year, I avoided, as instructed, products made in Japan.

Maxine and Jay, her pilot husband, had been stationed in the Canal Zone. Now Jay was being sent to the Pacific, so Maxine returned to Houston. (He was to return a much decorated hero, only to be killed on a training flight in the states.) Ray, Aunt Marie's husband, joined the army. Little Jack joined the marines, though he was very near the upper age limit, leaving Audrey alone on the ranch. Soon the few young men one saw on the streets in civilian clothes wore little emblems indicating that they were 4-F and so were honorably relieved of service. One stared at these young men, rejects, and wondered what was wrong with them. New shipyards grew up around Houston and were booming, with both men and women working three shifts a day.

✦ ✦ ✦

A new version of *Dr. Jekyll and Mr. Hyde*—with Spencer Tracy—came out when I was fourteen. I remember sitting on the grass in the backyard in the afternoon after I saw that film mulling over an image that inflamed Mr. Hyde as he went through the process of transformation. In his dream a stallion reared and sliced his hooves over a cringing lightly-clad woman. The image stirred and disturbed me strangely. Though I knew it was erotic, it evoked for me a world of manhood into which I knew I could never fit. Girls had beat up on *me* in our rough play, and I didn't find that erotic at all, and I could not imagine myself beating up on a girl or enjoying cruelty. I was a good boy.

✦ ✦ ✦

One of my favorite memories of Mother is of her biking with me and Stew to Galveston. In her biographical note she seemed to associate it with recognizing that we were "not having much fun anymore" together. It was the summer of 1942:

> . . . the two boys and I rode to Galveston on our bikes—50 miles. Nowadays that isn't a spit in the ocean, but with the old bikes with the big tires, it was quite a trick. I loved it—such freedom with the two I loved best. That highway is now a super freeway and it's dangerous for bikers. We stopped by the railroad one day. The brakeman, I guess, asked us to come up into the switch house for a cold drink. He explained all the workings and switches. Stew had forgotten to grease so we had to walk his bike over the causeway into town to get it to ride. We stayed two nights in a cottage. The trip back was sorta uneventful except it rained on us a few times and we had to seek shelter. And I remember it took us eight hours back and we thought that was pretty good time. Jud and I thought it a wonderful trip. Stew wasn't too convinced. He didn't take exercise as joyously then as he does now. He was nine, Jud fifteen, and I thirty-five.

That memory must have meant much to her: she devoted nowhere near so many words to any other incident in the five-page summary of her life. My chief feeling—then and now—was pride to have such a mother. She was still a quite attractive young woman, and it made me feel important to be seen with her. And I admired her spunk. I had taken fifty-mile bicycle trips before, but it seemed an outstanding thing for a *woman* to do, especially one's mother.

We were actually out three nights—the first in a cottage owned by a friend on a lake near Texas City, the next two in a tourist camp near the breakwater. One of the few times that food figures prominently in my memories of childhood was a meal at our favorite seafood restaurant. The odors of the cooking shrimp and fish whetted my appetite. And I was impressed that she would spend so much on a meal. (Mostly she cooked our meals in the tourist cottage.) I remember very few meals in restaurants in my youth—and those usually when an uncle was paying the bill.

154

I had forgotten the switch house and the grease problem, but I remember painfully that trip home. Stew's bike had a flat, and he had to push it, walking, for many of the final miles, sometimes in the rain. No wonder he lacked enthusiasm. But he *was* a moody boy in those days. I don't remember his often being happy.

✦   ✦   ✦

I gave little thought to my father in those years—a period when he was, I later learned, living as a derelict in the Reno Street district memorialized in a song of the times:

> Down in Oklahoma City
> On deep Reno Street
> That's where Small Town Mama
> Really turns on the heat.
>> Small Town Mama!
>> There's nothing she won't do.
>> She's got them big city ideas.
>> She's sure to satisfy you!

In Houston I was concentrating on becoming one of the boys. I recognized my problems in this regard. I was a shrimp, and I had not developed physically the way my buddies had. I overcompensated, throwing myself into *Boy's Life* (the name of a magazine I read regularly, along with *The Boy Scout Handbook*) with gusto. And I was doing pretty well at it. No one thought me a sissy. No one knew how bookish I was in private. In my own way, in spite of the failure I felt in my heart, I was passing myself off as a junior edition of a real man—albeit one who was rather too verbal and exhibitionistic to fit the type—for fear I would not be noticed otherwise.

Yet ahead lay the problem of defining for myself what a man *does* in this world. That process was to take me on a tangent from the values of my immediate environment—and, eventually, to take me back into the shadow of my father's influence.

9

Spirit and Flesh

A man needs, I thought, to believe in something so strongly that he would be willing to die for it. I'm not sure where I got that idea. Probably from books. Certainly not from anyone in my family. I thought that growing up meant discovering what you believed in, what you could commit your life to. And I set about this quest armed with skepticism that would prevent me from achieving it. Nothing had prepared me to believe in anything.

At about age fifteen Edwin, who was a year older than I, got himself saved. At his insistence I began attending the Sunday School of the Riverside Baptist Church. Occasionally he would persuade me to stay for the sermon. Those days I had to have two nickels, one for Sunday School, one for church. In the barnlike church with walnut pews, with sliding doors behind the altar concealing the tub (that's where they *do* it, explained Edwin, and described how the preacher in a white gown stood in the water and ducked the saved, in white gowns, and how you could see through the girls' gowns when they were wet), we sat listening to the incomprehensibly winding rhetoric of guilt. I was never sure of the line of argument, but I understood the central truth, which only needed to be pointed out to me, that I was slimy, and that I could step outside the church and be hit by a car, unredeemed. The final hymn was endless. Just one more chorus, the preacher would call, and we all stood singing with our heads bowed, peeking right and left to see if anyone would buckle.

Sometimes they did, explosively—with a shout of Lord save me! and palms flying and tears running as they moved up to the altar in a state of exaltation. These were mostly the old-timers, who had been saved again and again, and had had a wild time the night before. When the new ones went, as I felt I would surely go some day, it was shyly, with a kind of guilty embarrassment, as though they were planning to slip in by fraud. I could never get it out of my head that perhaps they were, that they weren't saved at all, but were so afraid of the imminent automobile accident on the church steps that they figured they might as well gamble on a lie. (I learned later about Pascal's wager.)

✦   ✦   ✦

The Unchosen

I guess I have a deficiency. God never
said boo to me when as a boy I stood
straining in church with muscular endeavor
for the sweet squirt of Salvation. I never could
see why He spoke to this and that old lady,

sending her, hallelujah, down the aisle.
Was I alone in the congregation vile?
Or was their claim of spirit something shady?
And now, when I read poets who simply Know,
drinking their imagery from God's own cup,

whose poems "just come" and then, like Topsy, grow,
whereas I always have to make them up
with never a tremor saying, "Break this line,"
or "Save this phrase, regardless of its beat,"
hear no obscurities that seem Divine,

and knowing not God's measure, still count feet,
I yearn that reason give me some relief
(besides those lapses when my mind—not soul—
is not so much inspired as out of control).
Non-Linear God, help Thou my unbelief.

✦　✦　✦

The preacher explained repetitively what the feeling would be
when it came. He put much emphasis on believing *on* Jesus Christ
as opposed to believing *in* Him—a distinction I never understood.
It would be a sensation of delicious certainty slightly left of center
of the rib cage. (I kept feeling the spot; nothing was happening.)
When they passed around trays with little glasses of grape juice
and crackers, I was not allowed to take any because I was not a
Christian. I always developed a terrible thirst as the tray came
down the pew—each standing person, head bowed, taking a shot
with a head jerk, returning to piety, and passing on the tray, being
careful not to rattle it too much—and I nearly joined the church
just to get refreshments. The mystery of grape juice that symbolized wine that, in turn, symbolized blood teased me out of thought,
as did the attitude of my friends and neighbors toward canni-
balism. Was a simple want, an obsessive desire for that magic swallow, salvation? I especially resented that children younger than I
went up to the altar, were baptized, and could participate in com-
munion. I added suspicion of their motives to my sins.

I wish I could say that I refrained from joining because of sin-
cere doubt or honesty, waiting for the true sensation of salvation
to overpower and compel me, but I was such a sinner I would have
done anything to get in if it hadn't required walking down that
aisle to the front of the church, everyone watching beneath lowered lids, and having that waxy-handed minister make a fuss over
me. I detested him instinctively, in spite of the truth of his message; he had the toneless earnestness of a salesman, a flat-faced
East Texan type of young man with an unctuous twang. He made
mistakes in grammar and used words I didn't know. I would not let
him triumph—and I especially wouldn't do it in front of a lot of

159

self-righteous, floury-breasted, and mealy-minded grown-ups and kids I didn't trust. It is hard to sort out my feelings, but the strongest seems to have been a horror of public exposure.

✦ ✦ ✦

One Sunday I told Mother I didn't want to go to church anymore. "I don't believe in praying in public," I said.

"That's a rationalization," she told me—and had to explain the word. I might, had I been less of a good boy, have called her a hypocrite. I had never known of her—or anyone else in my family—to go to either church *or* Sunday School, but she thought that since I had started, I should keep on going to either.

Thus I was deeply agitated by the problem when Reverend Moon came to the First Baptist Church downtown, with a one-week, nightly series of "Sermons from Science." Edwin, tall (I came to his chest), shuffling, big-nosed and ugly, continually whistling through his teeth in sheer spiritual contentment, was an initiate of science as well as of religion. He was building a ham radio and was an amateur chemist. He was saved no matter which side won.

The two of us would take the bus downtown each evening and wait on a windy corner (by a Catholic church looming sinister and dark) for the 11:35 bus to take us home. Though I was fourteen I could still get by for half-fare—most of the time. When the bus driver questioned my age I would explode in lofty indignation that I was *ob*viously eleven-and-a-half because I had dropped only a nickel in the glass-sided fare box. I would sit in the church for a couple of hours of agony and fear for my soul, imagining that blinding moment to come, the drunken driver veering around the corner, bumping right over the curb and hideously climbing the church steps, the grate and bang of metal and shatter of glass and then Hell Fire. Then I would make it safely off the steps (which *did* seem to be the most dangerous spot), and cheat on the bus. I was impossible:

✦ ✦ ✦

160

Revival

Sermons from Science! Reverend Moon, a man
from Moody Bible Institute, began
in Houston to convince us of his view:
the Bible, word by word, was scientific,
a world not good nor beautiful, but true,
the myth all tucked away, the soul aloof
from mysteries reduced to certain proof,
for agitated youth a soporific.

His stage was full of beakers, tubes, and wires.
He could prove anything with a slide or movie.
He prayed demonstrably; his hymns were groovy.
He handled all the elemental fires
and in a week did most of Genesis.
He could extrapolate a wife for Cain,
explain what Noah didn't know (for he
founded the Flood on sound geology).
His sparks jumped gaps, chemicals made a hiss,
and time-lapse films showed vines grope toward the light.
His climax was to stand on a coil one night,
a million volts spurting from his finger tips.

My sins poured forth from adolescent lips.
I cried, I cried, for fear I would not be saved.
Even my yearning for goodness was depraved:
I finally lied to be saved with the rest,
claiming I felt the spirit in my breast
and that I heard a Voice I could not hear.
I wrestled with the worm beneath my skin,
then, worm and all, I joined. They let me in.

I did not stay revived. The flesh is weak.
My Youth Group, so impassioned, throbbed out of church
in spiritual adventure. Mostly my search
was one of kissing every other cheek.
We listened to the sermons with our legs
crossed tight and sang our hymns like troubadours.

Oh hallelujah! how emotion begs
for any outlet, turn it out-of-doors.

Science, meanwhile, bequeathed the true to faith
and took up beauty and goodness. So did I.
Our times are cool—and Reverend Moon may boil
with certainty and passion, like a wraith
with fiery fingers on his surging coil,
but he looks foolish. I can verify
neither my friendly worm nor my damnation.
One can be burned by mere spark-gap salvation.
Electrons are uncertain; so am I.
For any act I know not any cure;
more facts, above all, make me more unsure,
and though they would forgive me, I will not
permit my sins—my self—to be forgot.

✦ ✦ ✦

Whether Genesis was absolutely, scientifically, word-for-word the literal truth did not much concern me. We learned that when the earth cooled the water all remained in the atmosphere, like a great steamy canopy enveloping the ball, and that was why it rained upwards before the Flood. But then a spark of lightning or something caused sudden condensation, and *whoosh*, all the water fell at once, or, rather, for forty days and nights. We learned how widespread were stories of the Flood in other religions, heard the geological and anthropological evidence that this Flood actually occurred, supplying all the water to form the glaciers. I accepted all such information with weary wonder. Didn't science beat all? But the gimmickry of science fascinated me. Reverend Moon carried a kind of telephone dial on a strap around his neck, and when he dialed a particular number, sparks would fly on the other side of the stage, or the lights would go out, or flasks would start bubbling with colored liquid. How I would have liked to have one of those telephone dials!

This seemed a long way from salvation, which was what we were there for, but by scaring us, he got us jumpy enough to visualize the careening car (was I wearing clean underwear?) and preparing the ground generally for violent emotional experience. The climax was the business on the coil. He climbed barefooted on what looked like a great cable drum, took all metal objects off his body, then they darkened the auditorium and turned on the juice—literally, he said, a million volts—lighting up Reverend Moon like a giant sparkler, sizzling and popping and streaming light until the long stick he held in his hand over his head burst into flame. Then they cut off the juice, turned up the house lights, and Reverend Moon climbed down off the coil, smiling and unhurt, and put his socks and shoes back on. He said it had something to do with purity of spirit. When the endless final hymn came the sinners streamed up in dozens. Each day he would announce the score for the preceding evening. "Now while we sing that last chorus one more time I want to see you turn to your neighbor there in the pew and introduce yourself, and ask him, 'Brother, are you saved?' and if he isn't, won't you tell him kindly to come forward and speak for Jesus?"

This would mean several frightening moments, singing like a stuck record, eyes burning the floor, wondering whether that sweet-smelling, lard-fleshed, pillow-bosomed lady next to me would turn and ask me whether I was a Christian. Suddenly there was a fist—Edwin's fist before my lowered eyes. His thumb was extended in the gesture of a traffic cop, indicating I should get the hell up front. I looked up at him, and his face was grim. I never expected it of Edwin. I looked down the long aisle, at one after the other of the congregation succumbing like fruit dropping from a tree. Moon was down in the aisle, his telephone dial still dangling from his neck, sweating and singing like it hurt, shaking the hand of each as he came forward and sending the sobbing sucker backstage where, no doubt, a team of aides performed some weird initiation rites. I could not do it.

That night I cried by the Catholic church, waiting for the bus. I was furious with Edwin. I was scared. And though I was still wiping tears when I got on the bus, the driver caught me dropping only a nickel and added shame and expense to my misery. The next day I went around the corner from the Baptist church to the Epworth Methodist Church, a dignified brick building (much tonier than the clapboard Riverside Baptist) and talked to the Nordic, handsome minister, a soft-voiced educated man of reason. I quizzed him in detail about the ritual of joining. No, I would not have to come forward after a service. All I had to do was sign a card. Sometime later there would be a baptism ceremony—a sprinkle of water, not full immersion as in the Baptist church— but this could be done privately, at my convenience, perhaps with my family present. Well, okay! I hadn't realized there were churches you could join in the back room.

So I saw less of Edwin, going now to a different Sunday School, meeting a more prosperous and refined class of people, listening to sermons like lectures in the respectable dignity of a thin, sedate chapel. I even persuaded my mother to go to the back room and sign up. But I here record that Reverend Moon, wherever he may be, should chalk up one more (two, if you count Mother) on his scoreboard. It was he who scared me into it—with the help of Edwin's imperious thumb.

✦   ✦   ✦

I was soon drawn back to the Baptists on Sunday nights, though, to attend their Youth Group, whose activities were much more in- teresting than anything the Methodists had to offer. The "teacher" was a rather stupid, stumpy, jolly man, interested in boys and girls, who owned a moving van in which he would take us all to neigh- boring towns and rural areas for revival meetings. Closed in the dark cavern of the truck, we would pull down the padded blankets used to pack furniture, spread them on the floor, and neck (a word that used to mean making love above the shoulders—with a rare squeeze of breast for the bold) while the truck rumbled off to Jesus. Edwin did not go to Youth Group. He was too moral. Mike went with his family to some other church entirely.

Thirty miles away in a tiny village we would sit on benches in a shack or tent while the preacher bellowed, eyes like running sores, throat knotting and bulging like a spastic python. The revival

164

meetings one can find on AM radio Sunday mornings are much the same, but on a grander scale. After a reasonably coherent beginning, the preacher begins pounding the pulpit to emphasize his *words*, and gradually the rhythm becomes more *regular*, and he is answered by scattered shouts of *amen* from the congregation, and with this en*cour*agement the preacher begins to suck *air* and blast it *forth* in the rhythm of cop*ula*tion, his body *sway*ing, the fist *slam*ming, the words becoming indis*tinct*, but with frequent clear *ref*erences to the terror of *Hell* and the sins of the *wick*ed, which are generally *item*ized and luridly con*sid*ered, how these young boys and *girls* in the drive-ins and *honky*tonks permit their tender *bod*ies to be abused and de*fil*ed, and watching the preacher's hair swinging loose around his sweating face, which is gasping and twisting in tortuous ecstasy, and hearing the sob in his chanting, the rhythm laborious with pumping, we could easily imagine what he was referring to, crossed our legs and squirmed, pulsing with his rhythm, until the last sinner for the night was saved, and we could go streaming back into the groaning hell of the moving van. When we reached our neighborhood in Houston we insisted that the amiable dope drive around and around the block to delay breaking up our play.

✦   ✦   ✦

Would I ever outgrow play? Still on my study shelves are the coins and stamps I collected in Houston in those years. A fellow has to have a hobby. Stamp and coin collecting were my hobbies. My collecting days culminated while I lived in Idlewood but began much earlier. Hubbard had started my coin collection with a whole boxful he had gathered in Europe during World War I, and a sense of the arbitrary cruelty of the great world beyond the family and within it lingers for me as I look at them today.

Two of the coins were ancient—Greek or Latin, I believe. They were paper thin, light gold in color, and had worn images of gods or heroes or emperors on them and almost indecipherable lettering. I took these along with some other coins and stamps to a coin shop in downtown Houston to have them identified and assessed. I was about ten at the time, and probably looked no more than a small seven.

✦　✦　✦

The door of the stamp and coin shop is in the narrow space (perhaps four feet wide) between two large buildings. There is just room inside for a counter and the proprietor behind it. The counter has yellowing transparent tape on a long crack in the glass.

I show the man behind the counter my stamp book—stamps stuck with transparent tape to lined notebook paper in a ring binder. "Please do not use that tape on your stamps," he says in a sad voice. "I'll show you why. Do you see that tape on the glass— how yellow it is? That is what will happen to the tape on your stamps. Besides, you cannot remove them. You've ruined them." He shows me the light little tabs you use to attach stamps to a stamp book. I buy a packet for a nickel.

Then I show him the two wafer-like coins. I ask him whether he can identify them and tell me their value.

He seems like a friendly man. He says he cannot immediately recognize the coins. It will take him awhile, he says, to look them up in his reference books. Could I leave them with him?

I am going to a movie, so I tell him I will stop back for them after it was over. When I return, a different man is on duty. He knows nothing about my coins.

That was, of course, the last I ever saw of those coins. I went back the next day when the proprietor was there, but he said he had never seen me before, and he knew nothing about my coins. I went to the corner and asked a policeman to come back to the store with me. He did, but what could I prove? I didn't even know where the coins were from.

I still feel in my gut a profound sense of loss—not of monetary value but of precious objects desecrated—regarding those coins. But I also felt outsmarted. I had been naïve. I had to outgrow that, I knew. I must keep on my toes. I must never let a swindler get to me again. Swindlers *have* got to me again and again. But always, after the wince, after the pain, comes renewed resolution. Wise up, Jud. Don't let emotion, trust, ingenuousness, blind your eyes. And yet I trust and trust again. I spend trust like Monopoly money—which may mean I am not deeply committed to what I risk or that I am overly eager to wager on being loved.

✦ ✦ ✦

My first real stamp album—eight and a half inches tall and eleven inches wide—was published in 1935, but I probably acquired it about 1940. On the title page (*The Modern Collector's Postage Stamp Album*, Whitman Publishing Company, Racine, Wisconsin) I had written in pencil "Rm 326" and "This Book Belongs to Judson Jerome." I wonder whether Rm 326 was where the stamp club met at Austin High. I didn't go to that club's meetings often. I noticed that some students went to them to meet new people, socialize, to make dates. Some seemed to have been pushed into philately by parents who thought stamps would teach them geography. Some had dreams of buried gold—thinking they might find rare stamps worth millions in their uncles' attics.

There was probably not a lot of social or sexual action in that club, however. Not much geography (or any other academic subject) was being learned there. I never heard of anyone actually finding a rare stamp and becoming rich thereby. And a lot of allowances were being spent in response to comic book ads that lured neophytes with introductory offers of packets of gorgeous triangles and rectangles from French colonies in Africa.

But I thought I was different from the other collectors I met there. I really loved stamps, especially the dim old canceled ones, each thin tissue that I knew had borne a message from one part of the world to another many years ago. I liked those better than the colorful new ones from exotic countries that one acquired by sending for those introductory offers. I even stopped looking up my stamps in the Scott catalog to find their mythical "market value." I liked stamps for themselves, not their monetary worth.

Then I met someone who *really* liked stamps. An elderly gentleman learned from an acquaintance that I was interested, so he invited me to see his collection. One evening I located his elegant apartment, was invited in, my stamp book under my arm, with its childish decorations of pictures cut from magazines, especially one of a large burly burglar in a red cap and red-striped sweater, and a huge, square, hairy jaw. The burglar has a stamp book open in front of him, and, with a beatific smile on his face, he is looking through a magnifying glass at a stamp he is delicately holding with tweezers. This illustration was from an ad for Dutch Cleanser that used as its slogan the phrase, "Tough, but Oh, so gentle."

The man I was visiting spread one volume after another of his collection on a table in the lamplight. There were dozens of albums under lock and key in a glass-faced case. The old man spoke sadly of the time when his heirs would auction his collection off for the thousands of dollars it was worth, as none of them were interested in continuing to build it. But it was obvious that he had not lavished his love on stamps for financial speculation.

And though he enjoyed sharing his hobby with me and would no doubt have relished getting together with connoisseurs, he was not using philately to satisfy some social urge. He must have learned a great deal of geography and history, not to mention the chemistry of paper and glue and the secrets of printing processes, but he was not collecting stamps to satisfy some scholarly or technical interest. He just loved stamps. Each one in his tweezers under his magnifying glass was a cherished object.

He was generous, too. He gave me several dozen U.S. stamps that were far more rare and valuable than any others in my collection. (Indeed, I was to get a second album, especially for U.S. stamps, to accommodate these.) Had he found in me the spark of a true collector, he might have put me—a virtual stranger—into his will. But his greatest gift to me was one he did not intend to give and might have regretted had he known about it. By his kindly example he showed me that I was not really a stamp collector and would never be one. I could not imagine myself a half-century later with a collection comparable to his—even if I were assiduous and lucky. And though I admired him for having achieved what he had, I knew I did not want to emulate him. He intended to inspire me. What he did was liberate my energy from stamps and allow it to move on to other things. Those stamps he gave me were among the last added to my collection.

His example was important in another respect as well. He made me burn to discover what it was in this world I could care about in the way he cared about stamps. I am reminded of a poem by Don Marquis's creation, archy the cockroach, who types out his poems on Marquis's machine each night. In one of these he is talking about a moth who had no desire greater than to fry himself on a light bulb or flame. Archy (who used only lowercase letters because he wasn't heavy enough to push down the shift key on the typewriter) concludes:

> i do not agree with him
> myself i would rather have
> half the happiness and twice
> the longevity
>
> but at the same time i wish
> there was something i wanted
> as badly as he wanted to fry himself

What the old man taught me was the importance of finding such a focus for one's efforts. I tell that story in *On Being a Poet* and add, "For many of the millions, young and old, who dabble in poetry the way adolescents of Houston used to dabble in philately, I would like to serve as that kindly old man."

I have never found salvation, not even in poetry. There is nothing I want as badly as the moth wants to fry himself. To believe in anything that intently, one would have to surrender reason, and since before I could remember I have been reasoning my secret way through an irrational world. Reason became my protective shell. If you can't outfight 'em, outsmart 'em. If you can't command 'em, outtalk 'em. Unpredictable adults provide a child with a certain immunity from religion, lay or otherwise. But in later years a vision of communalism brought coherence into my life: a vision that combined spirit and flesh, social and universal order, purpose and direction. It was a dream of Eden, unrealizable but nonetheless compelling, growing out of a child's experience of being intimately accepted and learning to accept and live with the contradictions of experience in the world.

10

Another Dollar

After my largely unsuccessful efforts to sell *Liberty* magazines at age five, I didn't give much thought to gainful employment until we set up that unsuccessful lending library when I was nine. That was a very important venture, representng definite progress toward elusive manhood, though it never turned a dime as a business.

But I knew a fellow had to work for a living, and, at age ten, in 1937, I took a job delivering advertising circulars to people's door-ways. I remember that job clearly because I discovered later that Stew, who had turned four in November, followed me, picked up the circulars, rang the doorbells, and tried to sell the free circulars to the occupants for a penny. He made five cents—clear profit, as Hubbard pointed out.

Then I got a *real* job, as a carhop. I went to Mr. Hemphill, who ran a small drugstore in the neighborhood, and asked whether he would hire me. "Well, you're pretty little," he said. But he took me on. I was to show up after school and sit out front in an apron to wait on cars and occasionally to run errands for Mr. Hemphill. I worked until nine o'clock five days a week and all day Saturday.

For that he paid me a dollar a week. Of course I got tips, but there were few customers for curb service—many days none at all. I do remember getting a fifty-cent tip once. I also remember asking for one Saturday off so I could go with the family to Galveston, and Mr. Hemphill very reluctantly agreed. He docked my pay a quarter.

Much has been made of the parsimoniousness of spirit of those who grew up in Depression years, but I am grateful for having had my first experiences with money and material things occur in a time when a cent had purchasing power, when losses and gains of even trivial amounts had meaning. I am obsessive about using leftovers, reusing paper towels and tissues, straightening used nails. I think I am lavish with love—and am inclined to share bountifully what I have saved with others. I have never been acquisitive, materialistic, a hoarder. But life taught me early the habits of economy, of making do, the aesthetic satisfaction of achieving results with minimum waste. There is grace and beauty in the lean line, in shimmering efficiency, in the elegance (just another word, here, for economy) of mathematical proof, the precision of satisfaction of need. I have advised poets, "Spend syllables as though they were dollars," an injunction that reflects my association of art with economy. Earning a living is, in its best sense, a metaphor for hanging in the cup of necessity's tall wave.

After my tenth year I seem to have been unemployed until I was twelve and living in Idlewood. In those lean years I lived on my allowance of a dime a week (plus the subsidy of free room and board). But then a friend of Ott's gave me an old hectograph. I was familiar with the hectographs teachers used—and, indeed, one could make a hectograph at home. All it takes is a tray of gelatin mixed with glycerine. You write or type what you want to reproduce on a sheet of paper with an upside-down carbon of a special type on the back. Then you press the carbon image—the writing or drawing in reverse—onto the hard gelatin. The image is taken by the gelatin and will transfer in mirror-image to a clean sheet pressed over it. It will make about twenty copies before it sinks below the surface—enough, say, for test papers for a school class. If you leave it for a few hours, the old image will sink, and the surface is ready for a new master. Many teachers used such hectographs in their classrooms in the thirties.

But I have never seen or heard of a hectograph like the one given me. The gelatin was on a belt long enough to take about twenty legal-sized sheets. That meant one could reproduce one page, then roll to a fresh place and make another without waiting for the old image to sink. Obviously I had to go into the publishing business. I began bringing out a neighborhood newspaper I called the *Idlewood Oomph,* named for Ann Sheridan, who was then regarded as the Oomph Girl, as Clara Bow had been the It Girl before her.

I was not much of a journalist—and the news of Idlewood was not very exciting. My method of reporting was to go from house to house with the latest *Idlewood Oomph* (I made the first issue up out of whole cloth) asking whether the woman (it was usually a woman) who answered the door wanted to buy a copy for a nickel, then ask whether she had any news for the next edition.

❖   ❖   ❖

The lady said she had no news herslf, but that some tulips had recently been stolen from a house across the street, which she pointed out to me. I went to that house, noticed that, indeed, the blossoms had been snipped from the lines of tulips on either side of the sidewalk.

I went through my sales and news pitch, but the lady at the door didn't want to buy and said she had no news. Then I told her I heard that someone stole her tulips. She jerked open the door, grabbed one of my ears, and pulled me inside and asked what I knew about her tulips. Risky business, being a reporter.

❖   ❖   ❖

Easier were features, editorials, and cartoons. I had invented a cartoon character, Elmer, based on Edgar Bergen's hick character Mortimer Snerd, and I turned this into a regular comic strip. To draw a comic strip you have to be able to draw characters over and over the same way, and I practiced until I could turn out dozens of almost identical copies of Elmer's face. The only problem was that I could draw Elmer only in left or right profiles—no frontal shots at all. And I wasn't very good at doing any of him below the neck. And though I could draw a lot of other faces, I had few I could repeat convincingly. So one saw a lot of Elmer in conversation.

Having made some dozen legal-sized pages of masters, I would go to the garage, where the hectograph was, and make about twenty copies (back and front) of each page, and set out on my rounds. If I sold twenty copies, I made a dollar. This was no way to earn a living, but the experience did make me begin thinking of myself as a journalist.

✦   ✦   ✦

More practically, Edwin, Mike, and I earned money by patching screens. This, like selling and gathering news for the *Idlewood Oomph*, required going door to door—in this case to ask whether people needed any screens patched. Most did. If something else had not punctured their screens, they had probably punctured a few themselves getting in when they were locked out of their houses. They would make a hole near the hook, push in a nail or small stick, and unsnap the hook of the screen. Most houses seemed to have these holes. Two of us would carry a roll of screen with us, cut a patch from it, pull out strands of wire to sew it on, and then, with one of us inside, the other outside, we threaded the wire back and forth through the patch and screen making stitches all around the edges. We charged a nickel a patch.

I also worked at the golf and archery range. Orpha and Louie had bought this business near us (their home on Shakespeare was on the other side of the city), and they hired me to work for them. I would rent buckets of balls and go out to pick them up in a burlap bag when there were no customers (most of the time). I could also practice driving and putting on the small putting range. Then I was put in charge of the archery range, so I got a lot of practice at archery, too.

I first learned about marijuana while working at the golf range.

Aunt Orpha had hired a Mexican laborer to do some painting around the place. But, his first day on the job, he was climbing a ladder to paint the highway sign and some brown paper "sticks", as they were called in those days, fell from his pants' pocket. Orpha spotted them on the grass, and she fired him on the spot as I stood by. She never explained what *marijuana* was or *sticks* were—words she used angrily as she sent the man away (without pay for the few hours he had put in), but I deduced their meaning from the context. I heard her tell Louie that the man was carrying *dope,* and so learned another word.

I did not realize at the time that this substance—used world-wide since ancient times and common and legal in Mexico— had been made illegal in the United States as recently as 1937. During Prohibition twice as many were imprisoned for drug offenses as for liquor offenses, and many a federal treasury agent was building his reputation in these years on a record of capturing users and dealers of common hemp.

✦   ✦   ✦

A huge green grasshopper has landed on the sign of the archery range just as I am about to shoot at one of the balloons I have put on the bullseye of each target. I divert my aim to the grasshopper and shoot. Before I know what has happened, a man comes raging out of the little café next door, my arrow in his fist. He drags me into the dining room to see what happened. The arrow had gone through a window screen just at the level of the table where the man and a woman were eating. It slithered across between their plates and dropped to the floor. He says I should be careful, and I agree. The next day I go to the café owner and offer to patch his screen for a nickel.

✦   ✦   ✦

The fellows and I also earned money by picking strawberries. A few miles out on the highway was a farm where anyone could pick for a nickel a quart. We would ride out early in the morning, spend all day stooping to the endless rows, and take carton after carton to a table in the field where a woman marked a credit by our names. We earned as much as a dollar a day that way.

I got some perspective on this in the seventies, at our communal Downhill Farm. One of the communards, Tim, was a giant hippie in his thirties with long red hair and beard. He and I were picking strawberries in our garden patch. "I used to do this as a kid in a commercial patch outside of Perryopolis, Pennsylvania," he said. "We were paid a nickel a quart." His experience was in the late fifties—some fifteen years after I was paid at the same rate. Stoop labor is your hard dollar.

✦ ✦ ✦

Merwin's family acquired one of the newfangled motorized lawn mowers, and it seemed only natural for us to go into business with that, offering to mow people's lawns for half-a-dollar. But the first customer we found, our next-door neighbor, pointed out a new tree he had planted, warning us to avoid it. We hit it, so we did not get paid—and were quickly out of business.

✦ ✦ ✦

Edwin and I occasionally took jobs delivering the *Shopping News*, a free paper distributed door-to-door on Sundays. This required getting up in the wee hours, going to a specified corner, and waiting for a truck to bring the papers and our assignments—usually in an unfamiliar neighborhood. We worked in pairs, one on either side of the street, which was reassuring as we went down the dark streets, encountered strange dogs, and took the papers up to strange doorways. Apartment houses were generally a break, as you could walk along dropping papers rapidly at each door. One, though, had no lights in the hallways. I remember feeling my way along, bumping knobs, and, once, having a door suddenly opened in my face bathing me in light, a startled man in his underwear staring from inside.

Then I got a regular paper route for the *Houston Post*, which came out in the mornings. Ott built a wooden frame to attach to the luggage carrier of my bike. The frame held canvas bags on either side to carry the papers. I would ride before daylight to that same corner where the *Shopping News* was delivered, receive a bundle of *Houston Posts* for Idlewood, roll each and fold it into a locking triangle, stuff my bags, then go back to my neighborhood to ride along spinning the triangles onto porches. The Sunday papers were too fat to fold into triangles, so I had to roll them and hold them together with rubber bands. Both bags would be stuffed with these heavy rolls. I rode weaving with their weight, and it took quite a heave to get them across the yards and to the doors. Rainy days required covering the papers with a tarp, carrying each one and depositing it inside the screen door. And if I failed to deliver the paper dry, or failed to get it close enough to the door, I heard about it when I went round each month to collect. There were always a couple of extra papers in each bundle. I would stand on busy street corners and hawk these for immediate cash.

Included in my route, right next to the Hughes Tool Co., owned by Howard Hughes, was a trailer park—a new wartime phenomenon. Families moved in, seeking jobs in industry, and needing quick housing, so entrepreneurs opened lots with electric, water, and sewer services for mobile homes. The trailer park was a great place to deliver and collect for papers because the trailers were so close together. Collecting in the afternoon I would thread my bike through the kids and tricycles and wagons in narrow lanes. The place hummed with music from radios, laughter, screaming arguments, crying children. Men would sit in their tiny yards in their undershirts, cooling off after work, while women hung laundry on crisscrossing lines.

Another welcome variation on the route was the convent. The nuns and fathers had boxes in their mail room, so I could go in and dispose of a stack of about thirty papers I didn't even have to fold.

✦ ✦ ✦

It is a cool morning just after dawn. Delivering papers, I am coasting round the curve by the woods along the bayou just beyond Merwin and Betty's yard. A red fox is sitting beside the curb. I stop. It does not run away. I carefully, quietly lay down my bike, and, very slowly, cross the street toward the fox. It merely looks up at me, as though it were a pet. I sit beside it and pet it. After a while I figure I should finish my paper route and so I leave it there.

Deer showed up several times in those woods. They escaped from the grounds of Jax Brewery, a couple of miles down the bayou from us, and wandered along through the woods until they reached our area.

✦　✦　✦

Having learned of the *Idlewood Oomph*, Dad, after being in and out of sanitaria frequently and now, apparently, considerably recovered from his most desolate period, had begun sending me books by and about journalists. From this point on he took an active interest in helping me shape my career. First he sent me biographies of some of his heroes among political and humor columnists such as Arthur Brisbane and O. O. McIntyre. But, most significantly, he sent a book by Clyde Brion Davis, *The Great American Novel.* This is the story of a reporter who went from job to job around the country working on various newspapers. His great aim in life was to write "the great American novel," but he died without writing any fiction at all. The implication was that the story of his life was itself the great American novel (hence the self-serving title of Davis's book). This novel had a powerful effect on my growing sense of what it might mean to be a man: roving, recording experience, living a story tinged with melancholy. The men around me, like Ott, took jobs and settled down to mundane routine. But others, like this hero, had some mysterious drive, some mission, some hopeless destiny. Since I could not be like the men I knew, I figured that I had to become one of these. I would commit my life to wise, sensitive, lonely failure. . . .

Dad's letters were humorous, thoughtful, loving, giving me a sense of his earthy and philosophic style. He was the father to me

178

Ott could never be, influencing my thoughts, helping me define myself as a journalist, if that's what I wanted to be. He wrote about the books he sent and made me begin to see books in a new way—as challenges, as ideas, as products men wrote for good reasons. He engaged my intellect more than any adult I had known.

✦　✦　✦

At any rate, I thought I had found my career. Toward that end, I worked some on my high-school paper, but, more importantly, I got a job as a copyboy for the *Houston Post* (and gave up my paper route). I worked after school, starting at four and getting off at nine, and spent my hours among genuine newsmen. The copy editor was all-powerful, seated behind his semicircular desk in a corner. Other editors worked at the other side of the desk, facing him. Around the rest of the large newsroom were a dozen typewriters where the rewrite men pounded out the raw words that editors tidied into publishable stories. Rarely were the real reporters, the guys with notebooks on the scene of the crime or disaster, in the newsroom at all. They took notes out there in the brawling city and called in their stories to the rewrite men. The newsroom seethed with the clacking of tall, square Underwoods from the banks of news desks and the mumble of male voices from the ranks of wall phones (each in its booth up from chest height) around the room. (There were no women in the newsroom—or in the building, as I remember—except for the operators on the second floor taking classified ads.)

Part of my job was to tear off the news coming in on the teletypes: AP, UP, and INS (International News Service, later bought by United Press). It was thrilling to watch the keys clatter on the roll of paper hacking out words that were being entered into the system in some distant city—New York, Washington, Chicago, Los Angeles—instantaneously feeding them into these automatic typewriters (like player pianos) in our Houston office. Headlines! The latest! I tore off stories as they tapped out their final -30-s and took the sheets of uneven lengths to the copy desk.

There I picked up edited copy for the composing room. In that

179

vast dark inner sanctum were tall rattling linotype machines where men set the copy I would deliver. I remember these men typing with unbelievable speed on huge ninety-key keyboards that picked up matrices of type and dropped them into sticks, a line at a time, that were then cast and transferred to frames for the pages. If type was spilled or scrambled it was called *shrdlu,* a general word for a mess. In the recesses of that room were other men composing headlines in hand-set type. I marveled at their ability to work in mirror images of the print that would finally appear. And scattered around in pairs were the proofreaders, taking turns reading aloud to one another the proofs taken from the massive trays in which each page was set. Across town, at the *Houston Press* building (where I often went to deliver or pick up copy), Lois's husband Hubbard must have been proofreading in just such a compos-ing room.

My errands often took me to the morgue (where photos and bios of prominent people were filed—for reference when they died), the photography studio, and even to the thundering press-room where the gigantic reels of paper fed into tall machines, slithered through an intricate system of rollers, printed from huge arcs of metal masters on drums, and emerged as cut, folded, bundled newspapers right at the loading dock. Trucks backed up to the dock and hauled the bundles away—to drop them at cor-ners around the city where boys with paper routes—like me, only months before—would roll them and stuff them into bicycle bags to deliver to homes in their neighborhoods. I felt, for the first time in my life, that I had an overview of a complex process in which I might find myself a permanent slot.

The *Houston Post* building was downtown in what was becom-ing a black neighborhood. While I was working there race riots broke out in Detroit, Chicago, New Orleans, and other cities owing to tensions caused by the influx into these cities of South-ern blacks seeking wartime industrial jobs. Each night as I left work to catch the bus home I felt uneasy about mingling with the blacks—conscious for the first time that the color of my skin might put me in danger. The very idea that blacks might mob to-gether and attack police, as they were doing on Lake Michigan beaches that summer, was a shocking revelation to the reporters I heard talking around the office. So far as I know there had not been a significant black uprising since Nat Turner. It seemed like a rebellion of rabbits, so unexpected (to whites) was it that blacks might become violent in the streets.

I suppose I shared the attitudes toward race that were common in the Southwest at that time. Mother said to me early in life, for instance, that I should never put a coin in my mouth "because a nigger might have touched it." The contradiction between the as-sumption that a black's touch could contaminate and reliance upon blacks for cooking, cleaning, and child care did not occur to her until much later in life. I remember Audrey having a fierce loyalty to her black servants, Rob and Lily, and an interest in their family and personal lives very much like the interest she had in her own family members. Peggy related to Ruth much as to a white friend. But I'm also sure their attitudes included one ex-pressed by Ott regarding a black who had gotten "uppity" at the refinery where they worked: "I think a nigger can do anything he wants, so long as he knows his place."

✦   ✦   ✦

Behind the copy desk was a row of cubbyholes with pebbled, translucent walls from a man's waistlevel to the ceiling. These were the offices of special editors, such as those who wrote edi-torials, the fashion editor, the society editor, and, my favorite, the film critic. This thin, cynical, temperamental man, Hubert Rou-sel, reminded me of my father as I idealized him. He had a thin black mustache and used big words like *balletomane*. And his cri-tiques of movies were generally scathing. I think that his columns gave me my first taste of intellectual analysis and critical judg-ment. My contacts with him were very slight, but he was none-theless a star for me. And Merwin, home from college for the sum-mer, was envious of me for having actually met Rousel, as he considered his movie columns the most interesting thing in the newspaper.

◆　　◆　　◆

In the fall of 1941 I had started at Stephen F. Austin High School, about a two-mile bike ride from home. After finishing my paper route I would stop at the park in the center of Idlewood and run a few laps around the park, chin myself a dozen times on the bar by the swings, do some push-ups, then ride home to shower and get ready for school. Before leaving, though, I made notes on the wind direction and its estimated speed, the kinds and heights of clouds, and other weather observations for a merit badge I was working on in meteorology.

No doubt as a consequence of all this exercise, I tended to fall asleep in classes. Time after time I would be wakened by bells, getting the homework assignment from another student, then going to another class to sleep again. I had plenty of energy after school. To amuse myself I sometimes carried a screwdriver and pair of pliers in my pocket. During class I would surreptitiously remove the nuts and bolts from the chair I was sitting in. Done correctly, this operation enabled one to sit through class, leave the chair carefully, and wait outside the door to watch it collapse when the next student sat in it.

I don't remember making friends in high school. I went and came home with my buddies, chiefly Edwin, who was in the class above me, avoiding the kids who gathered in the parking lot with their cigarettes and lettered sweaters and saddle shoes and talk of dates and cars. My habit was to bring as few books home as possible. I was able to do most of my homework in the ten-minute breaks between classes that liberated me for the day.

Instead of gym I took ROTC in my last year at Austin, and I became very good at close-order drill. Each day we were issued a facsimile rifle of light wood: it looked very realistic. We learned fancy routines—I believe this was called the "Butts Manual"—for swinging our rifles around in unison—an act we performed at half-

182

time at one of the football games. I suppose we had ROTC in high school because the U.S. had entered the war in 1941. An army officer and sergeant were assigned to the school and had offices in a temporary building behind it.

Ironically, in view of my later career, I loved most and got my best grades in algebra, plane geometry, and physics. I had a crush on my physics teacher, a young, sad-eyed woman with long dark hair who seemed to take a special interest in me. I loved learning how things worked—mechanics, electricity, gas, heat. And the "thought problems" were challenging, though if there was a lot of arithmetic I was likely to make mistakes. I was challenged by problems in algebra and geometry because they had few numbers in them, but I was sloppy both in figuring and penmanship. Sloppiness earned me my one D—in mechanical drawing. I loved doing the ingenious three-dimensional projections, developing views of complicated objects from above, below, and each side. But when it came to inking in my drawings with india ink and those pincer pens draftsmen use, I made messes.

✦   ✦   ✦

I am sitting in Miss Melville's American history class staring at the lamps hanging from the ceiling, burning though the room is filled with afternoon light. Miss Melville is a baby-faced, somewhat chubby lady in her forties who looks perpetually astonished behind her glasses. She asks me what I am thinking, staring at the lights, and I tell her that the lamps are like kings visiting our country. They have all this power, but it isn't needed, because in a democracy the people have power that makes the power of kings seem weak.

Miss Melville tells me I am a philosopher. I don't know what that means, and she has difficulty giving an explanation except to say that a philosopher is a man who thinks.

On another occasion in this class we read an essay by Francis Parkman on the closing of the frontier. In response I wrote an essay saying that the frontier had gone inward, and now it was in scientific discovery, invention, and in artistic achievement, but the spirit of the frontier still carried us onward. Thoughts like that brought tears to her eyes.

She also wept when she discovered that she had spilled coffee on her lace bib in the faculty lounge, and no one told her about it. Why, then, did I pick that particularly sensitive and supportive teacher to terrorize? I had discovered that I could cut into the skin of my finger tips with a pocket nail clipper of the spring variety. I could make a little strand of skin stand up by itself. I did this in history class, by long and careful work, on each finger and thumb on both hands, three or four strands on each, each strand about a quarter of an inch long, so my hands looked as though they were sprouting toenail clippings. Holding my hands down at my side I approached Miss Melville's desk and said, "I wonder if you know what is happening to my hands." I held them out suddenly before her face. She screamed, of course, and nearly fainted, and I was immediately sorry. Did I learn such cruel humor from my father?

✦　✦　✦

When we studied Shakespeare in English classes (*Midsummer Night's Dream* and *Macbeth*), I enjoyed wrapping my tongue around those long and difficult sentences, those delicious and often archaic words, and dramatizing feelings. I remember being bored by *Silas Marner*, thrilled by *The Return of the Native* and Galsworthy's *Strife*, a play about an industrial strike that made me think for the first time about such matters as social class and justice.

My speech teacher, Mr. Andrews (brother of movie star Dana—who turned out to be an alcoholic), coached me to win a declamation prize, for which purpose I had written a patriotic speech all about what a wonderful country we lived in. (I think I had been inspired by the movie version of *Our Town* that came out that year.) Then Mr. Andrews wanted me to join the debating team. I said I wasn't interested. I knew the debate team had to do research about current events, and that seemed like a lot of extra work.

Apparently Mr. Andrews thought a good bit of me. In one speech class he asked for a definition of *poise*. No one answered.

He told the class that to know what poise was they should watch me. I remember lowering my eyelids as he said this, having no idea what the word meant. He pursued this matter of the debate team earnestly. Once he was driving me home from school (my bike must have been broken that day) and brought the matter up again. I again refused, and told him I wasn't much interested in current events. "You're not interested in what's happening in the world?" he asked, appalled and disappointed. I said I guessed I wasn't. Some journalist I would be!

✦ ✦ ✦

Houston at that time had an eleven-year system, no twelfth grade. Since my grades had generally been high, I did not have to take study halls and so had been able to squeeze in extra credits. By taking two courses in summer school in the coming year I could graduate at sixteen and start college. The idea was to get into college early so as to rack up as much credit as possible before being drafted. And Dad had agreed to support me at the University of Oklahoma, so that was the plan.

✦ ✦ ✦

The news from Oklahoma City, meanwhile, was that Dad had finally gotten his life somewhat stabilized—and had married his secretary, Evelyn. He wrote long letters to Stew and me for about a year. (I remember Ott's disgust when a letter for Stew would arrive with a six-cent airmail stamp on it—such a waste of money for a letter to a *child.*) When school was out in 1942 Dad sent money down for train fare to bring Stew and me up for a visit. Evelyn was a girl of twenty-six—eleven years older than I was. She was tall, quiet, gaunt, and big-boned, having been raised in bleak exposure on farms in the panhandles of Texas and Oklahoma, durable in body and character, yet tender, loving, childlike in her milk-fed and long-footed way. She was quiet, with a girlish, innocent wit, incredibly patient, understanding, accepting—and yet not indulgent—just what Dad needed, I thought. She had been a secretary in the oil business for some eight years. She knew what some men were like—and that they couldn't help it. When I think of her sweet clarity and shy, gangly, colorless but loyal love, I wish her life had been uncrossed by my father's tragic shadow. She gave him some half a dozen years of her life.

They had married with fifty dollars and a car, rented half of a duplex and a good office address (in a mid-city skyscraper), and began putting a life together. Stew and I would go to the office with them and amuse ourselves as best we could around the city. Sometimes we ran errands for Dad, such as taking his large plats of oil tracts down the street to have Ozalid copies made. I recall the sharp ammonia fumes from that huge machine turning its wide felt-covered rollers—a common method of copying before the invention of photocopies.

Dad always had an interest in our intellectual development. His own literary heroes included Elbert Hubbard, Robert Ingersoll, Robert Service, O. Henry, Mark Twain, Alf Landon, Will Rogers. He was impressed that I had taught Stew, who was nine, to play chess, though Dad had taught me the game when I was much younger than that. He beat each of us in turn and then turned the board back over to us to play together. He was annoyed that I still read the comic strips. Otherwise, he was enormously enthusiastic about whatever we said or did. And day after day he was sober. We had a fine visit until I, in the midst of my brief career in Methodism, perhaps priggishly suggested that we all attend church the following Sunday, which was Father's Day. Dad said he would go, but whether it was the promise I had elicited or sheer excitement at having us there that broke him down, when Stew and I got up on Sunday morning we discovered that he was dead drunk. Evelyn swiftly arranged for us to catch a train for Houston.

Between Dad's benders he became a gentle Dr. Jekyll. He had told me that in the period after the divorce he would often end up in a cheap hotel on skid row, sending the porter out to the bootlegger for gin and to the grocery store for orange juice, trying, he said, to drink himself to death, though the orange juice kept him alive. He showed me how a drunk gets the glass or bottle to his lips when he is too shaky to do it unaided. You wrap one end of a towel

186

around the hand with the glass, put the towel around your neck, and slowly pull the other hand to bring up the one with the glass. Eventually the porter would find him in such a state of deep unconsciousness the police would be called. They would take him to a sanitarium, where he would stay till he dried out. Sometimes he would show up in Tulsa at the apartment of Marie and Mammaw, behave rowdily, pass out on the couch, wet himself.

Now, though, Evelyn was his sanitarium. After a bender she would nurture him to sobriety, and he would stay dry for months at a time, and his letters to me would again be full of loving intelligence and concern.

✦ ✦ ✦

I was surprised to find myself in the National Honor Society (which I had never heard of) in my senior year and to receive a little gold emblem to wear on my key chain. Boys all wore key chains in those days. Girls wore skirts to their ankles, bobbysocks, and saddle shoes. I remember biking to River Oaks, the rich part of town, and seeing the girls spinning on their toes, their skirts belling, on the deep dark green lawns in front of the mansions under the bearded oaks. There was a senior prom, which I didn't attend (I had my job at the *Houston Post*—and no girlfriends), and a senior picnic at a park outside the city. That park had a game I never saw before or since: a kind of combination of golf and bowling. One rolled enormous balls—something like hard medicine balls—from a starting pad to a distant hole. The holes were laid out like those on a golf course with similar hazards—sand traps, water, and woods.

Summer school was held in the downtown high school, which I reached by bus. I had two courses but remember only the one in English. I was accused of plagiarism. We were to write a review of a movie, and I chose *The Young Mr. Pitt*, starring Robert Donat. I no doubt saw other reviews of the film, and no doubt did some background reading, but I know I didn't copy words from anyone, and I was outraged by the teacher's judgment that I had. The simple truth is, my writing seemed professional to him by comparison with writing by other students. No matter. Even with an F on that paper, I got an A in the course.

Curious memory: the teacher asked a boy sitting across from me in the back of the room to read Burns's "A Man's a Man for a' That." What's a *that?* I wondered. The tall boy stood and read it very movingly—and I discovered that if you pronounce "a'" as *aw* (for *all*) the poem, which had been incomprehensible to me, made sense and was really quite beautiful. My admiration for that boy, a stranger to me, was not only for his ability in elocution but for his knowing the trick. For *a'*, saw *aw.*

✦ ✦ ✦

So much for schooling, but nothing that happened in school affected me so deeply as the reading I did on my own. I remember, for instance, when I was about thirteen, Stew and I, because of the heat, often slept out in the screened room Ott had built in the backyard. I was reading *Northwest Passage* or *Arundel* and learned about no-see-ums, a biting gnat that plagued Benedict Arnold in his expedition through the northern woods. One night I woke with sharp drilling, prickling pains on my legs and arms. Frightened, I ran into the house and woke Mother, crying, saying I was being bitten by no-see-ums. She looked over my skin carefully and told me to wash with a cold washrag. It was, she said, growing pains, a term she used for almost all of my few physical maladies.

Mention of those books reminds me that I read *all* the historical novels by Kenneth Roberts and several by Walter D. Edmonds (such as *Drums along the Mohawk*), all of the Bounty trilogy by Nordhoff and Hall. As I look back on it, *Pitcairn's Island* probably had a great deal to do with the utopian streak that drove me into the educational reform movement in the sixties and seventies and then into communal living. I shared the dream of the mutineers, who wanted to build Paradise on a lost island, and I was deeply grieved that their perfect plan was spoiled by the men's tendency to drink and fight—over women!

I think I must have found out about such books by seeing movies based on them. Children were readers in those days. Movies were

188

teasers to draw one into the books on which they were based. As long as I can remember being able to read I went through one after another of the Big-Little Books—fat little volumes on pulp paper, with thick cardboard covers, costing a dime apiece. They were about two inches thick, three-and-a-half inches square, with versions of children's classics (or those adapted for children, such as the Tarzan stories of Edgar Rice Burroughs) as well as many narratives based on such figures as Disney and comic strip characters. *My Book House* was a multi-volume set of hardbacks filled with tales and poems of adventure, fantasy, exploration of other lands and cultures, history, love stories, and much else, many of them illustrated by full-page reproductions of paintings. That collection stayed with me throughout childhood.

We tended to read whole series of books. One series I grew up with was by Laura Lee Hope, about a dozen books with bright yellow covers, each a tale of toy animals and dolls that came to life when people were not around (as in the Andersen tale of "The Little Tin Soldier"). I read my way through the Booth Tarkington books (the Penrod series and *Seventeen*) and The Hardy Boys series (produced by a syndicate headed by Edward L. Stratemeyer, who "wrote" over four hundred novels for adolescents, including the Rover Boys series and the Nancy Drew series—series produced by the syndicate, though he wrote three of the Drew books and eight of the Hardy series). We read all of Baum's *Oz* books, all the Doctor Doolittle books, the Bobbsey twin series, and many others.

Edwin introduced me to the Little Blue Books, published by E. Haldeman-Julius—hundreds of titles one could get by mail for a nickel or dime per title containing everything from the atheist tracts of Robert Ingersoll to the poetry of Keats. I must have read dozens of them, learning about sex, politics, philosophy, science, and introduced myself to many literary works not mentioned in schools.

But if I were looking for the source of my true education in the written word during adolescence I would settle upon a few key books. I carried two of them from home to home for thirty years, having bound them in boards and canvas, the *Pocket Book of Short*

Stories and *The Story Pocket Book,* which I read again and again and which taught me most of what I know about short stories— and much of what I know about life. From Hemingway's "The Killers" to Willa Cather's "Paul's Case" or Dorothy Parker's "Big Blonde," stories that ranged through the techniques and themes of modern fiction in a way that thrilled many an adolescent (or adult) imagination.

Add to that *The Pocket Book of Verse,* which introduced me to five hundred years of verse in English. Looking again at a battered copy (the third printing, October, of the year of its issue, 1940), I thought that one could build a civilization from this blueprint. I remember having an Armed Services edition of it on Okinawa. Think of the millions upon millions of Americans who saturated themselves in this poetry: Chaucer (a poor selection), Shakespeare (songs and sonnets only), Donne, The Bible (delicious excerpts, including "The Song of Songs" presented as drama), Milton, Pope (no Dryden!), Blake, Wordsworth, Byron, Shelley, Keats, Tennyson, Browning, Whitman, Dickinson, Housman, Yeats, Robinson, Frost. . . . The most recent poets represented are Padraic Colum, Joyce Kilmer, Rupert Brooke, Orrick Johns, Elinor Wylie, and Stephen Vincent Benét.

And I remembered what qualities I responded to in these poems in my teens. For one thing, wickedness, as in Suckling's "Out upon it, I have loved / Three whole days together! / And am like to love three more, / If it prove fair weather." Majestic thought, as in Gray's "Elegy Written in a Country Churchyard": "Some mute inglorious Milton here may rest." The rich sentiment of Goldsmith's "The Deserted Village." The lusty joy of song: "Here's to the maiden of bashful fifteen; / Here's to the widow of fifty; / Here's to the flaunting extravagant queen, / And here's to the housewife that's thrifty." (Sheridan.) Terror and wonder, as in Blake's "The Tyger": "What immortal hand or eye / Dare frame thy fearful symmetry?" Democratic faith, as in Burns: "That man to man the world o'er / Shall brithers be for a' that." Poignant humor, as in Leigh Hunt's "Jenny kiss'd me when we met, / Jumping from the chair she sat in." Here's one I memorized because it made me weep: Thomas Hood's "The Song of the Shirt," beginning: "With fingers weary and worn, / With eyelids heavy and red, / A woman sat, in unwomanly rags, / Plying her needle and thread." How I was stirred by Emerson's "Here once the embattled farmers stood, / And fired the shot heard round the world"! I began to understand love "to the depth and breadth and height / My soul can reach," as described by Elizabeth Barrett Browning. I identified with Longfellow's lilting "A boy's will is the wind's will, / And the thoughts of youth are long, long thoughts."

Professors later taught me to sneer at poems that meant a great deal to me as an uninstructed reader. Kipling's "If" helped define manhood for me: "If you can trust yourself when all men doubt you, / But make allowance for their doubting, too." They used Kilmer's "Trees" as the paradigm of a bad poem. Little did I realize that I was attracted to it by its sexiness. In those days we didn't often encounter mention in print of hungry mouths being pressed against sweet flowing breasts or bosoms upon whom "snow has lain; / Who intimately live with rain." How I thrilled to the rhythms of Alfred Noyes' "The Highwayman," of Masefield's "I must go down to the seas again, to the lonely sea and the sky, / And all I ask is a tall ship and a star to steer her by." Children's poems such as Eugene Field's "Little Boy Blue" (another one I memorized because it made me weep) are in there cheek-by-jowl with Edwin Markham's "The Man with the Hoe," probably the poem that politically radicalized me in my youth. I learned from Oscar Wilde's "The Ballad of Reading Gaol" that "each man kills the thing he loves," and, though not yet a man, sighed, "How true! How true!"

But even more overpowering, because more comprehensive, was one of the Book-of-the-Month selections my mother acquired, *This Is My Best*, edited by Whit Burnett. Ninety-three living American authors chose what they regarded as their best work for this anthology, and what a roster they were: Theodore Dreiser, Ernest Hemingway, John Steinbeck, Henry Mencken, Stephen Leacock (American apparently includes Canadian), Conrad Aiken, Archibald MacLeish, Willa Cather, Sinclair Lewis, Mark Van

191

Doren, Bernard De Voto, Dorothy Parker, Stephen Vincent Benét, Van Wyck Brooks, Robert Frost, Edmund Wilson, Erskine Caldwell, John P. Marquand, Marjorie Kinnan Rawlings, William Allen White, Upton Sinclair, James T. Farrell, Richard Wright, E. B. White, Langston Hughes, Maxwell Anderson, William Faulkner, Katherine Anne Porter, John Dos Passos, Booth Tarkington, Edna St. Vincent Millay, James Branch Cabell, Robinson Jeffers, William Carlos Williams, Marianne Moore, Muriel Ruykeyser, H. D., Wallace Stevens, Edgar Lee Masters, Carl Van Doren, Joseph Wood Krutch, Eugene O'Neill, Thornton Wilder, William Saroyan, Clifford Odets, E. E. Cummings, Cornelia Otis Skinner, Robert Benchley, Ogden Nash, S. J. Perelman, James Thurber, Ludwig Bemelmans, Pearl Buck, Lillian Hellman, Edna Ferber, William L. Shirer, Stuart Chase, John Dewey, and Carl Sandburg. I list only a few of those whose work I continued to read, who are still part of the furniture of my mind. Each selection is preceded by a statement by the author, dated 1942, indicating why he or she chose the piece. I don't see how anyone could read this anthology at age sixteen and not become a writer. My impulse is to close down my word processor and reread all eleven hundred pages right now. If I sometimes dismiss the role of schools and colleges in my education, review of that list helps me understand why. Before finishing high school I had read and reread most of the selections in this book.

I was confident, as I picked it up again in the process of writing this, that one more selection formative in my life was included, but it is not, and that makes sense because its author is Scandinavian, not American. It is My Little Boy, and it was a short book, too long for an anthology. Some years after I read it, Helen Hayes recorded some selections from it for the radio. My Little Boy, from its title on, is an egregiously sentimental account of a father's relationship with his son, ending with the sad day he had to relinquish the child to his first day of school. It struck my heart. I remembered especially setting out for my first day of the first grade. My Little Boy influenced my view of remembered childhood experiences and is probably reflected in the early chapters of this book.

The mother is a shadowy presence in the background. It is the father whose gentle caring nurtures the boy's impulses toward freedom and originality and love of life and who sees the world, symbolized by the school, as the threatening external force to which the child must be tragically delivered. When I was far distant from my own father and did not have to deal with him in daily life, I was able to think of him as a man like that, one who nourished my inner being and regretfully turned me over to a world that probably would *not* nourish it.

✦ ✦ ✦

We had the *Encyclopedia Britannica* at home, and I thought I ought to educate myself about this alleged incipient dictator, Franklin D. Roosevelt, and politics in general. I read the entry on the Democratic Party. The Democrats were, it said, for the common man. I read the entry on the Republican Party. The Republicans were on the side of big business. The *Britannica* did not, of course, put the matter that simply; its language was complicated for me to understand. I thought I must have misunderstood, so I read the entries again and again. The book sounded so authoritative, so *sure* of itself, but I could not believe what I could no longer deny it was telling me:

My father—and all the adults I had grown up with—were on the *wrong side!*

✦ ✦ ✦

Aside from my D in mechanical drawing, a course that might have helped me earn a living, as it helped my father, the next lowest grade I was given in high school was a C in typing. My lack of neatness was, again, my undoing. But typing turned out to be the most practical course of all. You had to type to be a journalist, after all, though the legend was that *real* reporters used only two fingers. When I was drafted, the combination of my two years of college and my typing ability caused me to be given the M.O.S. (military occupational specialty) of, if I remember correctly, 502— administrative assistant. That put me into the orderly room of our little phototechnical unit on Okinawa, and because of that I was quickly made acting first sergeant (as soon as the veterans who had been in the unit during the war were all sent home). Discharged, and on my own in Chicago, my first job was as a typist, hired on the basis of my ability to type over sixty words per minute, mostly error free.

Typing is something a little guy can always do for money. Put that together with a knowledge of grammar and punctuation, and you will always be in demand. And put *those* skills together with the reading that filled my free hours and you have the makings of a writer, if not a journalist. I did not realize at sixteen how well on my way to a career I already was.

11

The Search

I have saved for last my major interest during my Idlewood years—camping out. Six of us in Troop 50 (six regulars) had organized ourselves as the Trailblazer Patrol. With burning pencils we made special leather emblems for our uniforms. We went camping on every occasion. Camping out in the Houston area was a challenge. It meant striking out on foot or bicycle as far as one could go in a day in a straight line, along shipworker-infested highways, until, say, a tree, or on lucky days a stagnant bayou, served as an example of nature—perhaps out of earshot of the highway. There one could open cans and bat mosquitoes till morning.

I'm sure I was unclear about my motivation at the time, but I now see that camping had two purposes: to escape the world of adults and to seek purity of spirit. Camping was a much more satisfactory way to do this than going to church.

✦   ✦   ✦

At some point after we moved to Idlewood, Peggy and Douglas sent us one of Tarbaby's descendants, and I named the cocker pup

Sissy. She was *my* Sissy, for some reason. I was to take her to college with me. In my Houston days I often had her along on our camping trips. I would put my bedroll and camping gear in one of the bags for newspapers on my bike, and into the other would go Sissy.

One trip we took in this fashion was to San Jacinto Battleground, down toward the coast. Mosquitoes drove us out of the woods and up to the monument itself—a tall obelisk something like the Washington monument. The base of this monument consists of some three square levels, each a story higher than the last. By standing on shoulders of buddies and hauling one another up after, we got all of us and our bicycles to the top level of the base and spent the rest of the night riding round and round it to avoid mosquitoes.

The next night we spent on a street in a small town between San Jacinto and Houston. We simply stretched our bedrolls on the sidewalk in the dark shadow of a café on a side street and, with Sissy standing guard over us and barking at everyone who passed on the main drag some ten feet away, we finally slept. We were awakened once by a policeman's flashlight, but, after looking us over, he left us alone. At dawn, though, came the shipworkers, piling into the restaurant for breakfast, hooting, honking, yelling at us, so we got up and pedaled on our way.

Shipworkers were our symbol of evil. They went roaring past in endless streams, first one direction and then the other, as their innumerable shifts replaced one another, wearing steel helmets, honking at our little file to get off the damned road, banging their fists on the car doors and shouting obscenities as they screeched and swerved to avoid us. We were sure they made not only ships in those acres of off-limits factories, but schools, diseases, bosses, landlords, bicycle chains that broke when you were miles from home and had no repair links along, mosquitoes, lawn mowers, newspaper routes, Latin assignments, and girls.

To fling oneself deliberately into such hardship and agony out there in steamy flatland on searing highways to dwell among the mosquitoes and shipworkers—this was surely not something we did for fun. We had been called. It was our mission.

◆　◆　◆

One Friday afternoon after school Edwin, Mike, and I decided to go camping. We packed up and set out for a neighboring town and were well on the road when I remembered that I had not left a note for Mother. So when we reached the town I went to the post office, bought a penny postcard, and told her where I was.

That night we came to a river near a small gas station and grocery store. We asked permission to leave our bikes there and hiked in through the woods that lined the creek, set up camp, then went back to the store—probably for pop. When we started back to the camp it was dark, but I had a flashlight. We walked and walked and finally realized that we had wandered away from the river and were lost. No matter. We'll follow Sissy, I said. Dogs *never* get lost. For a half-hour or so we trailed along behind Sissy—until I realized that if I flicked the light a bit to the right, Sissy went to the right. If I flicked it left, she went left. She was following the light, and we were following her!

There's a metaphor in that story for something—our tendency, in science and elsewhere in life, to see what we want to see, what chance throws before our eyes. When I realized what was happening out there in the woods, I thought of one of the little moron jokes that were popular in those days. A man finds this little moron searching the gutter under a streetlight. "What are you looking for, little moron?" the man asks.

"My quarter."

"Where did you drop it, little moron?"

"Down the block a way."

"Why don't you look down there, little moron?"

"It's too dark."

We did find our campsite eventually, rode on through several more towns the next day, camped again, and continued, making about a fifty-mile circuit in all. As I pedaled up to the house Sun-

197

day evening, Mother was standing in the front yard in a skirt and bare feet watering the lawn. "Hi," she greeted me warmly. "Where you been?"

"Didn't you get my card?" I asked. Of course not. No mail on Sunday.

"I figured you went camping," she said. "Your bike, Sissy, and your camping gear were missing." She did not scold me.

In one of my poems—for our son—I call the parent's capacity to permit a child to flourish without interference "the gift of letting go." Such a gift from Mother was one of her major contributions to my life. In a poem for her I talk about how we resembled one another more and more as we aged (she was sixty-six; I was forty-six at the time I wrote it), and yet she had generated an independence in me that I believe Marty and I generated in our five children:

> Five lines have sprung from mine, from ours, and each
> like a stubborn weed of some Southwestern strain
> asserts its independence of all nurture,
> stretching its own green vine, replete with thorns.
> I try to remember how you allowed that growth
> and how it cut you, remember that your pride
> could never be in worshipping resemblance
> but in the sinew that sustained all difference,
> glad as it twisted, rambled: "Just don't whine."
>
> Each time I wince and sigh and try to keep
> from interfering, I think of how you must have
> ached and yet refrained. I thank you for
> the things you did not save me from: They saved me.
> That is the heritage I can pass on
> and watch ironically how after all
> the breed affirms its strength in spite of wild
> diversion: Our pictures show us all alike.

✦   ✦   ✦

Camping, we were always looking for the Source. Water was our symbol of good. We spent days climbing through blackberry vines and canebrakes following the sluggish course of water in the direction it seemed to be coming from—a bayou, or, better, a small tributary (since the smaller the stream, the more likely we were to find its source). A source would be, we knew, if we ever found one, a limpid spring of potable, icy water pulsing eternally out of Texas soil. We forgave water for being corrupt as we found it, for we knew it began clean, around some bend and beyond some drainage ditch.

Most streams actually begin, I found—whether on the Continental Divide or in the Kiamichi Mountains or on Okinawa or in the plains of East Texas—in swamps. Suddenly the ground goes soggy underfoot as you are following the stream, and you find yourself desperately trying to trace the current in a field of weeds and muck. We tried to believe that this was just a phase the water was going through and would forgive it. The true stream, the real water, came from beyond or within. After sloshing around a while we would give it up. Perhaps that pure source, that hole in the ground, was out there in the middle of the swamp somewhere, overwhelmed by its own abundance. Or perhaps the stream entered the swamp at some point on the periphery that we had not discovered. But our failure was owing to our own frailty and in no way discredited the water, which worked in a way that passed our understanding.

Our faith was most nearly shaken in a large, wild park near Houston where a certain irregularity and rare rockiness of landscape seemed to us about like Colorado ought to look, and therefore any mystery was possible. We found a little runlet splashing down the bank into the central bayou. It was clear and cool—and we scrambled up the bank like bloodhounds, literally chasing it upstream as it twisted and spilled, running brightly over rocks, standing clear in tiny pools, and we began laughing in spiritual delight as we raced along, paddling in it, stopping to dash our faces, even wash our dry mouths (afraid, still, to swallow it, though

199

the temptation was maddening). For its size, it was incredibly long and persistent. Finally, of course, our hearts sank as we realized that it had led us out of woods onto a headland, and though it still babbled on clearly through the meadow, we felt the hot sun, the mosquitoes in midday, caught the heavy, muddy Houston odor, and knew that a swamp was inevitable. We could see houses across the fields, a road, cars. We were approaching a long ditch, where we found weathered signs clearly marking the source: "Old Latrine, 93rd Infantry, October, 1940."

Only twice did we find a source in the classical mold: just a hole in the ground with a stream trailing from its lips. And these were both in the vicinity of New Braunfels, where my family had vacationed in 1940 and saw where the exquisite Comal River welled up out of limestone in pristine clarity—a definitive source, marked with official plaques! In 1942 the Trailblazers—or at least Mike, Edwin, and I—went back to New Braunfels and explored the area thoroughly—and found another source.

We were not really nature-lovers. Oh, we could identify rabbits and squirrels and birds and trees (that is, we could tell birds from trees and either of these from rabbits or squirrels). We were reverential concerning growth and naturalness, absolutely anal about burying campfires and waste, never cutting green unnecessarily. We had an engineering bent, loving to make stepping-stone bridges in difficult crossings, a lean-to, a fireplace, stairs down a creek bank. We hadn't the least interest in those days in hunting or fishing. We liked hiking and biking to get places, but not for their own sakes, certainly not for exercise. Basically (like literary scholars) we were source-hunters: it was always up, up, up, always following water, always searching for what the English call "the unspoiled." We would break through the brush and come upon a vista in which there was not a single visible evidence of human life. No houses through the trees, no cleared fields, no barbed wire, no Kleenex or condoms underfoot. We stood there gasping, afraid to move or gaze an inch to right or left—until (this literally happened near New Braunfels) a beer bottle came bobbing down the limpid creek.

On that trip the three of us had taken to New Braunfels and hiked through beautiful Landa Park, where the Comal River rises, but where we could not camp. So we hitchhiked on to San Marcos and up above to Wimberley. Our family had discovered Blue Hole the year before, so I knew where we were headed. Near Blue Hole are some scrawny woods where we camped for a few days, spending our days around the swimming hole.

One night there was a frightful thunderstorm, and we woke up in soaking bedrolls. Nearby was a privy that had been built by the WPA, a substantial little two-holer with walls of corrugated steel and a concrete floor. We headed for that, squeezed together inside, and shivered. Finally Edwin had a bright idea. He dashed back to the campsite and returned with his hatchet and a rather large log. Bringing these into the shelter, he took the floor while Mike and I stood up on the seat platform. Edwin split the log, then split the dry wood inside into finer and finer pieces, ultimately coming up with some long splinters. He started a fire outside the door with these and toilet paper, protecting the young flame with his tarp raincoat until it was burning well. Then we could put on wet sticks and hunks of logs. We spent the rest of the night huddled by a bonfire in the open door of the privy.

Then there was the matter of the lightning and the mules. Mike stayed behind, but Edwin and I were determined to scale the highest mountain in the area (it was marked on the map—something over a thousand feet high, which meant maybe a couple of hundred feet above the flatland around it). This meant a day or so of hiking out on the treeless, arid landscape to where low scrub-covered hills rose above the generally flat terrain. We picked out the one we believed to be the tallest, tore our way through mesquite, scrub cedar, sage, and prickly pears and climbed to the top. And we whooped in celebration when we were on the bare knob. We would camp up there, we decided. Summits were, of course, like sources, definitive of something spiritual. We spread our bedrolls, scrambled down the side of the hill to find some firewood, then cooked a supper. Sitting there in the evening, after dinner, we enjoyed watching distant lightning striking hilltops like our own.

Then we began to think. Or Edwin the scientist began to think. Why, he asked me, are these hills covered with brush right up to the top, but the tops are all bald? I didn't know. Why, he pursued the matter, does the lightning strike only the tops of those hills? I didn't know. Lightning strikes the highest point in a low-pressure area, he explained. I was impressed by the elegance of his explanation.

The implications for us, as the storm rapidly blew our way, were apparent. We grabbed up our stuff in panic and ran scurrying down the mountain. We were in such a hurry that we didn't get things put away properly, and Edwin was carrying in his hand a fork and knife and can opener that had been in his empty pork-and-beans can. A crossed fork, knife, and can opener were to become part of the Trailblazer medallion in honor of this occasion. In our haste to get off the top of the mountain, we ran down the wrong side—the side *away* from the road. That meant that we had no alternative but to walk *around* the mountain—no doubt a couple of miles. That wouldn't have been so bad if it hadn't been for the mules.

At the bottom of the mountain we found ourselves in a pasture where there was a herd of the biggest, most beautiful mules I have ever seen—about twenty of them. They all looked identical: soft black fur except for their big white noses. And they had great curiosity concerning their human visitors. Neither of us was afraid of horses and mules, but the curiosity of the mules got to us. They formed a ring around us, sniffing us, especially the utensils in Edwin's hand. Whichever way we moved, the circle of mules moved with us—and we were beginning to get spooked. At last we reached a very sturdy barbed-wire fence—a high one with strands so close and tight we could not get through them. Eventually we got ourselves, our packs, and bedrolls over the top and made it round the mountain to the road, and, the next morning, back to where Mike was camped.

Then we decided to follow the creek that ran through Blue Hole to its source. Believe it or not, we found it, pure and beautiful as the eye of Heaven.

✦   ✦   ✦

A Handful of Grit

We camped upon the limestone lip four feet
above the artesian well, and by dawn light
we watched the fat bass rise. By night these dwelt
in a cavern at the bottom, off to the right,
an artery of the earth's clear water pulsing
beneath those knubbly hills.
                    From here a creek
flowed twisting east toward Wimberley (shallow
except at deep Blue Hole—a chill expanse
of current in cypress shade where we would swing
screaming on ropes and drop from dizzying heights).
Off to the west the channel formed a pond
of murky backwater, sluggish and warm, mud-bottomed,
its surface thick with lily-pads and bugs.

Up there was where those bass did business. They
would glide up from their cave as from a subway, ride
the invisible stream of the well and stately rise
like paunchy capitalists on an elevator—
up, up in silence, trembling not a fin,
becoming huge and huger in our eyes,
the size of muscled forearms—four stories up
the widening shaft, that hole in nature, then,
at the well's rim, a boy's length below
the glassy surface, they one by one would slide
off to the pond to make their busy deals.
Soon the backwater scum would break with geysers
where bass gulped down their breakfasts,
                          leaving the well
to us. Our campfire crackled on the cliff
beneath the overhang of yet another cliff
stairstepping up above the well. A Boyscout
skillet spat with lard, ready for eggs.
Mike had the little pot from his mess kit steaming
with Carnation for our cocoa. Edwin toasted
slices of bread on a green twig. I spread
our dewy bedrolls on branches of brush to dry.
Our business for the day required the sun

straight up above the well, illuminating
dark sides clear down to the glint of golden gravel
over forty feet below.
                              A throat. (A vagina,
though we were too young to think of that.) A tube
into the interior of the hills. Its steep
rock walls were green with velvet moss, and as
the morning passed the violet depths grew greener
until we could see down there the yawning black
of cave—opening into Wonder. Today,
this half-century later, scuba divers
take lights into the entrails of central Texas.
But our goal back then (the locals said *impossible*)
was simply to reach the bottom of the well.

This competition lasted several days.
The trick was to get enough momentum. A four-
foot dive from the bottom ledge was not enough
to carry a hundred-pound boy down very far.
When impetus from the dive gave out you breast-
stroked frantically straight down in the noon streak
of sun. Your ears would ache, your chest be bursting,
until your breath was gone. You twisted and kicked,
seeing the yawn of walls above, the shapes
of buddies on the cliff waiting their turn.
You shattered the surface, breaking out, and swam
to the bank. Over your trailing feet a body
arched from the cliff, using the precious sun,
while you flopped flat on the rock floor, panting,
gathering breath to take your turn again.

We needed a higher dive. The second lip
was over our heads, but back so far we had
to leap out to clear the first, and then correct
trajectory to go straight down without
bumping the wall of the well. And even that
was not enough, we found, as each of us
plunged to the limit of his breath and squirmed
kicking back up the column of rising current.

In all my more than sixty years have I
but once been cast as hero. It was there
at Jacob's Well, not from Wimberley,
at the leaking crotch of Texas, where the cold
clear purity wells up to find its way
downhill into corruption, there where we
gaped at the pit, were haunted, terrified
and lured down into unknown depths of manhood,
that I, smallest and lightest of the three,
climbed to the third step, surveyed the ledges
fanning below me. I leaped and dove, my belly
skimming the brink, and I was plummeting
past darkening walls, stroking and kicking on down,
the pressure like a vise against my ears,
the water dark and thick, a fluid wall—
until my reaching hand grabbed bottom gravel.

I squatted a moment, in horror of the hole
that blackly yawned by my knees, looked up the flue
that spread to light above me, then shoved away
and kicking rose as an angel floats to heaven
borne on a hyaline stream.
                                    I clutched my gravel
in my fist, handful of proof, my Ph.D.
While Mike and Edwin whooped an Indian dance
around me on the ledge beside my knapsack,
I wrapped the gravel in a brown scrap
of paper bag and tucked it in a pouch.
Now I could show them, show anyone, show Mother!
No one else in the world had a handful of gravel
from the bottom of Jacob's Well!
                                    And when at dusk
we watched the sated bass returning, counting
their killings, all unaware of the day's drama
in their elevator, and languidly descending
one by one to secrecy in the depths,
I proudly remembered that packet safely stowed,
still having failed to grasp that, as gravel goes,
it looked like any other. What did I

have in mind? Frame it—with an inscription?
Invite girls to my room to see my gravel?
Like another Ph.D. I came by later,
it was acquired with some effort and some risk.
Yet there it lay, hidden and useless, like
a poem waiting to be written, like
the stuff of manhood dormant in the groin,
those shards of Texas, tailings of time, once seized
by an adolescent in over his head.
Where it is now I can't imagine. I
would guess that after I left home my mother,
coming upon debris among my treasures,
just threw it out. I show it to you now,
bones reassembled:
                    My creased palm opens in lamplight,
those glittering flakes of quartz, feldspar, and limestone—
jewels for a hero's diadem. May their
shimmer in words commemorate forever
the dive of innocence in Jacob's Well.

✦ ✦ ✦

We arrived in New Braunfels too late for the noon train to
Houston. We had our tickets, but we would have to spend the
night in the little depot to wait for tomorrow's noon train. We had
nothing left in our packs to eat—and thirteen cents between us.
At the bakery we bought a hot loaf of bread for a dime, then, next
door at the grocery, three Tootsie Rolls. Back in the depot we
shared these, marveling at the good fresh taste of the hot bread.

We knew we should have saved a nickel to call one of our parents to pick us up when we arrived in Houston, but we were too
hungry. It would be a long hike from the downtown train station
to our homes in the outskirts of the city.

✦ ✦ ✦

What we sought as Trailblazers was progress. We wanted to *use*
that virginal land, and though we had no beer bottles and would
be tidy with our bean cans, our urge must have been partly to de-

file. We wanted to go out there in nature and live in it. We wanted to be the first. Nature for us, as it must be for everyone, was something ultimately to overcome.

Of course we also wanted to cleanse ourselves—with fright, labor, exposure, weathering. To cleanse oneself and to conquer, with nature as antagonist and material to be worked: how far it all was from any sentimental love of nature!

Let me dwell a moment on fright. "Oh, let's go up the hill and scare ourselves," Robert Frost begins "The Bonfire." Fright is one of the most stimulating and purifying emotions available, and the desire for it must motivate a lot of religion and camping trips: pushing into the Mystery, the spooky and inexplicable. As you go plunging through the woods the experience of back-crawling dread is most conveniently provided by snakes. I am scared to death of snakes and so is everyone else. (How wise was God to know that an alliance with a snake was the definitive betrayal of human essence!) Actually I have encountered very few in the woods, but I travel continually alert, stepping onto logs rather than over them, avoiding sunny patches of leaves or pine needles (in Texas the sluggish little fat brown copperhead that suns itself in such patches is the most common of the poisonous snakes). I sometimes think the desire to go camping is a desire to go out and be scared by snakes, to go deep into the woods and survive the night and come home again without being bitten.

I have never seen the bite of a poisonous snake, either, though I was vigilant in my boyhood and prepared to make X marks with my penknife and suck. Once upon a path alongside a bayou a sleepy cottonmouth dived across our way to reach the water and encountered the boot of the fellow in front of me. For a minute or so the boy hopped round and round on one leg, swinging the other, from which flopped about three fat feet of snake, whose teeth had gotten embedded in his rubber heel. The boy was thereafter changed. He had a kind of distance, a distracted, spiritual dignity that set him off from us, and we no longer included him in our adventures. There is a close link between fright, especially by a snake, and salvation.

Fright and pain. Deliberate exposure to discomfort is only on the face of it a curious way of having fun. Look how far the Pilgrims traveled to camp out and find fulfillment.

✦　✦　✦

I could take Sissy to college because Dad and Evelyn, his new wife, drove down to Houston to pick me up. The plan was that the Trailblazers would go to Oklahoma by train. We would pick them up at the Idabel train station and take them to Coleman and Willy's place in the Kiamichis for one last camping trip before I started college. We were there a week or so—on the far side of Mountain Fork from the Wards'. We dug a huge, deep hole for food storage and put a fifty-pound chunk of ice in it to preserve our food; then we piled it deep with brush to keep out critters. Injun, Coleman and Willy's fish-and-game warden son, brought us a quarter of venison (out-of-season, of course), and we stored it down there—under the ice. In the morning it was gone. The pigs that the Wards let roam wild in the woods had rooted it out and left the bare bones littering the campsite.

I showed the fellows how to noodle for fish and tried to show them how to use Coleman's Indian club to knock down squirrels. We were more effective with rocks. We were most effective with the .22 Mike had brought along. One day we decided to eat only what we could gather from the woods—a twenty-four-hour regimen. Noodling proved ineffective, as did fishing with worms. We got no squirrels. We did get a lot of berries, but we didn't know any other available, edible plant life. The only game Mike bagged with his rifle was a blue jay, which we plucked and roasted, but it wasn't very satisfying, divided among six guys. Another night we decided to go off separate ways and each sleep alone in the woods. You could take a flashlight. I thought I had a great advantage, as I had Sissy for company, but she woke up and barked at strange noises every few minutes, and I began to wish she would go off and sleep elsewhere, but I supposed she was scared to be alone. I brought her into my bedroll with me, covered her head, and she settled down.

Our camp was near low falls stretching clear across the wide Mountain Fork River. Much of my early swimming had been just above those falls. About twenty feet from the side where the Wards' complex was located was a flat rock about six inches below the surface, and it was an adventure of my young childhood to be able to make it (at first, of course, in Mother's company) from the slick pebbly shore out to that rock—without being swept into the falls. It was safe. There was a declivity *behind* the falls, so one would not be swept over in the inch of current that spilled down the slanting curved surface. But swimming out to that rock was an adventure.

On this trip I was swimming for it underwater, my eyes open, and there coiled on the rock was a cottonmouth, its head beneath the surface. I had often seen moccasins floating by in the river, their heads like black knobs with their open mouths, indeed, appearing to be full of cotton, but I had never seen one under water. If I had been swimming on the surface I might well have come down on the snake with a stroking arm. Having spun round and beat a retreat to the shore, I felt the tingling of lower-back muscles that told me I had, once more, been purified.

✦　✦　✦

That trip was a kind of farewell to childhood. I was seeing most of those guys for the last time. I remember their faces—Chester, Punky, Edgar. All, including Edgar, agreed that Edgar was the dope of our patrol. He once fell from the balcony of our second-floor meeting room at Riverside Baptist and landed on his head, but that was an effect, not the cause, of his dopiness. Our scoutmaster taught us close-order drill on the lawn in front of the church. (War-readiness was a major theme of the scouts in those days.) "Fall *in!*"" called the scoutmaster. "I *fell* in," called Edgar. "I fell in a *goopher* hole."

For relaxation at Trailblazer meetings we played War. We played civilized games and uncivilized games, and War was one of the latter. It consisted of trying to grab anyone's balls you could. You danced around the yard, your own balls cupped for protection in one hand, reaching for those of someone else with the other. We played one memorial game of War at our camp in the Kiamichis, then said goodbye.

That game reminds me that the Trailblazers, not counting an occasional obscenity like this game, had little to do with sex. I don't remember our even *talking* about sex, though I suppose we did. None of the Trailblazers went out with girls. My infatuation with Shirley was the only case of one of us even imagining he had a girlfriend.

✦ ✦ ✦

I wrote about all this in my first book, *Birds in the Wilderness*, a title taken from the song we sang at the Boy Scout camp while waiting for food. Book? It must have been about thirty pages long. It was meant to be funny, for we saw our adventures as funny at the time. I had unconsciously taken on the role of chronicler. At some level I assumed already that experience was no more than the raw material of literature. You went out in the woods, indeed you lived, to have something to write about.

There was one more big camping trip to come in my early life— with Mike in the Rockies, in the summer between my two years at the University of Oklahoma. Or perhaps the climax was my year in a tent on Okinawa, that ultimate scout camp, while I was serving in the United States Air Force. Marty and I took to camping out after we were married, and again after we began having children. On our last camping trip—once more in the Rockies—she was in her latter months of pregnancy with our third child. Camping out was for much of my life an end in itself. If we fished or hunted or engaged in any other activity, that was incidental, for survival. It was being out there facing the discomforts inflicted by nature that counted. In one poem on the subject I say, "Life lives a self-willed test." Though I've never been an athlete, and certainly would not compare our feats of endurance with those of mountain climbers or hangglider pilots or others who deliberately put their lives at hazard, I suppose the satisfactions are similar in kind if not degree. You pitch yourself against some limits; you slam hard against

210

the world until you finally find that there is, indeed, something *real* outside yourself. The world slams back. The punishments that people inflict on us, deliberately or not, seem relatively arbitrary, compared with those Nature so casually administers.

> . . . if in the granite State of Maine
> by the clear cold sea you wrest some campfire comfort
> from driftwood, scrubby spruce and rocks, or rain
>
> cutting around a stretched tarp does not
> quite penetrate, or if, at Fundy, where
> the headlands loom all shaggy in the fog,
> the coffee perks, and in your duffel a pair
>
> of dry socks waits your weakening, you know
> my recluse ecstasies. . . .

"Who knows what fun / is any more?" the same poem asks. I didn't. It had been a theme of my life to find out. And the search continued to take me down strange avenues.

12

Freshman

In the summer of 1943 I had left the most secure and permanent home I had known in my life for the big world, and though I did not realize it at the time, I would be adrift until I settled down in Chicago with Marty in 1948. Mother and Ott had been my parents for nearly four years—a fourth of my life. Now I would be a college boy (five feet tall, weighing a hundred pounds, looking as though I were eleven) living away from home in a dorm, reporting in, if at all, to a new set of parents—one of them, Dad, a questionable support at best, and my stepmother, Evelyn, largely an unknown quantity.

Dad and Evelyn had rented a one-room log cabin in the country. A large asparagus bed came with the property, and I learned to harvest that delicious vegetable by using one of those long dandelion weeders with a V point. At sixteen I was old enough to get a driver's license, so Dad began teaching me how to drive—and, sure enough, before I started college, I not only could drive but had smashed up the front of the car. Still on my learner's permit, Dad on the seat beside me, I was approaching an incline for a railroad crossing. The car in front suddenly stopped as the signal arm lowered and began drifting back. In my panic I could not remember where reverse was.

Dad was supplying me with the necessary skills for coping as a man. I remember once following him into a butcher shop and watching him, waiting for service, dangle his keys. When we went back to the car he told me I should get in the habit of jingling keys that way. "It lets people know you are important and in a hurry."

During the next two years I saw a lot of Dad. For sometimes months at a time he would be sober before another week-long attempt to find obliteration in drink. There were times when he was too drunk to drive and would insist that Evelyn or I take him to the bootlegger's. Oklahoma's prohibition made liquor no less available there than elsewhere, but it was more expensive and more directly associated with crime and seediness. Dad could force one or the other of us to take him by threatening to go alone and weaving out the door with the car keys.

Dad's bootlegger in those years operated from a clandestine bar up a flight of steps in a shabby building in the slums. Evelyn or I (or both) would sit out in the car, sometimes for hours, waiting for him to come staggering down the steep, dark stairs of that hideous building, a bottle tucked in the pocket of his flapping, vomit-stained, blue topcoat, and reel across the street to be driven back to the cabin out in the country.

Home again, and the long night interrupted by his trips to the kitchen to get another drink. While going to the university I stayed weekdays at the dormitory in Norman, twenty miles away (reached by an interurban train), but I spent a good many weekends with them in their tiny cabin. I hiked miles in the surrounding woods that year chasing Sissy through the snow, dreading the house, the long single room with a bed in a nook at one end and a kitchen in a nook at the other. I slept on a trundle bed that pulled out from under their bunk, so that Dad stepped on my mattress whenever he crossed to go to the sink. Evelyn never argued. She protested only weakly, in whispers in their bed. She rarely cried or showed the incredible strain, though some mornings I would find she had slipped down to sleep beside me on the trundle bed.

"What would you do if I came home drunk?" I asked him once.

"Slug you."

"Suppose I should slug *you*, now?"

(To imagine the outrageous humor of this you must remember that I titillated the scales at a hundred pounds—a cocky little snot. And Dad, though by no means a big man, was about nine inches taller than I was, with a ropy muscularity, unshaven now, with bloody-rimmed eyes and a heavy slur, leaning against the refrigerator and drainboard as in the corner of a ring. . . .)

I lifted my chin proudly and did not stoop to fight.

Perhaps I should have, though. It would have done me good to be beaten. But, of course, he would not have fought. He would have cowered, as I found him once huddling on the floor in the back room of a bar. A geologist friend had called us from the bar to say that someone should come to pick up Ralph. Evelyn had a new baby to take care of, so I set off to get him at about one in the morning. Rob, our friend, was waiting in the bar. "He's back there," he told me, pointing at the kitchen's swinging doors. "The bartender thinks Ralph knows where his floozy has gone, but Ralph doesn't know a thing about it. He was sitting here with me the whole evening."

I drew myself to my five-foot height and pushed through the swinging doors. Dad was lying there in his overcoat, his knees drawn up to protect his stomach, and the bartender was standing over him with a lifted butcher knife, kicking him again and again. "Let me take him home," I pleaded, and I dragged Dad out to the car and somehow got him into the passenger seat, then started the car, threw it into reverse, and backed fast out of the diagonal parking space. Our bumper caught the fender of the car beside us, making a loud ripping sound. No one came out of the bar. I thought, "I've got to be careful. I could mess this up. It doesn't do to mash up fenders of strangers." I shifted to first, went forward, freed our bumper, and set out for the highway.

I think I may have felt heroic. This is what big fellows do—go into bars in the wee hours of the morning and confront gigantic armed bartenders and rescue their fathers. I can reconstruct the emotional mechanics of that situation. My moment of anger and fear had gotten me into trouble. Got to shape up. Got to control this machine. Got to complete my mission. Dad, slumped beside me on the seat, barely conscious, was cursing—at me or the bartender, I couldn't tell which. There simply was no room for any number of other things I might have been justified in feeling: resentment, disgust, righteousness. Evelyn met the car behind the cabin, and the two of us got him into the house, out of his clothes, and into bed. I probably went promptly to sleep. I had by that age thoroughly learned how to close down responses that interfered with survival.

As for Dad, his collapse on the floor was indicative of his view of himself. True, the bartender was a powerful fellow, but that was not the reason for Dad's complete, submissive surrender. Innocent in that case, he somehow felt he was wrong, no matter what the circumstances—and feeling wrong made him snap but not strike; his resistance was verbal—sarcasm, obscenity, picking, sneering, snarling. And even drunk he could talk rings around most people who argued with him, slicing away with cutting truth at their personalities in the process. But he hated himself, wanted to be stopped, and would have welcomed, I suspect, physical punishment and restraint.

Looking for limits. The era of repression, rigidity, and moralistic restrictions in which Dad grew up gave way in the twenties to one in which people suffered the ills of expression, of freedom without meaning, of permissiveness and indirection. These, too, can drive one mad. I would not claim, of course, that punching my father in the jaw would have cured his alcoholism. Mother had tried that long since, and it didn't work. But it was difficult to know how to be kind. Mother's way was dangerous: not for her, but for him—as she surely knew that by leaving him she was risking killing him. But her way at least cast him back upon himself and forced him to discover his resources if he was to live at all.

216

"You're insecure," I once informed him with collegiate glibness.

"You're goddamn right I'm insecure."

"Well, Dad, that's the sort of thing a psychiatrist can maybe help you with."

"You tell me how the hell a psychiatrist can make me secure."

"But it's not that you're *not* really secure. It's just that you *feel* insecure." Just listen to me.

"Listen, Buster, I *am* insecure." Listen to him.

And of course he was, and however seriously I took my father it was never seriously enough to grant that his ruin had some meaning. Sober, he was sane, penetrating, witty, tender—albeit Elbert Hubbard and Arthur Brisbane did not, perhaps, provide him with enough ideas to understand his world. One of his mottoes was, "I never lie unless it's absolutely convenient"—ethics I seem to have inherited. He understood too little to express or contain the rich possibilities of his own sensibility. And through that gap ripped the currents he could not swim. His ethos had no use for his capacity for love and vivid response; rather, it demanded toughness and cleverness in pursuit of what it defined as success—a rather narrow definition, too: money. Whatever of his verdant being could not be sold for cash was left to rot on the vine or sour in the soil, to ferment and decay, to lie in darkness until some rotating bit cut through the cap and all spewed in a wild black fountain. Minds not permitted to answer dull themselves so that they will not question. Hearts that opened themselves have been ignored or injured. One tends to wise up, get smart, and pickle the tender parts exposed. How well I know.

Aside from his uneconomical personal habits Dad was also cursed with generosity and spontaneity—as when he got drunk and bought out half a toy store for that emaciated little black boy he picked up out in the country (while trying to make a royalty deal on the farmer's scabby patch of cotton land). We ate steaks when there wasn't money to fill the gas tank—not because he liked eating (he, like most alcoholics, avoided food) but because of his sheer joy in good things and a pathetic urge to make up to his family the pain of enduring him. He was too soft to survive: he once set off on a bender because—while Evelyn was in the hospital for the birth of their daughter—my cocker Sissy, at home, had pups. Otherwise, he claimed, he would have been all right.

He gave me that explanation in the sanitarium where I found him when I came over to see the new baby. He was in his pajamas, robe, and slippers, and we sat in a sunny day room to talk—Dad seeming at the top of his sober form. He said he wasn't ready to leave the sanitarium yet, but he would certainly like to be out for a while, if I would take him for a drive in the country. So he got dressed, I signed him out, and we drove, and he persuaded me to stop at the bootlegger's so he could have "one beer"—and an hour later I supported him as he staggered back into the sanitarium.

The open heart, closing, clamps tight. He became vicious, sadistic, sneaky, cruelest to those he loved. (Oscar Wilde's "Ballad of Reading Gaol," which says, "each man kills the thing he loves," was one of his favorite poems, a theme revived in a popular song of the times, one he liked to croon, that had as its refrain, "You always hurt the one you love, / The one you shouldn't hurt at all.") He never got smart and didn't know anything else to try to be.

"But intelligence isn't a virtue," I told him prissily, fending a compliment.

"The hell it isn't," he said and told me an intricate story of how a friend had made a clever deal, substantially cheating the government of tax money, and cleared several thousand dollars. "Now I tell you," he concluded, punching his finger on my pigeon chest, "intelligence is a *virtue*." One of his favorite books was O. Henry's *The Gentle Grafter,* and I think he must have seen himself as that variety of frontier hero who swindled his way through life.

However, intelligence in that sense—the ability to outwit—he never really acquired. In spite of his outrageous self-centeredness when drunk, he never developed a proper sense of self-interest, and his last act of charity was, in 1947, to weaken his condition sufficiently that virus pneumonia could, at last, relieve us of him.

✦   ✦   ✦

Alcoholic

My father (didn't everybody's?) drank—
the Dread Disease, plague of his generation,
and we were patient, swallowed down his spite,
and understood him as he thrashed and sank,
and all forgave, with whining and evasion,
and all refrained from saying wrong or right.
We knew, in dry, bright Oklahoma City,
the only cure for drink was love and pity.
We knew the flesh was frail, with delicate breath,
and so indulged each other into death.

But when he dared me, cursing me, demanding,
and shuffling scrawnily down halls of the mind,
sagging his jaw, speaking with tongue gone blind,
should I have answered him with understanding?
He cannot help the things he does, we said.
(He grinned and snitched a ten and drove off, weaving.)
His heart, we said, is spotless—but his head
disturbed. (Late I would hear him: racketing, heaving.)

Years after he was gone I think I saw
how we insulted him, drove him along:
his spirit we called nerves, said nerves were raw—
denied his holy sanction to be wrong.
The sonofabitch (God bless him) drank and died
because we understood away his pride.

✦   ✦   ✦

   Now, over forty years since he died, he continues to stalk my
imagination. The two people I have learned most from, both of
whom I loved dearly, have been the two who caused me the most
pain—my father and our brain-damaged daughter Jenny, now,
also, deceased. They are the only figures who recur in my dreams.
Jenny is always comic in those dreams, full of mischief as she was
in life, and I always wake feeling better about life for having
dreamed her back. My father appears in his overcoat with up-

219

turned collar and felt hat, its brim down over his eyes. He stands at a distance, his hands in his coat pockets, and says nothing, but I know he is saying, "I'm sorry," and though I say nothing I am hoping he can hear my thoughts: "I know. I know." All his life he *was* sorry—for what he was, for what he couldn't, I suppose, help being. From my dreams of Jenny or Dad I wake with a sense of profound loss of relationships I would not relive for the world.

◆   ◆   ◆

Before driving me over to Norman to start college Dad took me to town to buy a suitable wardrobe. The most spectacular items in it were six sleeveless sweaters, wool and rayon, each a different color. He explained that these took the place of a vest: you always had something over your shirt when you took off your sports jacket.

One September evening, then, he drove me to my dorm (a Jewish fraternity house, Sigma Alpha Mu, the Sammies—all fraternities were inactive since so many men were in the service, so the university operated their house as a dorm.) "I'm glad I don't smoke yet," I said in that car filled with deep thoughts and long silences. I remember especially one piece of advice Dad gave me on that trip: "Remember, it's not *what* you know, but *who* you know that counts." He explained that sons of some of the wealthiest and most influential families in Oklahoma would be in my classes. Knowing such people was, he said, how college men got ahead. Years later I was to see a deeper significance in what he said—a significance that I'm sure he never saw. Human relationships are infinitely more significant and valuable in our lives than any knowledge we acquire.

I was ridiculously far from the manhood I should have been approaching: a runt moving into the Sammies' fraternity house—a journalism major, starting the next day. The first evening, before registration, the dorm members met to socialize in the living room—a long, elegant room with plaster stalactites painted silver hanging all over the ceiling. I noticed that most of the fellows had National Honor Society medallions on their key chains, so I took mine off that night and never wore it again. The pond was larger, and so were the fish around me.

✦   ✦   ✦

I was sitting on our living room floor with Mother, studying the University of Oklahoma catalog. She would turn to the pages relating to geology or engineering and say, "Oh, look at all *these* nice courses." Growing up and becoming a man in the Southwest meant getting into the oil business. It meant I should prepare to take my place standing with other real men in the kitchen drinking bourbon and talking cars, or sports, or taxes, or profits. None of those things interested me.

Single-mindedly I would turn to the journalism section and say, "But these are the ones I want to take." I ended up, in my two years at the University of Oklahoma before I was drafted, as a major in the new School of Letters—a combination of English, philosophy, and history. But back home in Texas I could think only in terms of career. You went to college to learn how to make money. I knew what a journalist was. But what was a letterist? (Actually, the School of Letters major was not in that catalogue. It began during my second semester, and I was one of its first recruits.)

What I was really thinking of was not so much writing for newspapers as living a life of beautiful failure like the hero of Clyde Brion Davis's *The Great American Novel.* Life is a novel, I thought. Experience is art. What one must do is suffer gracefully and unostentatiously, and his heart will become an epic. At sixteen, one has a fearful need of committing oneself to the tragic way of life. Or at least I had, and perhaps that was why I did not major in engineering.

I knew that I was not like the other students. They happily accepted their lot in conventional society, in a world for which I was unfit. I was an outcast, and that made me special, though I knew I would be a failure in the world's terms. Where does one pick up from our culture an ennoblement of suffering, of sickness, of failure? Surely I got it from my reading, as it was not around me in the

221

Southwestern milieu. I remember, in freshman English, reading a short essay by Deems Taylor about Richard Wagner. Titled "The Monster," it depicted Wagner as a monumental egoist, a vain, petty leech who subjected friend after friend to torturous displays of his work and relentless litanies of his needs. Yet, for Taylor, as, Taylor said, for most music critics in the world, the supernal beauty of Wagner's music redeemed him. The world must suffer such monsters in its midst if it is to have great art.

I bought this line, and though I wasn't up to being a true monster, I could try. I cast myself as a great artist *manqué*. As I later learned more about the literary life I found variations of this conception of the artist or poet in the lives of Edgar Allan Poe, Hart Crane, Sylvia Plath, Dylan Thomas, and other monsters who made life miserable for themselves and those around them in the name of art. There must have been thousands of us in the twentieth century who, at one time or another, set out more-or-less deliberately to destroy our lives in the belief that that was somehow the path to aesthetic insight and achievement. Perhaps I read Taylor's essay as an apologia for my father's life—and as a license for my own destructive and self-destructive behavior in later life. But for the nonce it provided a rationale for a new posture—I would *seem* tragic, even though nothing in my life really warranted it. In such attitudes flourished the widespread tendency to cherish an unhappy childhood, as though such a childhood set one apart as a somehow more delicate, refined, superior being, like an eighteenth-century lady with the vapors.

Sometime during my freshman year, no doubt grubbing in the library for material for my radio program, I discovered another author whose life and views influenced me greatly at the time. In the latter half of the nineteenth century, at age sixteen, Arthur Rimbaud had left his provincial hometown to go to Paris, the cultural center of Europe. Well, the University of Oklahoma at Norman was not exactly Paris, but I saw a certain resemblance between Rimbaud's story and mine. And he became for a time my literary hero. Rimbaud had set out deliberately to be a poet, and he soon devised a program for achieving that end:

I say one must be a *seer* [*voyant*], make oneself a *seer*.

The Poet makes himself a *seer* by a long, gigantic and rational *derangement* of *all the senses*. All forms of love, suffering, and madness. He searches himself. He exhausts all poisons in himself and keeps only their quintessences. Unspeakable torture where he needs all his faith, all his superhuman strength, where he becomes among all men the great patient, the great criminal, the one accursed—and the supreme Scholar!—Because he reaches the *unknown!* Since he cultivated his soul, rich already, more than any man! He reaches the unknown, and when, bewildered, he ends by losing the intelligence of his visions, he has seen them. Let him die as he leaps through unheard of and unnamable things: other horrible workers will come; they will begin from the horizons where the other one collapsed!

This credo, expressed in a letter to a mentor, was manifested in *Une Saison en enfer*, or *A Season in Hell*, a book I carried under my arm for weeks and ostentatiously displayed to my fellow-students and professors. It was filled with incomprehensible but inspired ramblings:

One evening I pulled Beauty down on my knees. I found her embittered and I cursed her.
I took arms against justice.
I ran away. O witches, poverty, hate—I have confided my treasure to you.
I was able to expel from my mind all human hope. On every form of joy, in order to strangle it, I pounced stealthily like a wild animal.

And so on. I took this vision of the artist to my heart and set about, in my innocent way, to drown myself in excess. Drink, drugs, and sex were unavailable, so I took up cigarettes and in one evening thoroughly deranged my senses to the point of nausea.

✦   ✦   ✦

223

I set out quite deliberately that evening to learn to smoke. At first, during a bull session in the dorm, I begged a cigarette from one of the other fellows. They took delight in corrupting me and gladly supplied me with that one, then another and another. I tried a pipe. I tried a cigar. Suddenly the room was spinning. It was about two in the morning. I staggered down the stairs heading for fresh air outdoors and collapsed full-length on the lawn. I could hear a couple approaching along the sidewalk. If I just lie still, I thought, they will not see me. But I couldn't help myself, and they must have been startled, as they passed, to see a form rise from the dark lawn on stiffened arms, heave onto the grass, then pitch himself to the side and fall flat onto his back, staring at the wheeling stars.

✦ ✦ ✦

Most of my excess, though, was in the realm of ideas and rhetoric, pursuing things to their limits, shocking my dormmates and professors with my willingness to outrage. Or such was the image of myself I cultivated in private. I generally lacked the nerve to indulge overtly in such behavior.

Meanwhile I repressed the remainder of Rimbaud's cautionary life story—how he was burned out by age twenty or so, abandoned poetry and literature entirely, and lived an unrenowned life in Africa, gun-running and probably slave-trading, in a newly found dedication (never to be achieved) to get rich. He died impoverished at thirty-seven with a cancerous leg.

✦ ✦ ✦

I was crossing campus in short pants. A woman stopped me to ask the way to the university's demonstration elementary school. I didn't know where it was, but I knew why she asked me. I did not wear short pants on campus again.

✦ ✦ ✦

My journalism course was chiefly concerned with writing the same story over and over with different leads, emphasizing in turn

224

what, who, why, where, and *how.* For my beat on the campus daily I was assigned the Agricultural Science Department barn. There I pursued regularly the status of various pregnant cows. I became associated with the newspaper crowd, the upperclass journalism majors, who seemed to me a noisy, pushing, and vulgarly tough-minded bunch. I was rapidly becoming disillusioned with journalism.

Meanwhile I was having some surprises. I remember especially Professor Gustav Müller, my withered, tiny philosophy professor, with his giant hanging meerschaum, giving as his first assignment the first paragraph of Plato's *Republic.* Read a paragraph? I could read it in a minute. Philosophy appeared to be enormously easy stuff. But the next day we tried to discuss that paragraph in our little seminar of eight, and Professor Müller, inexplicably, was outraged that we had found so little. The next day's assignment was to read it again. As I spent a couple of hours that evening asking myself what the little man wanted me to see in that short narrative paragraph—involving, I remember, festivities and religion—I began to comprehend something of what it means to think—just to sit down and think. After poring over that paragraph twenty times I decided to draw a chart of what it meant. I don't remember what was on the chart, but it was a spider web of terms with lines connecting them in curious ways, and Professor Müller was so elated with it that he copied it on the board and spent an hour lecturing about it.

Scrawny Professor Müller, with his thick accent and erratic humor and jerky gestures, replaced Clyde Brion Davis's journalist as my ideal. Looking back, I realize I had had a crush on Herr Professor not unlike the one I had on Shirley in high school. I spent many fall evenings walking up and down outside his home, seeing him occasionally cross his study in the lamplight, puffing his huge pipe, hoping that he would just happen to come out for a walk and, on the way to the corner drugstore, tell me the Meaning of Life. He was a remarkable little man, often spending afternoons in college hangouts drinking beer and playing chess with students. No one had ever heard of his losing a chess game. He explained to me once how he won: "I listen to the chess pieces," he said. "I ask them what I should do next. They tell me how the board looks from where they stand."

✦ ✦ ✦

Though the radio programs I was writing for the campus station consisted mostly of patriotic cant (those were patriotic times), I was coming to see the function of the writer in a different way. Instead of the melancholy ineffectual journalist, I now wanted to be Jean Paul Marat, the French revolutionary who wrote in sewers against all authority. My dormitory mates called me "the Little Radical," from the title of a biography of Marat—another book I carried around ostentatiously. Marat, Rimbaud, Professor Müller— my mind was becoming cluttered with models. The main thing was to be a rebel. I cannot remember all I was against in those days, but among them were government, society, proctors, industry, commerce, manners, creamed dried beef, military science, and journalism.

One of the faculty was a professional writer, Walter Campbell, who wrote under the pen name Stanley Vestal. This stout man with a grey moustache and red cheeks referred to literature as "the writing game." His courses (which I never took) were characterized by realism about markets and slick techniques. His students studied ten different periodicals at a time ranging in intellectual quality from *Woman's Day* to *Saturday Evening Post.* Adrift from journalism, finding the heights of Professor Müller's mind inaccessible, poisons of Rimbaud hard to come by, the sewers of Marat romantically distant, but still in search of a model, I went to see Professor Campbell to find out whether I should study to become a professional writer. I left his office with two or three of his books about how to write, which I could return or pay for at my convenience. I felt embarrassed and cringing. The books were full of formulae for breaking in, getting ahead, knowing what and how to sell. After riffling through these books I gave them to his secretary the next day. Whatever it was I wanted to do or be, I suspected, it wasn't very pro.

Sometime that first semester I wrote a poem. Now, I had written poems long before, as everyone does, at about the age of eight or nine, but poetry, when I was sixteen, did not seem to me a very effective means of reforming the world. I am not sure what impelled me to write this poem, but judging from its vocabulary, it must have resulted from an incessant study of the dictionary. I remember being proud to have worked in the word *ephemeral.* And I learned that *rime,* besides being an alternate spelling of *rhyme,* was a term for the hoarfrost on winter windows. That pun probably prompted the poem; it pops up in the first stanza:

Window Painters

A finger on the window pane
   Sketches in rime that follows rain,
The idle thoughts of a youthful brain.

Youth knows that what he draws will stream
   No other soul will flay his dream;
A vision to vision but not to deem.

So free, he sculps whate'er he will
   To melt upon the window sill
Reverie veiled by ephemeral rill.

Fantasy falls in the duel
   Of youth and social ridicule.
Maturity makes man a stoic tool.

Escape cannot be found again.
   'Tis, then, a sin—it is not sane
To scribble on the window pane.

It embarrasses me to reprint it, but it illustrates the struggle going on as I sought a posture to assume as I moved from childhood to whatever lay ahead. Ah, the lamentable sacrifice of imagination on the altar of maturity! Bad as the poem was, it was accepted by a little regional poetry magazine called *Red Earth* and appeared in

227

print, with my name—not in a campus news story about the cow-barn, not in a campus magazine, but in an honest-to-goodness real live adult literary periodical. I tasted blood.

✦ ✦ ✦

English Composition. Professor Walcutt. Once in class discussion I made a comment to the effect that animals don't think, and a terrific controversy erupted. He called me to his office later to warn me about such statements. He told me he had once said something like that in class—specifically about dogs—and one of his students had apparently repeated his remark at home. There was first one letter of protest, telling an anecdote about a thinking dog, then a flurry of others, in Oklahoma City's *Daily Oklahoman*, and Professor Walcutt was nearly fired.

He assigned a description: that is, we were to write a one-page description of anything. I didn't stop at one page, but wrote a complete short story, "A Broken Fence," based on my memories of Jack and Audrey's ranch near Haskell. Professor Walcutt liked it so much he read it aloud to the class, and, after class, was praising me privately.

"Well, I copied," I told him.

Alarmed, he took me to the privacy of his office and asked what I meant.

"I just wrote down the things that are really there and made up a story to go with them."

He assured me that that kind of copying was not cheating.

The story is about a lazy hired man who doesn't want to walk down to the highway in the hot sun to fix a fence that's down. Throughout the story, alone, stalling, goofing off, he mutters his resentment of the woman who owns the ranch. Her husband is off in the service, so she is running the place alone. At the end we see her briefly. She turns out to be the antithesis of the snooty, domineering, bossy person depicted by the hired man—with a touch of pathos about her: "She scuffed off toward the barn, dragging her feet a little with the weight of her husband's boots." Audrey was much amused by that when she read it. True, her son Jack was

228

away in the marines and she had to manage the ranch by herself, but to her mind having Jack gone was good riddance.

But the core of the piece of writing was the description, my "copying," and rereading the story now evokes for me a sharp memory of the ranch:

> Pushing back his hat he walked into the tool house. A hot gust of air scented with animal dips and sprays met him. On the floor were piled bags of feed and salt. The man shuffled inside and sat on the roller-top desk that served as a filing place for the greasy papers covered with dates and figures concerning breedings and doctorings, sales and purchases. He began to clean a curry brush with a comb. "Whut do *wimmen* know?" he said.

A couple of my stories had already been published in the campus humor magazine, but now some of the students and the English department were starting a new literary magazine, *Bluestocking,* so I submitted "A Broken Fence" to them. It appeared in the first issue, Spring 1945, and a second story of mine—"The Death of the Bread-and-Butter Woman," based on our experiences picking up goat milk from a farm outside Oklahoma City—was in the following issue, coming out when I was already on Okinawa.

✦ ✦ ✦

I was taking discernible steps toward becoming a writer, but most of the time I was not thinking of my career at all—the career that had been the great concern of everyone before I came to college. As the courses piled up—Spanish, algebra, physics, geology, American, modern European, and ancient history, government— there was little sense that they were *for* anything, that they were leading anywhere (except to lead me out of my own narrowness). I wasn't feeling any wiser. I only knew that someone had let me loose, like a weak-kneed pony, in the bewildering rolling fields of thought. I was less interested in facts than in ideas, less interested in skills than in wonder. And I wanted to say, say, say it all—often before having it very clearly in mind.

229

My major discovery was of the library, which research for my radio program drew me to. At first I felt some suspicion and fear as I found my way through the card catalogue into some unlikely range of books on subjects I had never known of. And then I caught on. You can find out *anything* in the library, nearly. I looked up *Sex* and found a whole drawerful of cards about things I hadn't known one was allowed to write about. I had learned another new word, *pornography*, looked that up, found D. H. Lawrence's brilliant essay on "Sex and Censorship," and was temporarily liberated from pornography. I began to discover the intricacies of reference and cross reference, how buried in a dusty and unlikely book in a strange part of the stacks was apt to be the very fact or idea that would open a new experience for me. I was insatiable. I learned for the first time that you don't necessarily have to *read* books. You *use* them. You start at the back, with the index, and read no more than the relevant pages.

Other books demanded swallowing whole, and I was sorry I could swallow so few of them. I discovered magazines. At home I had only known those that my mother bought, such as *Ladies Home Companion,* or the *National Geographic* that an uncle subscribed for in my name every year. A friend once showed me a stack of *Esquires* in his garage with off-color jokes and Petty and Varga girls. We always had the *Reader's Digest*—and its jokes and sayings. But *Harper's! The New Yorker! The Nation! Progressive! Science! The Journal of English and Germanic Philology! Politics! Golden Goose, a literary quarterly! Mainstream!* I was elated by a sense of being in communication with everyone—and depressed that I knew so little, and had so little time to find out, with these periodicals flooding in, week after week, month after month, a constant outpouring of the bewildering and thrilling products of the human mind!

✦ ✦ ✦

College, as I remember it in those first couple of years, was only incidentally classes. I joined an intramural swimming team and swam the fifty-yard dash. I took and passed senior Life Saving—

the only male in the class, that was given in the women's gym. (Ah, the pleasures of the cross-chest carry—with a woman a head taller than I was!) I worked for meals, chiefly washing dishes at a sorority house and learning to detest lipstick-tipped cigarettes squashed in gravy. I played (badly) too many hours of pool. I acted in a play that we took to a number of army and navy bases, so I was at last doing something for the war effort. All these diversions overwhelmed in my mind the courses I happened to be taking.

The girls were all taller than I was. Our dorm had a house-master, a Milton scholar named Professor Kester Svendsen, who lived there with his wife, Matilda. They taught us table manners and other elements of social behavior, including proper deportment at dances. Girls from the sorority houses (which were still operating) would come on Saturday nights, and we would dress up in suits and ties and ask them to dance. I would lay my head on their bosoms. They thought that was cute. But they weren't interested in dating me. Finally a near-midget girl, a Theta, showed up in one of my classes. She was the first girl I met on campus who was my size, so I asked her for a date. What would she like to do? Go to the basketball game, she said. I had never been to a basketball game, but I figured I could cheer when the others did and took her there. But in those days I was spending most of my free time in the library doing research for my radio programs and would study into the wee hours. I dozed off at the game and fell through the bleachers. She was embarrassed and would never date me again. Girls, I decided, were pretty much a lost cause.

Boys, too. One raped me during my first semester. One of the fellows in my dorm had bought a grass skirt and bra for his little sister while he was on a vacation in Hawaii. He was showing it to a group of us gathered in his room one evening when someone speculated that the costume, which was very small, might fit me. On a dare I tried it on, and, sure enough, it was just big enough. I began prancing around through the dorm, swishing, rotating my hips, sometimes sitting wiggling on various guys' laps. Then I took the outfit off and went back to my room.

My roommate was out. I had put on my pajamas and stretched

out on my lower bunk to read, when the knob twisted, the door opened, and a student I barely knew—and didn't much like—stepped in and shut the door behind him. He was a huge fellow, heavy-set, pig-eyed, wearing his customary blond stubble. With a sinister grin, without saying a word, he opened his bathrobe, came to the bed, shoved me flat and climbed on my stomach, almost smothering me with his heavy body. His rough face scraped mine. His big, muscular arms pinioned me. And he began humping and continued till he was satisfied, got up and left, still without speaking. Thereafter, I am happy to say, he avoided me.

✦ ✦ ✦

Lester, one of my dormmates, was always the first in line for meals in the dorm—by a good half-hour or so. Once a rowdy gang came in during the wee hours of the night, and their noise woke Lester. He jumped up, got dressed, and hurried downstairs to stand by the dining room door, waiting for breakfast, as observed by a half-dozen of us suppressing our laughter while we watched him from the stairway. It was five hours until breakfast.

Lester was a Muslim, having been converted by reading. (I don't think he had ever met a Muslim.) He carried a small rag rug with him wherever he went, and several times a day he would lay out the rug, kneel on it, and bend his body, with hands stretched over his head, toward the West. "Shouldn't you bow to the East, Lester?" I asked him. He said Mecca was closer if you went west.

✦ ✦ ✦

I got expelled—first from the dorm at Sammies, and, in my second year, from the university. Our housemaster, Kester Svendsen, kicked me out of the Sammies' house because I threw a clock at the dorm proctor. At two A.M. one morning I had just gotten to sleep after a night of heavy study. Then a gang of students, including the proctor, came in drunk, singing, and they deliberately woke me, so I grabbed the clock and hurled it. I was transferred to another dorm—a high rise.

232

That building seemed more like an apartment house than a dormitory. It had elevators, and a huge cafeteria—and so many boys and men that I felt infinitesimal and anonymous. One day I decided that I should wash my hair. Usually I did this at Dad and Evelyn's cabin where lemon or vinegar were available; I had been taught that, after washing your hair, you always put a bit of lemon juice or vinegar in the rinse water to get your hair really clean of soap. Where was I to get lemon or vinegar in the dorm? In the middle of the afternoon I went down to the cafeteria and back to the vast institutional kitchen, where I explained my needs to one of the workers. He sent me to the administrator in charge of the kitchen, who had never heard of using lemon or vinegar to rinse one's hair. Nonetheless, he gave me a quarter of a lemon, which served my immediate needs; but I was embarrassed by the incident. I must have seemed a sissy to want to wash my hair the way Mother had taught me. I don't think I bothered with adulterating my rinse water after that.

Expulsion from the university grew out of a conflict with the Military Science Department. I had had R.O.T.C. in high school, so I already knew close-order drill. On this basis I was made a kind of acting sergeant, assigned to march outside the ranks where the others could watch me as a model. But I stopped going to drill. We had to wear scratchy wool uniforms from four to six on Thursday afternoons, which meant I had to leave campus, walk the half-mile or so to the rooming house where I was then living, change, return to campus, then, after drill, walk back to my room to change again, as I couldn't stand the idea of eating dinner in that hot, uncomfortable uniform. If you missed drill, you were given fifteen demerits, to be worked off at the rate of five per hour—three hours work in place of two miserable hours of drill, plus another hour of coming and going.

Drill, I figured, was a bad bargain. I would just show up at the supply room once a week to put in a three-hour stint studying in the cool building, as there was never any work to be done. It was a very pleasant alternative to drill until one day I brought in my uniform and handed it to the supply sergeant. I wanted my ten-dollar deposit back because I was flat broke. The supply sergeant, like the officers, was a regular-army man, too old for combat duty. He said I couldn't turn my uniform in the middle of the semester: I would need it. "But I don't go to drill," I explained, and told him what I had been doing—as he very well knew—for the past several weeks. Though he had been glad to have me regularly behind the counter so he could leave for errands or other activities, he had not asked how I happened to be there. Now he was outraged and took me to the captain. The captain was outraged and took me to the major, who was a squat little man behind a big desk that he liked to tap with his riding crop while he talked. (He was always in jodphurs, perhaps thinking he was playing the role of Eric Von Stroheim.) When I again patiently explained what I had been doing and why, he puffed up red in the face and said, "You can't do whatever you like. That would be anarchism!"

That was a new word for me, so when I got back to my room I looked it up. I have considered myself an anarchist ever since, and I am grateful to the major for that. But the major also nudged me into crime. I began going to the clinic claiming to be sick and asking for excuses from drill. This worked for a few weeks, but the clinic sergeant began to get suspicious. He said he thought I was malingering. (I had to look that one up, too.) He gave me a little bottle of something called Red Devil and insisted that I drink it down right there in the office. It brought on a violent diarrhea that convinced me of the unwisdom of further malingering.

At finals time I knew we would have to write out the ten General Orders from memory. These are the rules for being on guard duty, like "A guard never leaves his post," or "A guard never falls asleep," and so on—only longer and more complicated statements that one had to memorize word-for-word. I knew my General Orders all right. But, the hour before the military science exam, I finished an exam in Shakespeare early, and, waiting for the end of the hour, I wrote the first words of each of the General Orders (from memory) on a brown bookcover, just for practice. During the exam the major marched up and down the aisles switching his jodphurs with his riding crop while we wrote. In a moment of hesitation I glanced at the book on top of the pile in the seat of the chair in front of me. I couldn't see it—and didn't need the prompt, really. But the major had followed my glance. He snatched up the book, saw what was on the cover, and marched me right out of the classroom, across campus to the office of the president of the university. After some moments we were admitted to a huge, luxurious office and seated at a long conference table, where we were joined by the president.

The major and I each told our versions of what happened, then the president turned to me and asked me to recite my General Orders, which I did flawlessly. "Well," he said, "I'm sure you *didn't* need the crib. Nonetheless, I think you should be taught a lesson. You will receive a failing grade in military science and be expelled for one day." What the lesson was I am still not sure. I hadn't cheated and, as the president determined, hadn't needed to cheat. But I had gotten caught glancing. Don't get caught glancing again!

The following summer, after I had received my draft notice and was waiting at home for the final call, I wrote the president a long letter about this whole incident, hoping to expunge what I regarded as a shameful blot on an otherwise commendable record. His reply taught me some more new words, such as *sophistry, duplicity,* and *tendentious.*

✦   ✦   ✦

I had walked back to my room after drill and flung myself on the bed without even taking off my uniform and had fallen into a deep sleep. I woke, stifling, suffocating, and trying to get up, but I could not rise. I slid to the edge of the bed and slipped to the floor. Laboriously, slowly, slowly, I drug my flat, sweating body across the floor to the doorjamb and pulled myself up. I was standing. I looked back across the room at the bed, and I was still there—stretched out, asleep.

The shock woke me. This was merely a dream, unlike what

seems to have been an out-of-body experience when I was about three. But it haunted me and stirred my imagination.

✦ ✦ ✦

But my chief memory of those two years was of reading. I suppose I read the things assigned me in courses—for I made good grades (except for military science)—but that is not the reading I remember. Rather, I relished the odd books pulled off the shelves deep in the stacks, read squatting in the aisle under a weak ceiling bulb. The universe was opening before my eyes.

Next to reading I suppose my next major activity was talking. Dormitory bull sessions lasted, as they no doubt last in freshman dorms everywhere, on through the night. Is there a God? What do you mean by that? What is communism all about? And existentialism—yea, what? Well, what about it? And some poorly informed one of us, usually I, would advance some half-baked theory with great dogmatism, and others would fall to and pool their ignorance. In spite of our misinformation and bad reasoning, I am sure we all learned more in bull sessions than we ever learned in classes. We learned to express ourselves, to hold the floor, to find holes in the other fellow's argument, to qualify and define and theorize. Moved by Nietzche's *Thus Spake Zarathustra*, for instance, I argued that we should all strive to live as solitary Supermen and meet one another in the clearing to battle for our lives until only one reigned. We were in the lounge of the dormitory for this discussion, and I remember the wise smile of a professor who had joined us when he told me that as I grew older I would learn that man is a gregarious animal.

Upstairs, to the dictionary. *Gregarious.*

I remember that same professor, in another bull session, this one around the Coke machine in the hall of one of the classroom buildings, greeting a young woman. "Come join us," he said. "All of our sentences begin with 'Life is . . .'" Oh, how I yearned to be sophisticated enough to say things like that!

I remember concerts, exhibitions of paintings, foreign films including *Ecstasy* with Hedy Lamarr—the first commercial release

236

showing total nudity. I remember a cut from a close-up of lovers to a lily blossom dripping a slow drop of dew. I gasped. Symbolism! We'd just learned about such devices when we studied *Madame Bovary*. We carried on discussions of such matters on through the night. In spite of the shortage of manpower, the University fielded a sort of football team, and I discovered the excitement of sitting up high in the stadium and yelling like crazy about a lot of activity down there I didn't understand.

One memorable night I went out in drag. Another roomer in the house where I was staying had a date with a girl who was given a pass from her sorority house on the pretext of going to a prom. They didn't go to any prom; they went somewhere and made out together. But the plan included a way of getting back into the sorority house undetected. The girl's roommate, by a prearranged signal, opened a window and threw down a formal gown. The girl changed clothes in the bushes, went in in her gown, and the fellow took home her street clothes.

So, at his suggestion, I dressed up in them, hiding my hair in a scarf. We ambled along what passed for the Great White Way in Norman—a couple of blocks of campus hangouts—shot a game of pool, met several friends, and returned to the house, my disguise undetected.

◆　　◆　　◆

From the fall of 1943 until July 1945, when I was drafted, I seemed to bounce back and forth between the slamming intensity of campus life and the counterslap of weekend encounters with my father in Oklahoma City. That pattern was interrupted by the summer Mike and I spent in Colorado between my two years at the university—stress and excitement of another sort entirely. And my stint in college was followed by immersion in the army— basic training, Okinawa, Shanghai—one overwhelming experience piled upon the last until I was discharged—the word seems appropriately graphic—and found my way to Chicago in the winter of 1947.

Though my mind raced, I was too busy to think, certainly too busy to feel sorry for myself. Life was becoming a series of unfolding adventures. I was coping, wasn't I? I was generally happy, excited. I experienced no depression, no panic, no great sorrow, and perhaps felt shallow, unformed, because I had not seemed to develop the tragic mien that characterized my heroes. I was still in quest.

✦   ✦   ✦

In my second English course, again with Professor Walcutt, I wrote a paper on "The Love Song of J. Alfred Prufrock." That poem, I said, is about a man trying to make up his mind whether to ask one of the women at a soiree to marry him (or to have an affair with him). He comes from a poor neighborhood and knows he will feel out of place—indeed, like a pair of ragged claws on the floor of silent seas—at the party, though he goes to such parties regularly. But he is from a class inferior to that of the women and, besides, is getting too old for romantic ideas, so he decides not to ask her. He thinks she would simply dismiss him. Imagine her saying something like, "Would you fetch me another cup of tea, dear?" and he answers, "Did you call me 'dear'? Could that mean that you think of me as I think of you. . . ." And she would say, "That's not what I meant at all."

I knew just how he felt. I, too, sensed that I was outclassed among these college students. I, too, feared that I would only get a brush-off if I asked a girl for a date. I was no longer Marat. I was Prufrock. Watch me age!

13

Vagrants, Come Home

One summer evening in 1988, sitting in the backyard with friends, I began recounting a chain of anecdotes from the summer of 1944, between my two years at the University of Oklahoma, and our friends urged me to write them down. That was the genesis of this book. I started writing about how Mike and I worked as ranch hands and then went camping in the Rockies. But in the process I began asking myself what preparation enabled me to be so independent and adventurous while still so immature. Digging into my childhood uncovered many layers of experience I had repressed—to the extent that the tales I shared that night came to seem mere aftermath. The Jud I see here seems to me like the core of a golf ball: a solid mass of stretched strands of rubber band, not yet encased in its plastic shell. That summer was my first sustained venture out into the big world utterly beyond parental protection or supervision. What amazes me, on looking back at these events, is how well I had already learned to bounce.

Mike and I were the staunchest of buddies—and very different from one another. Mike, a swarthy, muscular, athletic type a head taller and a year younger than I, came from a conventional, stable family and was well on his way to becoming the sort of man that I recognized I would never be. A man like Ott, for example: non-verbal, practical, stolid, reliable. He wanted to be an engineer like his father. I was immature, mercurial, seething with rebellious notions, boyish in body and mind, with no clear notion of what sort of person I wanted to become. I was certain only that my life would be very different from Mike's. I didn't feel superior on that account; in fact, I was probably somewhat envious. But we understood and complemented one another. And, in a summer of amazing challenges, we both not only survived but thrived.

Mike's plan for the summer was that we should go to Colorado and work to earn enough for a camping trip in the Rockies. We had saved enough for train fare—one way. When school let out, Mike came up from Houston and met me in the Oklahoma City train station where we boarded a train for Denver. Trains in those years were full of soldiers and sailors, WACS, WAVES, and WAFS. Though I would join the ranks of those in service the following year, and Mike, who was still sixteen, expected to go the year after that, these servicemen seemed incredibly old and mature to us. I could imagine Mike as a soldier. But I hadn't grown since entering college. The idea of being drafted was terrifying. Living among all those men! Even more terrifying was the thought of being rejected for any reason. Citizens looked askance at those who were not accepted for the service. Did they have some mysterious physical or psychological disability? What was *wrong* with them?

There were no seats on the train. This seemed normal to us; for the last three years America had been on the road—or on the rails. Aside from the constant flow of military personnel on leave or moving between assignments, civilians were boiling around in the wartime energy trying to find jobs in shipyards or other industry, much like the earlier wave after wave of Oklahomans depicted in *The Grapes of Wrath* who traveled westward to find work and to populate California. It was sometimes difficult to find even standing room on the trains. When I was drafted the next year I took a train from Oklahoma City down to Houston and rode the whole distance—some twelve hours as I remember—leaning crookedly, so packed were the aisles with passengers—most of them, it seemed, servicemen—their duffels between their legs.

But we were lucky that June. We found space in what we called the "vestibule"—the noisy enclosure at the end of the car—where we could not only sit but lie down on the floor. Our vestibule was jammed with luggage, and I could find room for my knapsack only in the adjoining vestibule of the car behind us. We didn't realize how unfortunate that was until we reached Denver. During the night, while we were sleeping on the metal floor, our legs curled around piles of luggage (including Mike's knapsack), we stopped at Wichita. Our car went on to Denver. But the car behind us was switched off and went to California with my knapsack.

Mike had been told that we could be hired to pick cherries in Fort Collins. The cherry season had not started, however, and so Mike had arranged for us to work as ranch hands on an uncle's place on the plains east of Denver. Before leaving the train station I reported the loss of my knapsack. I had nothing but the pair of shorts, high laced boots, and short-sleeved shirt I was wearing— and Mike's clothes were too big for me. But this seemed no great inconvenience. Surely the knapsack would be located in a few days. The only thing I really needed was a toothbrush, which we picked up at a drugstore before boarding the bus that would take us to the edge of the city where we began hitching to Mike's uncle's ranch in the northeastern part of the state.

✦   ✦   ✦

Mike had never met this uncle, who turned out to be a wiry and tyrannical little man. He would pay no wages. For the two weeks we would be there before the cherry season we worked ten hours a day six days a week in exchange for upkeep. We slept on a couple of iron cots in a room at the rear of the house and were fed three plain but filling meals a day—a lot of beans. Up at dawn, to bed as soon as possible after the evening meal.

And, in between, hard work. Mostly we dug postholes, taking turns loosening dirt with a long iron prybar and scooping it out with a scissor-handled posthole digger, stealing glances at the dis-

241

tant mauve ridge of mountains, the shimmering goal of all our labor. Some days we walked along the green rows of mowed and raked alfalfa, pitching hay up on to the horse-drawn wagon along-side, or, on the wagon, stacking the hay that other hands pitched up, keeping the load evenly rising as great forkfuls came floating up from either side. When the wagon was loaded, like a giant loaf, rounded to the point that one more stem would slither down its side and fall off, the wagon swayed its way to the barn, and there we had to pitch it up into the mow. We were taught how to drive our forks in from the top, never trying to scoop the hay, but spearing it in massive bundles like the stork nests I had seen pictures of on European chimneys, and heaving it loose from the fork to sail to the slick floor where another worker would spear the same bundle and toss it to the pile. Balers were rare in those days, and hay was mostly stored loose. The wagon empty, we would roll the wide doors on the hay mow closed and ride the wagon back out to the wide yellow field, our dreaming eyes on the shadowy ranges of mountains that loomed in the distance.

This was an introduction to both of us of long days of labor, of man's work, and I remember thinking, as, after dinner, we dropped off to sleep in our cots in the bare little room off the farmhouse kitchen, "I made it! I made it again!" I had gotten through the day's work without complaining, without letting on that this life was any different from what I had always been accustomed to. My hands blistered, then calloused over the blisters, and I was proud of the callouses and silent about my pride.

There was no phone, so I had to return to Denver to check whether my knapsack had been returned. I made a couple of trips alone back to the train station, leaving after evening chores and hitching, shivering in my skimpy clothing. On the way back from my first unsuccessful venture I was given a ride by a businessman who took pity on my situation. This little man in his three-piece suit and Milquetoast mustache insisted on giving me not only a ten-dollar bill but a canvas windbreaker he happened to have in the trunk. It was much too large, but it kept me somewhat warmer. On a couple of other rides I encountered drivers who could not resist my bare knees. I learned how to remove hands forcibly and ride scrunched against the door. I sometimes insisted on getting out—into the icy darkness—if the man was too persistent.

✦   ✦   ✦

My knapsack finally showed up, and our two weeks at that ranch came to an end. Mike's plan had included transportation in the Fort Collins area. Our parents had shipped our balloon-tired one-speed bikes, each with a wooden rack and newspaper bags on the back, from Houston to Fort Collins. We arrived at Fort Collins in the late afternoon, picked up our bikes at the train station, and were spellbound by our first distant look at the foothills of the Rockies that swelled in a sienna and purple ridge at the edge of town.

We headed for these. That's what we had come to Colorado for—the mountains. We would camp that night in the mountains, we thought, and pumped on and on in gathering dusk, watching the foothills seem to recede before us. At last we realized that we would never reach them by nightfall, so we turned down the lane of what appeared to be an abandoned farm. A rotting barn leaned outside a dark farmhouse. We would sleep, we thought, in that barn.

But as we approached the barn, walking our bikes now on the rutted lane, we became aware of bouncing headlight beams on our backs. A Chevy sedan pulled up, and a man called, "Where do you boys think you are going?" He stopped and climbed out of the car, leaving the motor running, the headlights illuminating us but blinding us to him, though I could tell he was wearing a business suit and a felt hat. Mr. Metcalf, head of the agricultural program at the Fort Collins branch of the state university, told us this farm belonged to the university. We could not sleep there.

We asked for suggestions as to where we *could* camp. There was no park in town that permitted camping, so, reluctantly, Mr. Metcalf offered to let us sleep in his basement for that night only. He piled one bike on the front and one on the rear bumper and drove us to a middle-class brick row house in town. After we unloaded our bikes, we were told to put them in his garage, but as we were leaving the garage, Mr. Metcalf rolled down the garage door, and one side of it spun off its track and hit Mike in the side of his head. Mike collapsed on the drive in a pool of blood.

Mr. and Mrs. Metcalf were gasping in terror. Mike was stunned but conscious. We helped him to his feet and down to the cots we were to use in the recreation room while Mrs. Metcalf called a doctor. The scalp wound proved superficial, and well worth the benefits it brought us, for, after a second night in the Metcalfs' rec room, we had a job. Mike's plan, we learned, was unrealistic. The cherries wouldn't be in for some time, and when they did come in, they would be picked by skilled migrant workers, mostly Mexicans and Jamaicans. We wouldn't stand a chance of getting a job—nor would we be able to earn more than a pittance had we been hired. Pickers were paid by the bucket, and the migrant workers were so skillful that we would be unable to compete. But Mr. Metcalf could give us temporary work on the university farms. And where would we stay? On the very farm where he had found us. An old shepherd lived in the house, and we could share quarters with him.

Jake, as that ancient was called, tended the university's herd of sheep that grazed on a vast acreage stretching up from the farmhouse into the foothills. Mr. Metcalf said that Jake would be delighted to have company. So we rode our bikes into town and shopped for groceries, then pedaled the few miles back to the ranch. Jake wasn't there. We went in cautiously with flashlights, found and lit kerosene lamps, and looked around. The house consisted of a small kitchen and another large room with a table and three iron cots in it. The cots were lumpy and broken down, and the place was generally a pigsty, but we felt immensely successful. We had a home, a job, and maybe Sunday we could ride on up into the mountains. (We never did this.)

While I went outside to pump water, Mike started frying our hot dogs and opening our can of beans. Meanwhile Jake showed up, a bent little man with a blond stubble on his lantern jaw. He was soused, and hardly noticed our presence. He fell onto his cot fully dressed, his muddy boots on the tattered army blanket, while Mike and I had our dinner.

The farm where we were to report to work was surrounded by a high chain link fence near the campus on the opposite side of town from the ranch where we were staying. Each morning we would bike over there to arrive there by eight and work till six. Forty cents an hour: four bucks apiece! Six days a week! Between us we were taking in nearly fifty dollars a week. We were rolling in dough! We would stop for groceries as we rode through town, spending as little as possible so we could accumulate savings for our camping trip. That would be, according to Mike's plan, along the Los Pinos River in the San Juan National Forest above Durango in the southwestern corner of the state—an area where Mike's family had taken him on vacation and to look over the Colorado College of Mines in nearby Golden, which Mike hoped to attend.

At the university farm we were put to work digging a well—about four feet wide and already about four feet deep. We took turns digging, loosening dirt with a prybar and then shoveling it into a bucket that the one on top pulled up with a rope and emptied. Digging got harder and harder as the well got deeper. At about fifteen feet, water began seeping in, and we worked in mud up over our bare feet and ankles until the water was up to our shins, and we were told that that was enough.

The well finished, we scrubbed down cow pens, wondering how the calves that had recently been penned there managed to get manure above our head level. Another day we stacked chopped hay—standing in the back of a truck while a spout from a machine blew the fine, dry, dusty hay around our feet. I got sick that day, apparently from breathing the dust, and ran a high fever. So we were assigned to cleaning a silo—and were nearly nauseated by the sweet moist fumes of rotted silage that we had to shovel into buckets and carry to a compost pile.

Meanwhile we were enjoying the company of Jake in the evenings and before we set out each morning. He was full of tall tales and foul jokes. I remember that he picked up a novel I was reading—a paperback by a woman author about a woman who escaped from a concentration camp by appearing to be dead. (Reflecting on this, I am amazed that so much information about the con-

245

centration camps had already penetrated popular culture.) Some doctor at the camp gave her a potion that put her into a comatose state and so tricked the Nazis. When we came into the farmhouse that evening Jake slapped the book down on the plank table and said, "That woman's got an imagination longer than a whore's dream." This was the big world, Mike and I reassured one another with an exchange of knowing looks. That's how one talks out here. "Longer than a whore's dream." I've been waiting all these years to find an occasion to use that phrase.

Jake was our first intimate introduction to men in the real world—not in school, not even in business. He had been a bachelor all his life, growing up in Montana and, from his teenage years on, living with sheep in lonely outposts, herding them to high mountain pastures in the summer and back to ranches where they could be fed through the winter. "Ever fuck a sheep?" he asked us. We allowed as how we hadn't. "Women is for having babies," he said, "boys is for sport, but sheep is for bliss." He told us a story about a sheepherder who finally gave in and decided to have himself a sheep. He picked out a yearling ewe, bathed her and curried her, put a bow on her head, and took her into town to a bar. All the men in the bar dived for cover when he and the sheep entered. When he asked what the problem was they told him: "You're dating the boss's sweetheart!"

Tough as he was, though, Jake revealed to us the underlying sissiness of these Northerners—at least in regard to grapefruit. I started to dip my spoon into a half-grapefruit one morning when Jake screeched with alarm. It was a response appropriate to seeing a rattlesnake under my chair. "You forgot to put sugar on it!" he said. I had never heard of putting sugar on grapefruit. Some people, I knew, used salt, but I preferred grapefruit plain. Jake watched agog as I finished it off without sugar. I figured I had earned a merit badge in manliness that morning.

Mike and I were in our glory, collecting regular wages, shopping each day for groceries, living independently and doing, we thought, men's work. But after a couple of weeks of this routine we were sent on our way. Ever-solicitous Mr. Metcalf plainly didn't want us

246

around. We weren't much use at the university farm, after all, and our dependency made him uneasy. So he palmed us off on a friend who owned the Bar-D-Bar Ranch up near Grand Lake on the edge of Rocky Mountain National Park and who agreed to take us on for fifty dollars a month and room and board. Finally we would get to see the mountains!

✦   ✦   ✦

It was time to ship our bikes home, as we would never be able to ride them up to Grand Lake. That done, we set off hitching to cross the park, overwhelmed by the vistas. I had never seen mountains taller than the Kiamichis before. I remember riding with a family of tourists—a man, his wife, and two or three children, jammed into the back seat with our knapsacks on our laps, gawking as the car climbed up into the tall pines, then aspen, then the barren stretches above the timberline, along a highway that seemed to be the spine of the world up in the lonely silence of thin, cold air. We spent that night in a campground near the western park boundary and watched a herd of elk in a meadow across a deep valley where a silver stream twisted below us. The next morning we hitched on to become ranch hands.

Bar-D-Bar was a ranch right out of the movies we had seen (such as *Of Mice and Men*). There was a pipe cattle guard at the entrance (as there was at Aunt Audrey's ranch). We hiked the mile or so of drive to the ranch house where we met our new boss, the foreman, Mr. Sprague, a mustached young man in cowboy boots and Levi's who lived in a big modern house on a hill at the far end of the ranch. It was lunchtime, and our first job was to join eight other hands at the groaning table: plates with piles of chops, fried chicken, sausages, mashed potatoes, beans, spinach, and other vegetables we couldn't identify, tall pitchers of cold milk, tall piles of homemade bread. . . . Stuffed, we were next shown to our beds in the bunkhouse. Upstairs over a long work shed were rows of cots along the facing walls. Most of the other hands had footlockers. We stowed our knapsacks at the foot of the two cots appointed for us and went downstairs to report to work.

On the manure wagon. Our job was to clean a barn lot, forking the hoof-flattened manure onto the wagon, literally peeling it off the ground with pitchforks, then driving the team of two horses down the lane to a distant manure pile and unloading it. We did that for several days. Each evening we showered and changed clothes (saving our manure clothes for work the next day), but we could not get rid of the odor. The other hands insisted we move our cots to the far end of the room, a dozen feet from our nearest neighbors.

Before daylight each morning Cookie (that is actually what the cook was called) would thump on our floor from below with a broom handle. The hands would roll out of bed. Someone would get a lantern going, and we pulled on our work clothes. Downstairs we washed up in a trough of cold water ouside the shed, then started morning chores. That meant, primarily, milking, but Mike and I had never milked cows and were comically ineffective at that, so we were put to cleaning the cream separator. This was an immense shining metal machine with many parts, each of them sour with drying milk.

Breakfast came after morning chores—another groaning table: grapefruit, flapjacks, eggs, ham, bacon, grits, fried potatoes, milk, coffee, juice. . . . We marveled at the amount of food those cowboys could put away. By six or so we were back on the manure wagon. That barn lot cleared, I was assigned to run fences. Mike hadn't ever ridden a horse, so he was given another job, while, with another hand as supervisor, I rode along miles of barbed wire, replacing missing staples or broken wire. This was playing cowboy for real!

Other days we moved bales of hay from one end to the other of a barn loft, or hosed down and curried prize Herefords for photographs that would appear in a sale catalog. After a big lunch and big dinner each day we joined the hands in the yard for horseshoes or played penny ante poker with them on the dining room table or went with them into the little town of Grand Lake for whatever entertainment could be found there. Very little. There was no movie house. The women weren't interested in Mike and me, and we could not drink at the bar. At any rate, the evenings were short. Everyone was tired from the day's work and knew that Cookie's broom would be pounding early.

We lasted two weeks at the Bar-D-Bar. Mr. Sprague called us aside and told us that we were just too little for the job, and he let us go with half a month's pay. "Too *little!*" Mike objected to me as we hiked out with our knapsacks on our backs. "That's the first time I've ever been called too little for anything." Mike, still sixteen, his dark complexion shadowed by black facial hair, might have held the job if it weren't for his shrimp of a companion. But, anyway, we were eager to begin our camping trip and had saved enough, we figured, for provisions.

Though we were unused to the long hours, none of the work we had done was all that strange to us. I had been around and participated in some farm work at Aunt Audrey's ranch, and Mike's father, an engineer, had accustomed him to labor. But neither of us, of course, had had real jobs, nor had we lived on our own. We tried to behave casually about our new independence, taking it in stride, but we were no doubt much impressed with ourselves. We were laborers. We were acting like real men. And, no doubt, the *real* men around us were amused behind our backs at a couple of kids in beyond their depth.

✦　✦　✦

Thumbs up—and on down the highway to Walsenburg, then west to the Los Pinos River. I remember our ride up into the mountains on a flat-bed trailer carrying heavy machinery. The truck labored so slowly up the mountain one might almost walk beside it. The driver opened his cab door, stood on the running board, and peed as the truck groaned along. When we reached the river we got off and hitched north to the little town of Vallecito on the edge of the San Juan National Forest—a tiny tourist town stretched out along a lake. There we shopped for food and rented a burro—Matilda, as I named her, for Professor Kester Svendsen's wife. Matilda had recently had a colt that was still nursing, so we had to let the colt follow her, which was fine with us. She was a pet. And, as the human Matilda had recently had a baby named Jenny, we gave that name to the colt.

Mike had done a lot of research for this expedition, and he knew how to pack a burro with our gear and food rolled into a tarp, held to the pack saddle with a diamond hitch. He had brought his .22 along, and we had fishing tackle, so we would mostly live off the land, we thought.

And off we went, first along a flat trail under the pines, then up and up, beyond the pines into aspen and columbine, eventually to the timberline. We soon left behind the few other human beings, mostly fishermen, who were in the forest, and were walking single file—Mike, Matilda with her rocking load, Jenny, and I—along narrow trails. On our second night we set up our two-man tent beside a stream. The geodetic survey map we had with us indicated a shelter there, but there was none—only a first aid kit on a tree. But there was a fine little meadow where the burros could graze and a good swimming hole in the stream (much calmer and a little warmer than the swift cold river). But for now, traveling lighter, leaving the tent and some other gear behind, we set out to go up higher.

We were, of course, looking for the Source. Our trail roughly followed the river that tumbled its crashing, swirling crystal way down the mountain—and supplied us with trout and perch on a regular basis. We wanted to find where that river started. We wanted to reach the dotted line on our map marked Continental Divide.

It seemed endless as we climbed day after day, unloading Matilda each night and tying her to a tree where she could graze, with Jenny gamboling around our campsite, nosing into our gear, or returning to her mother to nurse. At one point, on a trail so narrow that Matilda's load scraped the cliff-face as she walked, Mike called back that he had seen dog tracks. A *dog*? He found more nail marks, and then finally a whole paw-print. It was about six inches in diameter—surely a bear. And, as we walked, we began getting the scent, a large-animal scent we recognized from zoos. There was nothing to do but hike on: we could not turn around.

Eventually we found what was apparently the bear's den, a cave-like little hollow in the side of the cliff with crushed debris in it where a large animal appeared to have slept. The scent was strongest there. But we never saw the bear.

One of the vegetables we had brought with us was green beans. Neither of us had ever cooked green beans, but we figured our little Boy Scout kettleful of them should be done in about twenty minutes. But after twenty minutes, they were still tough and crisp. So we poured out the water, left them in the pot, and packed them to cook the next night. They didn't get done on their second cooking, either, so we carried them on for a third night.

We had long left the aspens behind. There was no trail up there—just rocky wastes, but eventually we found ourselves wading through trackless, deep, tough meadow grass. The river had become a straight ditch in which water was flowing the wrong direction, so we knew we had reached the Continental Divide, and what we were following was an irrigation ditch carrying water from the east to the dry west side of the mountains. The meadow alongside the ditch became a swamp—no doubt the Source we sought.

One of our ambitions had been to camp on the Divide (pure as a Source or a Summit), so we found dry ground and settled down up there for the night, and, again, cooked our beans. After they had been bubbling for an hour or so it finally occurred to us what the problem was. I stuck my finger in the water, which was hot, but not scaldingly so. We were too high to cook beans. The boiling point of water was too low. So that night we munched on crisp green beans. Mike's feet were ominously swollen, and we were both somewhat nauseated with altitude sickness, so we started back down the mountain the next day for our base camp.

From there we took overnight hikes to explore the region, coming upon marvels such as beavers in clear cold pools, a live fox with its leg in a trap, a herd of sheep and two shepherds in a hut on a high meadow. Each night we climbed into our bedrolls early—and shivered. My bedroll, purchased when I joined the scouts in Houston, was especially thin, stuffed only with cotton batting. Around us loomed the silent lofty peaks.

251

One day we climbed the highest peak we could see, the one we took to be Needle Mountain, 14,087 feet—a climb that in retrospect still causes flipflops in my belly. It required scaling sheer walls of rock, moving along ledges more narrow than our boots, going up crevices we could climb only by pressing our hands and feet to either side. We may have seen movies of mountain climbing, but we certainly had nothing like the preparation that modern young people have, seeing often on television exactly how it is done. Had we known, we might not have attempted it without the ropes and equipment mountain climbers use.

We paused at each new elevation to gaze around the ever-widening vista. At one point another zoo scent struck our nostrils, and we came upon a freshly killed goat in a croft. A puma or other large cat was on the mountain with us, but it was obviously impossible to run away if we should come upon it.

By early afternoon (we had set out early, having camped part way up the base of the mountain) we reached the peak and swore we could see New Mexico and possibly Arizona and Utah as well. (One *can* see four states from Mesa Verde, where we were to go after we came down out of the mountains.) We sat up there on the high rocks with an unrestricted view in every direction, imagining that, perhaps, we were the first human beings ever to have been there—a mountain peak with no graffiti. We congratulated ourselves awhile, then figured we had better start down if we were to get off the mountain by nightfall.

We could not go back the way we came. It was simply too steep. But we spotted a better route from the peak, and, about halfway down, came upon a slice like a long, steep valley that appeared to be easy climbing. The valley was packed with snow for a few hundred feet, and I went out on it, digging the edges of my boots into its crunchy surface, while Mike climbed on down along the edge. I discovered I could ski on my boots (I had never skied before), so went glissading along in wide zig-zags. I realize now what would have happened if I had lost my footing. There was nothing below but what appeared to be a sheer fall for hundreds of feet. But, of course, I didn't think about that at the time. Now Mike had reached the bottom of the snow patch, and he began yelling for me to get off it. I completed my zag and did so, scrambling down the rocks, and when I joined Mike I discovered why he was yelling. The snow had melted beneath the surface and was hollowed out for yards under where I had been skiing on its ever-thinning lip.

In the woods near our base camp was the shitting tree. It was marked by a paperback book—a collection of short stories or a novel. We both read the book as we leaned back against the tree to do our business, worked our way through, using it as toilet paper, and the rule was you couldn't tear out pages ahead of where the other fellow had stopped reading. I don't know how many books we had along on that trip, but I know we used several. Paper was scarce. We used leaves and twigs to start our fires.

One day found us with our bedrolls in a dry niche under a stone ledge. As the rain ran down the ledge toward us, we made a wax line with the base of a candle to make it drip off, but water eventually crossed the line, and we had to make another, and another, farther back, until we were crouched in a tiny area against our bedrolls. We were hungry. We hadn't been able to catch a fish or shoot a squirrel for days, and our grocery supply was almost exhausted.

Well, we could make some cornmeal mush, couldn't we? There were only a couple of cupfuls of cornmeal left (the supply we brought mostly for coating fish before frying). We had no sugar, but we could eat it without that. We split a log to get at the dry wood in the center, chipped out some splinters for kindling, tore some pages out of our last book to get it started. Soon the mush was bubbling merrily, and we cheered up.

Then I remembered that we had some cocoa in the pack. Chocolate-flavored mush sounded swell. I stirred a couple of heaping tablespoons of cocoa into the mush, and took a bite. Unbearably bitter! We had to throw out our last cornmeal. We caught some fish the next day, but had to fry them without cornmeal. We were so hungry I doubt we fried them much at all.

✦ ✦ ✦

The trip was winding down. Even after the rain, which lasted for days, we were gloomy. I was disgusted with Mike, who now had a stubble and had not bathed for days. I realize now that what disgusted me was his adolescence, his emerging manhood—physical development that I was never, really, to experience. I no longer recognized this lumbering beast as the buddy I knew. After an argument over some petty thing I threatened to leave by myself, but Mike sheepishly and reluctantly decided to come with me:

Descent of Man

After a month in the Rockies Mike's arms hung,
his jaw hung, beard was matted black around
his stagnant mouth, his eyes, lumpish in membranes,
hung in their pods as he sat beside the fire.
Our burros, hobbled on the meadow, grazed like a pair

of Greeks relieved of animality—
but we had let centuries take us, sank
in the lunar ebb, the slime of the past. These blue
peaks had not brought the grandeur boys require
just at the age they sniff themselves in fear.

We had reverted: the fish we mostly fed
upon were fried, now, trailing intestines, pasted
with scales, and soon we would, with beak or paw,
lift them out wriggling, eat them raw. I broke.
A look at Mike at breakfast made me choke.

I shook my skinny arms and screamed (while silent
mountains averted their faces like polite
neighbors). I kicked my dew-damp bedroll. I
was going home. Home in my mind was sheets,
radio music, sanitary streets.

Bride-like, I had found exudation in
the exercise of life. I sought my dream,
where things were starched and done for one in kitchens.

Mike, huge in his blundering haste, packed up, agreed—
like one who had exposed what he should hide.

We rolled our stuff in tarps and scuffed the fire.
An hour later we were filing down
a cliff lip overlooking the glinting river,
Mike goading our two burros, their great packs
rocking their rhythm, winding past the rocks

with aspen epaulets—just like the books
said outdoors ought to be. Civility
regained, we watched the leaves—grace in their gold
going—and how the woods decayed with pride,
and nodding burros took their waste in stride.

✦   ✦   ✦

Back in Vallecito we returned the burros to the dude ranch
from which we had rented them, put on our knapsacks again, and
started hitching. When we reached the highway, we headed west
for Mesa Verde, saw the pueblo ruins, camped there one night,
and were brought down the mountain by a mad forest ranger who
drove around the hairpin curves at sixty, licking his cigarettes before he lit them to make their taste stronger.

We headed back east then, for home, by way of Carlsbad Caverns. At Durango we bought a loaf of fresh bread at a bakery and
begged a ride on the bread truck, which was just heading out. Two
men were up front, and the enclosed bed was loaded with bread,
its roof luggage-carrier filled with empty metal bread cartons, but
they allowed us to ride on the roof of the cab, which was all caved
in with a giant indentation that would make staying up there
easier.

So up we climbed. A drizzle had started, so we put our packs
and ourselves under our tarp, held on to the rail of the rack for the
cartons, and chewed warm bread as we rolled out of town. The
problem was that when the truck hit bumps the cartons banged
our knuckles badly, so we had no way of hanging on. But we managed to balance ourselves up there all the way to Pagosa Springs,

255

the truck weaving along the winding mountain highway while Mike and I, clinging to one another and the tarp that covered us (and the bread we were devouring) tried to stay seated in the middle of the indentation.

South, then, to Santa Fe. Our first ride into New Mexico left us at a little crossroads where a combined post office and grocery store was the only sign of life, and we sat out on the road waiting for a ride for twenty-four hours. We played chess. We scratched a board design in the dirt, found pebbles and twigs we could identify as pieces, and played game after game. "Hey, that's not your queen! That rock's a *rook!*"

By the time we reached Santa Fe we were broke, so I wired Dad, collect, to ask him to send us ten dollars. We left our knapsacks in the Western Union office, to which we returned at regular intervals to see whether the wire had been answered. All day we wandered around that lovely old city's low adobe buildings. One museum contained the office of Lew Wallace, who had been territorial governor of the state. I saw the desk where, the sign said, *Ben Hur* was written. I summarized for Mike some highlights of that haunting novel, marvelling that Wallace had been able to create the biblical world so convincingly while isolated in this New Mexican fortress. Just before the Western Union office closed, the money arrived. On to Carlsbad Caverns!

◆　◆　◆

At the edge of Santa Fe a wizened cowboy gave us a ride in the bed of his pickup truck (with a gunrack over his rear window). As the sun set bloodily over the wide, flat desert, he drove about forty miles south on the little highway toward Roswell. There he stopped and yelled back to us, "Well, here's where I turn off." We could see the lights of his ranch house off to the right on the horizon. Otherwise it was pitch black, and around us was nothing but cacti and sage and a deserted highway as we watched the truck's lights bob off and disappear. Well, we'd better camp for the night, we figured. There probably would be no more cars passing. We saw a culvert under the highway ahead and thought we might sleep there. As we approached it, though, we caught the scent of fresh meat. I fished out a flashlight and shined it into the culvert revealing a freshly killed lamb. On almost every fence post along the highway we had noticed a coyote skin. Obviously, coyotes were a major pest in the area, and we had come upon the den of one of them. So we climbed through the barbed wire and gingerly picked our way over the desert until, we figured, we were far enough to be out of sight of passing traffic, and settled down—no fire, just bed-rolls and sleep.

We woke to the sound of trucks and cars whizzing past—about ten feet away: we hadn't gone as far as we thought we had.

"Mike," I said before I stirred, "have you ever heard of snakes getting in the bedrolls of cowboys."

"Yes," he said. "I've heard they do that to get warm in the chill of the night."

It was some time before we moved.

✦ ✦ ✦

We were no sooner inside Carlsbad Cavern in the midst of a long line of tourists when I felt the runs coming on. All morning I walked in agony past the spectacular lighted chambers, our path always descending, while I held in my sphincter, my stomach rumbling, until we reached the cafeteria in the depths and I could go to the men's room. I had leaked. I cut my undershorts off of me with my sheathknife and flushed them down.

✦ ✦ ✦

We were on the highway outside of Sweetwater in western Texas, heading for Dallas, at dusk. A police car stopped, and the officer asked our names. "You're all right, Clevenger," he said, "but I think we have something on you, Jerome." He took us into the car and back to the station. They booked us for vagrancy. We had less than a dollar between us.

In the jail cell I started hollering. I demanded a lawyer. I demanded a free phone call to Mother. I waved my Boy Scout card at the policeman. Trying to calm us down, he asked, "Do you boys want to see a nigger woman who killed a man?" She was, he said, a couple of cells down the aisle. We didn't want to see her. Finally, to quiet us, they let us come out in the office, behind a wooden railing. They were waiting for a change of shifts. Meanwhile, they brought us what they call jailburgers—tall sandwiches with many pieces of white bread, a slab of bologna between each. I asked to use one of the typewriters and started writing indignant penny postcards to Mother and to Dad.

At last another policeman came on duty. "Didn't we have something on someone named Jerome?" the first officer asked the new man.

"Not that I remember," he said. "We did have a fellow in here from Jerome, Arizona, the other day."

"Oh, that was it. Well, you boys can go." He gave us our belongings and then a ride to the spot where he picked us up. It was pitch black, and there was no traffic. "Watch out for snakes," were his parting words.

✦   ✦   ✦

After reaching Dallas the next day, hiking all the way through the city to get out to the highway, spending a night under the carport of a deserted service station, and hitching on to Houston, we had a nickel left to call Mother to drive downtown to pick us up.

The mountains loomed in our imagination—beautiful and dangerous and hard. We felt very competent, I'm sure, with little sense of our foolhardiness, of risks we'd taken that still send chills down my spine. I told very little of our adventures to Mother. I am amazed at what she didn't know—and how capable she was of assuming that my life was my own, that I could manage. There is a toughness in her attitude that I believe I have incorporated into my own behavior as a parent and as a person. It can amount almost to indifference to the welfare of those I love, but it is born of a Southwestern respect for individual choice and independence. As I started off for my second year at the University of Oklahoma it was with confidence that I was—had been for some time—out of the nest and needing to trust my own fledgling wings.

258

14

Go West, Young Man

On every windshield during the war was a gas rationing sticker.
If you had an A sticker you were entitled to the normal family allowance. If you had a B, that meant your profession, such as that
of a doctor, required you to travel more, and you got more gas.
Dad managed to get a C sticker, commercial, which meant his car
was used for his job (hustling oil royalties), so he had a substantial
gasoline allowance. Inside the car, the back of the sticker asked
each citizen to consider, "Is this trip necessary?"

Elegy: Barefoot Boy

Lead soldiers once were lead, oh barefoot boy.
You sympathized with Ethiopians,
and Germans (in your mind confused with germs)
toppled in trenches in your garden wars,
but years, Spitfires and Messerschmitts made your
dirt digging and your tanks all obsolete.
Dive bombers dived to noises in your throat.
They rationed shoes right off your grateful feet.

A lock of hair pulled down, a comb upon
your lips, you made Sieg Heils into the mirror,
saved grease and hangars, paper, fingered a V,

and sang the notes Beethoven wrote to show
support of Churchill and the Allied Powers.
Air wardens were your generals when, unwary,
you smiled into a birthday and were taken,
nor wondered if the trip were necessary.

Children will play you with your quaint devices,
your GI boots and nylon parachutes.
Though jets outdate you, children will remember
some of the names of some of your enemies,
and though the name of Iwo or of Anzio
become a crossword, death become a toy,
and beaches wash themselves of leaden soldiers,
children will play you hard, oh barefoot boy.

Until I was drafted (remember those old posters of the young
man with goggles looking challengingly at the skies?) I was satisfied to be neuter, admitted to confidence of girls, cuddled, and
thought precocious. I was Peter Pan in high school, cocky in college. But the army made me feel fierce pangs of missing manhood.

For two years I had been writing patriotic radio programs for the
campus station at the University of Oklahoma, but somehow I had
not connected in my mind loving my country with going into
military service to defend it. Military service meant living with a
lot of guys who were bigger than I was. Of course, I had done that
in college dorms, but those were students like me. Ordinary guys—
from farms and factories and strange places outside of Oklahoma
and Texas—were another matter. I dreaded going, but accepted
the necessity, as I was coming to accept the other requirements of
manhood. Above all, I feared being rejected. People would think
there was something wrong with me. They might think I was a
homosexual.

Four of us from the dorm where I was living in the spring of
1945 were called in for army physicals on the same day, but I was
the only one who passed. The other three, all Jews as it happens,
were rejected because, they told me, they declared themselves to
be homosexuals. They were proud of having evaded the draft, and

I was shocked because no one *admitted* wanting to evade the draft. But I didn't disapprove: I thought they were brave. One of them, my roommate, often crawled into my bed at night and played with me. I just lay there and let him do what he pleased. He would bring me off and then go back to his own bed. We never talked about it. I didn't know what to make of it.

I *never* knew what to make of it. Sex has come up often in this book, and I mention it not gratuitously but in wonder. No accounts of childhood I have seen mention the pervasiveness of sexual experience in young lives, yet if such things happened to me, they must have happened to others. It seemed to have been a preoccupation of many around me—certainly more than it was for me. I don't remember ever taking the initiative or bringing the matter up—except in jokes. We exchanged a lot of jokes about sex, always. But after my splurge of masturbation in early adolescence, I remained physically underdeveloped and was for the most part sexually inactive until I was courting my wife-to-be. It just wasn't on my mind. Fellows in the dorms passed around the usual sexual literature: the last chapter of *Ulysses*, *Studs Lonigan*, Pierre Louÿs, "Venus and Adonis" (the last a poem I first discovered in our family's complete Shakespeare back in Houston; I wondered whether Mother realized that she had such dirty literature in the house). I read such materials but didn't find them especially arousing. It was interesting. I was learning what you could do in literature. I wasn't shocked by sex, nor did I have any moral objections to it. It just rarely occurred to me to *do* it.

Surely I knew what a homosexual was by that time, and knew what a Jew was, but I was unaware of anyone around me *being* in either category. One of these fellows regarded himself as a Zionist— a new term to me that he explained in hushed words. Zionism was revolutionary. The Jews were going to throw the English out of Palestine. It sounded exciting. The four of us were great buddies and played a lot of chess together, but they remained for me exotics, and it was no surprise to me that they didn't go into the army. They didn't seem American. Indeed, they themselves may not have identified with a war of a nation in which they lived unassimilated.

261

At any rate, I passed the physical—an ordeal, walking around nude in a long line of nude men, being picked and poked and measured and weighed—and was asked a lot of embarrassing questions by a psychologist. Before the college semester was over I was notified that I should report for induction in ten days in Oklahoma City.

Before I went off to war I wanted to visit Mother and Stew again—and my new baby brother, Dan, whom I had not seen. I was in the odd position of having a baby brother and baby sister born within three months of each other. My mother had one, I would explain to the curious, and my father had the other. I asked my draft board whether I could be transferred to a Texas draft board and be inducted down there, so I wouldn't have to make the trip both ways. Yes, I could do that. They sent my records to Sweeny, near Old Ocean, where my family was living because Ott had taken a job as supervisor of a catalytic cracker at a refinery.

So I bid Dad, Evelyn, and baby Judy goodbye and caught a train to Houston. That train, like all trains in wartime, was jammed with people; I arrived in Houston about one in the morning and learned that there would not be a bus to Sweeny until seven. I was exhausted, so I lugged my heavy suitcase up to the second-floor desk of a seedy hotel near the bus station and asked for a room. I had never before, of course, checked in at a hotel and had no idea what to expect. There were no rooms available. When I explained my plight to the old man at the desk, however, he rented me *his* room, as he wouldn't be using it until after my bus time.

Grateful for any bed, I nonetheless shrank a little from the unclean sheets on a narrow cot with coil springs and a mattress. Beside the bed was a stack of magazines for railroad retirees. The bathroom was down the dark hall; most of the doors of the rooms were open a foot or so, presumably for air circulation, and there were sounds of love-making coming out of a couple of them. Uneasy as I was about this weird and sleazy environment, I was nonetheless soon sound asleep—and, after all my worrying, I was not attacked by bedbugs.

✦   ✦   ✦

The odor of the refinery penetrated everything in the small town of Old Ocean. Expecting to leave any day, I spent most of my time reading novels and writing free verse, the kind of poetry we read in English classes in college, the kind that all the student writers were turning out for the literary magazine. Stew, then twelve, had a horse that he couldn't handle—and I couldn't do much with it either, so it was sold a few days after I arrived. Day after day of lazy summer passed—and still no word from the draft board. I was not eager to go, but I felt suspended. I couldn't get a job, couldn't travel, couldn't make any plans. Just wait. I did take Stew on a camping trip to Blue Hole in central Texas, hitchhiking both ways. Mother said she would drive up to get us if my notice came, but it did not.

Ott's son Bill was there—ten at the time—always a difficult and naughty boy. I never much cared for him—and was astonished when *he* initiated sexplay with me. I rebuffed him. Did he think I was a little boy? After all, I was about to become a soldier. Mother came into the bathroom once while I was in the tub and observed that I was developing "down there." I shyly acknowledged that I was. Finally I had a thin growth of pubic hair. But the personal sexual reference embarrassed me.

Finally I decided to hitchhike down to Sweeny to find out whether the draft board there could give me some estimate of how long it would be until my induction. They had never heard of me. The elderly woman clerk seemed alarmed that somehow I had slipped through their fingers, and she hunted around in her files until she found my folder—filed under Judson. Many confuse my names. The year before, my high-school diploma had been mailed to me in Oklahoma with my name as Jerome Judson, so my files at that school, if such exist, are probably in the wrong place, too.

✦　✦　✦

Having found me, the government was quick enough to act, and about a week later I was in Houston reporting for induction. That late in the war they were scraping the bottom of the barrel for inductees. Men as old as thirty-nine with up to three children

Scrub the barracks floor. Fall out for short-arms inspection (always in the middle of the night). Jump to attention and salute when an officer or noncom comes in. Then, when unsupervised, go back to penny ante, or short-sheeting absent soldiers. Weekends we could avail ourselves of the amenities of the day room (pool tables, Ping-Pong, drink and candy machines), go to movies on the base, and sometimes go into town. After three weeks of intensive training we began getting evening passes and so could go into San Antonio for the express purpose of picking up girls. This, it turned out, was easy to do—even for me. Teenage girls congregated in certain parts of the city just waiting for servicemen to come along. *They* whistled at *us!* On one occasion the girl I had picked up hugged me and pulled me to the floor of a canoe we had rented on the beautiful river that runs through the center of the city. Our canoe hit a dam and dumped us over—about a four-foot drop to the river below, which turned out to be only knee-deep. Giggling and drenched, we waded ashore and took a bus to her home in an outlying part of town. Her house was dark, so we entered quietly, sat on the couch, and resumed our necking. I had a hand under her wet skirt when her father threw open a bedroom door and snapped on a light, a signal for me to leap to the door and go running down the street.

We were at that base twelve weeks. For the last half of these we were assigned jobs. Because I could type I was assigned to the Separation Center to type out discharge papers. The war in Europe had ended in May, but men were coming back from the Pacific—wounded, disabled, sick, or with sufficient accumulated service points to have earned a discharge. The separation papers came in three colors—white for honorable discharges, pink for those without honor, and yellow for dishonorable. Most were pink, a large number for medical reasons, often enuresis, as many men apparently wet their beds as a way of getting out.

When V-J Day came, August 10, we were all given half a day off but could not leave the base. Free beer was distributed, and most of the men stood around on the streets hoisting beer cans and shouting in celebration. There were still black barracks and white

266

ones (Truman was to integrate the services the following year) and much tension between them. By nightfall there were gangs of each race standing on opposite sides of a street yelling insults and threats back and forth. Fistfights broke out. I remember a buddy observing that as a species we are most absurd when trying to express overwhelming grief or joy.

Meanwhile, following the lead of natty dressers around camp, I took my uniform shirts to the base tailor and paid to have them form-fitted so their tails would not ruffle around my belt. At last we were reassigned and given a two weeks' pass before we had to report to another camp. I was to go to one outside Salt Lake City to prepare to be shipped to the Pacific.

◆　◆　◆

One of the perks we had as soldiers was free air travel in USAF planes. I went from Basic camp to an airfield and hung around a Quonset office until a cargo plane with space for me was ready to take off for Ellis Field near Houston. I had not flown since childhood and now felt very military climbing into the barren interior of the camouflaged cigar. From Ellis I hitched down to see Mother and my family in Old Ocean, then caught another free flight from Houston to Oklahoma City to visit my other family there. Dad and Evelyn said they would drive me to Salt Lake City.

Before we went, though, I wanted to get in one more camping trip, this time to the Arbuckle Mountains in south-central Oklahoma, those gnarled, soft, old limestone hills where Dad had long before explained to me how underground domes captured prehistoric gas and oil. I had never camped in the Arbuckles, an omission I wanted to correct. A buddy from college and I hitched down to that area, spotted a woody area near the highway, pitched our pup tent, heated our hot dogs and beans, and climbed into our bedrolls for the night. That trip was memorable chiefly for what happened when we started home. We walked out of the woods and onto the highway and were immediately picked up by a businessman who skidded to a stop. "Get in fast," he said, "I'm in a hurry. I have to be in Oklahoma City in an hour." There was no way that was possible. Oklahoma City was at least eighty miles away, but he was trying. He sped down a hill toward a narrow bridge that a truck was crossing toward us, slammed on his brakes to avoid the truck, skidded, and his car toppled over onto its roof in the ditch beside the highway. None of us was hurt. My buddy and I stepped out onto the highway and put up our thumbs. "Hey, you can't run off!" the man yelled, but it was too late. There was obviously nothing we could do to help him. The first car to pass stopped for us, and we quickly climbed in and zoomed away—all this within five minutes after we stepped out of the woods.

✦ ✦ ✦

A couple of years earlier, when I was camping with Mike and Edwin near Wimberley, Texas, an itinerant movie exhibitor came to town with a small circus tent and camp chairs. He would set up a theater and show a film, then move on to another small town for the next night's showing, completing his circuit about once a month. I forget what the film was the night we went—some B-Western—but a short subject was memorable. It was a Disney cartoon about the Red Menace. Russia was depicted as a scarlet monster creeping up over the eastern horizon. The whole crowd broke out laughing. Even *I* knew the Russians were our *allies.*

Now here we were entering a barracks at the camp outside Salt Lake City. The barracks had been out of use for some time, so it was pretty dusty. On the wall was a poster showing a Russian and an American soldier shaking hands with big grins on their faces. We all jeered. We knew the Russians were our *enemies.*

✦ ✦ ✦

We were stationed at Salt Lake for only ten days and had no duties. Every night we had passes to town, where we generally went to the Trocadero, a large dancing hall—not to dance, but to pick up girls, who were as available as they had been in San Antonio. Maybe some of the fellows made out, but I certainly didn't. I didn't seriously try. The prospect of actual sexual intercourse intimidated me. But meeting a girl, taking her home, dodging her parents, going as far as she would let me and the circumstances permitted—all that was *de rigueur*. And back at the barracks one boasted of his conquests the previous evening. I didn't dare admit I was still a virgin (not counting my sexplay with Polly Popper), so my boasting was vague.

Orders came for us to ship off to somewhere in the Pacific from Seattle. I remember being rocked to sleep in my berth on the troop train, then waking deep in the night. Outside a bare mountainous landscape of Idaho was sweeping by. A bright moon fell on the snowy peaks as the train snaked through a deep granite canyon. I was awed by these northern wastes, aware that Texas and Oklahoma were flying away and away behind me.

In Seattle they gave us shots for flu and all kinds of tropical diseases and let us out on the town. I was aching and dizzy from the shots and fraught with melancholy. I could not be served in bars. This, particularly, seemed an indignity, as I wandered the misty November streets. Here I was old enough, I reasoned, to commit myself to treacherous seas and Oriental soil, my head reeling from shots, and the only appropriate manly entertainment was denied me. All the other soldiers, most my age but looking older, were in the bars, so, alone, I went to a burlesque theater. They had the same jokes, the same bumps and grinds, the same obscene gestures, that I had seen years before when Dad took me to see Sally Rand in Oklahoma City. Sweet violets . . . covered all over with dew. . . .

✦   ✦   ✦

The next morning a long line of us hauled our huge barracks bags up iron steps and onto the deck of a Liberty ship (a cargo vessel adapted to carrying troops)—the first ship I had boarded since I was six, in Galveston. We steamed out into dim fog, soon hitting high waves that tossed our half-empty Liberty ship like a chip. I lifted my beardless chin to the storm, thrilled by a sense of gloom and doom.

As we crashed and groaned through stormy northern seas, I tried to work up a tragic acceptance of my situation: young, exiled, in arms to fight a war that was already over. I was reading *Look Homeward, Angel* at the time, and I knew just how its author had felt. Thomas Wolfe's problem was that he was too big and old for his age; mine was the opposite: I was too little and too young. In either case, we were misfits, misunderstood by our families, and girls, and everybody else. The only thing to do about it was to write.

On that voyage I also read Aldous Huxley's *Antic Hay*. If Wolfe had described the bleeding heart of youth, Huxley described its sophisticated outer crust—the crust I was desperate to acquire. At one point a man and woman in that novel are comparing memories of their first sexual experiences. He says, "I thought, is *that* all?" She says, "Oh, *I* thought, that *is* all." There you are, thought I. People make a big fuss about it, especially girls, but it's really no big deal. I kept the army-issue copies of these books and, when we had landed, mailed them to Mother, telling her that she should read them if she really wanted to understand me. I'm not sure how she reacted (except that she wrote that the novel by Huxley was naughty), but I felt somehow clinically cruel in flaunting my intellectual growing pains, my growing cynicism, the delicious worldliness of my polluted mind.

As that rusty drum of a ship reared and dove headlong westward to the East and the seas flooded through the scuppers, I clung to a cable up on the bow, near the anchor, looking with the spiritual guidance of Thomas Wolfe for a stone, a leaf, an unfound door, exhilarated by my suffering, drenched, and the only one of the passengers or crew not to be sick (experience took no toll on *me*). It stormed for most of the twenty-one days of our crossing. I watched the crashing sea yawn below and then rush up to break over the plunging bow. I wasn't supposed to be on the forward deck, but none of the sailors was around to notice me.

Three times a day we stood in jammed mess lines in the passageway between the kitchen and mess room. From time to time one of the KPs would burst through the swinging doors of the kitchen and call out, "Hot stuff! Coming through!" That shout would be echoed by soldiers down the line as the KP progressed, our ranks parting to permit him to elbow his way to the dining room carrying a huge aluminum pot full of some kind of broth. Once, however, we heard that shout, heard it repeated, and turned and fell back to discover a blushing WAAC trying to make her way to the dining room. What a gauntlet she had to run! That was the only time I saw a female on the ship. As we weathered day after day of storm, meals were reduced to baloney sandwiches hurriedly shoved at us by green-faced kitchen staff. We ate at stand-up metal tables on which our trays slid from side to side and crashed into the aisles.

On calmer days we played penny ante on the deck of the huge cargo room converted to a barracks. Lights out! We climbed up onto the stretched-canvas bunks, stacked five-high, to sleep, row-upon-row of soldiers in the black hold of the heaving ship. We had no idea where we were going. At one point we were told that we were passing Hawaii, but it was too misty to see the islands. And then we docked at a strange island in the middle of the night and were trucked to Quonset barracks. In the morning we woke to look out the window and see passing washwomen who looked Japanese carrying enormous bundles of laundry on their heads. We yelled out happy greetings. The women swung their heads to look at us, clapped right palms on left biceps and lifted their fists at us yelling "*Fangu! A te! Ugatza la ming!*" I was told later that the arm sign was the Italian equivalent of our raised middle-finger, and the Italian words meant "Fuck you! Suck cock!" Apparently Italian-American troops had arrived before us. Welcome to Okinawa.

✦ ✦ ✦

Several of us were assigned to a fifty-man phototechnical unit that had recently been transferred to the island from India. Our outfit camped in a short valley between steep, pine-covered hills—two facing rows of twelve-man tents with a dirt road between them. At the bottom end of the valley were larger tents of the lab for processing and printing aerial photographs. In front of these was the motor pool. At the head of the valley, up wooden steps, on a ledge, was the officers' tent, for Captain Bland, our commanding officer, and Lieutenant Sirocco, our adjutant.

I had picked up the nickname "Peewee" as soon as I arrived in San Antonio for basic training, and a few who knew me then were with me still, so the name, which I hated, spread like a disease. But some have manhood thrust upon them. This happened to me because of my enviable MOS—military occupational serial number—which was 502, administrative assistant. I was given that MOS because I could type (and had two years of college credit). It meant I was assigned to the orderly room, working directly with Captain Bland and Lieutenant Sirocco. Within weeks of our arrival, as soon as the veterans left—those who had accumulated sufficient service points to be discharged—I was appointed acting first sergeant, and, though my actual rank was still private (later private first class, corporal, and finally sergeant), I was issued master-sergeant stripes to wear on my sleeves—three above, three rockers below, and a diamond in the middle. The stripes covered most of the distance between my elbows and my shoulders.

I took to smoking cigars. Here is Peewee making his daily inspection of the tents, bouncing dimes on the blankets of each cot to check for tightness. Fall in! Ranks of shambling soldiers lined up in the dusty road between the two rows of tents and Peewee, puffing his stogy, marching up and down to review them, his burred hair standing ragged in the sun. What was he inspecting them for? missing buttons? Listen to his moral lessons about dress and saluting and proper procedures for signing out vehicles, all in the voice of an adolescent Harry Truman, or Skeezix, or overgrown escapee from Our Gang.

Peewee was a wheel, with control over the jeeps, weapons-carriers, and six-bys (two-and-a-half ton trucks with six wheels and six forward speeds). Here is Peewee at his desk poring over personnel records, mentally classifying his men by AGCT and MOS. A lumbering oaf from Minnesota wants to check out a jeep for recreational use. "I can't let you have a jeep this afternoon, but there is a free weapons-carrier. Are you off-duty? Yes?" Away he goes to the beach. And, of course, because Peewee is a big shot, he can take a vehicle anytime he pleases.

Here is Peewee drinking beer at the NCO club. Soused. It was time to go back to camp, and I got the notion that I should drive. I was in charge, after all. We had come in a six-by, and I had never driven a six-by. It required double-clutching: you floored the clutch, got out of gear, let out the clutch, then floored it again before shifting to the next gear. I managed all that fairly smoothly, the huge truck weaving down the twisty highway alongside tall cliffs, a dozen men in the rear under a flapping canvas cover. I rolled into the motor-pool area of our camp and stopped, cut off the engine, opened the door, and slumped down the high step to fall on the ground—too drunk to walk. My loyal men carried me to my cot.

Peewee also got free film from the photolab, occasional bottles of booze, and other gifts—including a ride in a B-17 over the island, and, with an officer who was an anthropologist, a tour of the restricted northern end of the island where the Okinawans lived in their fishing villages. One Okinawan family conducted a traditional tea ceremony for us in their lovely rock garden.

There were still bands of Japanese soldiers in the mountains up north, undetectable to Americans because they blended in with the local population. Occasionally they would raid a naval or military base for supplies. One group of such soldiers, in the occupied southern end of the island, came out of a cave and surrendered some nine months after the war was over. They didn't know the fighting had stopped, and they had lived in hiding all that time— cramped, unable to sit up straight in the cave, picking their way past mine fields at night to steal food and drink from American field units.

Everywhere were signs of the war: twisted wreckage of two-man submarines, tiny narrow-gauge locomotives, aircraft hulls, demolished buildings and gutted tombs with their large bulb-shaped, concrete faces and black square entrances on surrounding hills. I had seen pictures of marines cleaning Japanese out of those tombs with flame throwers. Naha, the capital, deserted at the time I was there, had been quite a cultural center. Friends and I climbed over the wreckage of the city—including a bombed opera house, where I was amused by a row of urinals on a steeply pitched and broken concrete floor. They were about three feet high—urinals for children. On a battlefield near Naha I wandered alone in a litter of bones, occasionally coming upon little Japanese feet still in their boots, still wound in rotting puttees.

Our souls grew tough. One day I was being a tourist, out in a jeep all by myself, taking pictures to send home. I saw a Shinto shrine on a little hill with concrete steps leading up to it. I started to climb and suddenly stopped. A rifle was pointing at me over a concrete ledge. After some moments I continued my climb and discovered a mummified corpse of a Japanese soldier, still helmeted and in uniform, aiming the rifle he had been aiming for over nine months.

On another occasion I was swimming alone in shallow water over a coral reef, wearing a mask to look at the tropical fish. Suddenly I passed over the head of a Japanese soldier—a helmeted skull with tatters of gristle and flesh streaming from it. The sight was like a blow to my gut as I floated past, inches above the dangerous coral, and when I reached the beach I quickly drew myself up on the sand, looking back with a shudder. The encompassing mystery and horror of war settled around me in the silence. What does one do? Nothing. Whom does one tell? No one. You take it in. You learn to take it.

✦   ✦   ✦

One of our jeeps needed repair. Four men pushed it into one of the empty tents, lifted one side and turned it up to rest on the other. Flat sides have their advantages. A jeep, one of the soldiers said, is the best car ever invented. All the parts are simple, easily accessible, and replaceable. After the war, he went on to prognosticate, every family would have a jeep and a helicopter. People could live in the mountains or anywhere they wished, whether there were roads or not. Society will decentralize into little pockets of community, and neighborliness and equality will prevail. Being in the service had taught us to live simply, to share, to value what really matters in life. Now that we have stamped out totalitarianism the whole world will live in freedom and democracy. There was much to be learned, I thought, from repairing a jeep.

Nighttime, after a rain, we were driving jeeps, lights off so as not to be seen, on an abandoned dirt airstrip. The game that night was to speed along, slam on the brakes, then jerk the wheel hard to right or left, making the jeep slide in the mud and spin round and round to a stop. I am today a good driver on icy roads, and I think I learned the skills on the muddy strips on Okinawa. Next we were speeding straight down the runway. A guy yelled "Look out!" and then "Stop!" I stopped the jeep, spinning it in the mud. He hopped down and we followed him to retrace our tracks. He had seen an enormous square pit about fifteen feet deep in the runway. Our tire track passed straight along its edge.

We were driving high on a mountain along the lip of a rice paddy, our wheels crumbling the ledge that fell sheerly at our side. There was no way to turn around or go back the way we came, so we trusted there would be a way down when we reached the end of the paddy.

There was. Barely.

High cliffs along the sea offered the opportunity for daredevil highdiving from various heights. Jumping, not diving, for me. I once dove off a ten-meter board in an Oklahoma City pool, and I remembered the painful smack I had gotten when my body was just slightly off the vertical, so from a spot on the cliff that seemed much higher than that board I went feet-first, keeping my body as straight as possible—and managed to hit the water without hurting myself. Other soldiers *dived* from even higher spots.

Another day I watched, on these same cliffs, a string of jeeps being liquidated—literally. Soldiers put them in gear and sent them over the edge one after another. This, we were told, was to protect the used-car market back in the States. Jeeps were already selling for as little as fifty dollars each, and unless the supply were stopped everyone would have one. So went that piece of our dream of a decentralized society. The other piece, family helicopters, soon disappeared as well. In the postwar era technological development moved in the opposite direction from flexible, personal aircraft. Giant passenger jets were built. In the early days these could land only at the largest airports and so encouraged even greater growth of large cities.

✦ ✦ ✦

"Hey, Peewee," called Holloway, "I've got some sake." He invited me into the tent he used for a portrait studio. Holloway was old for a soldier—thirty-nine. He had been a photographer in civilian life, but drink ruined him professionally, so he made his living with a tripod and camera on a beach—a camera whose film could be instantly developed and handed still wet to a customer.

Holloway was like a wise old uncle to us younger soldiers. He was a thumping good jazz pianist and whiskey-voiced singer (accompanying himself on the upright in our day room). I associated him with the popular composer Hoagie Carmichael or with Doolie Wilson, the pianist-singer in *Casablanca*. He was also the only man in our outfit to go AWOL from time to time. After disappearing for a few days, he would show up drunk, having been living among the Okinawans in their off-limits villages. "*Why*, Holloway?" I asked, pained that I had to report him to the officers again and risk his court martial. He weepingly told me of the little two-stringed instruments the Okinawans played with a bow and sang for me snatches of their native songs. He was an eccentric, melancholy man whom I deeply loved. Somehow he seemed a gentler version of my father. I wonder how the army seemed to him, an alcoholic vagabond consigned to live for a period among teenagers.

On Okinawa he had access to aerial cameras that used twelve-inch film—perfect for portraits—and was selling these to soldiers and officers who came to him for sittings. It was from his tent studio that he called to offer me sake. Curious, never having tasted sake, I drank the clear liquid Holloway handed me in a beaker. "Bottoms up!" he said, and I drank it down, my throat scalded. I was instantly drunk. It was straight two-hundred-proof denatured alcohol I had swallowed. Holloway and another soldier helped me

276

stagger to the mess tent and got me fed, then to my bunk where I slept it off for the rest of the afternoon.

◆ ◆ ◆

Holloway was a regular at the camp poker table that ran perpetually in off-hours. A $18.50 savings bond was deducted from my check each month and sent home to Mother. I drew the remainder of my pay in army-issue yens, bought my month's supply of cigarettes and toiletries, and, without fail, lost the remainder at poker, usually within a day or two of receiving it.

Trying out various religions, I went to Catholic, Jewish, and several Protestant denominational services conducted in Quonset-hut churches around the island, and once I went to visit a Catholic chaplin in tears. "I can't stand all the bad language," I explained. Every phrase was about fuckin' this or fuckin' that. All the men talked about was sex. The plump, barbered, scented chaplin patted my knee consolingly. "I could give hours of lectures on sex without ever using an obscene word," he told me. "You just need better company. Come over to my tent this evening and meet a more refined group of men." I went to his tent as invited, sat around through the evening having well-bred conversation on intellectual topics with a half-dozen officers and enlisted men, and did, indeed, feel refreshed. But there must be a catch, I thought. Maybe this priest and his friends are all homosexuals. A young private of low IQ in our outfit had been discharged-without-honor for having been caught giving another soldier a blow job, so I was apprehensive of such people. Though I was invited to come any evening I wished, I never went back—and stopped going to churches, too.

I began studying Japanese in one of the texts supplied by the army—one of hundreds of titles, including great works of poetry and other literature, published in special editions for servicemen. I practiced as I studied by making conversation with the Okinawan girls who came to work in the tent that served as our day room. One of these, Una, became a special friend. Often I drove her (on special permit) to her distant village (otherwise off-limits) when she finished work, or I picked her up in the mornings. At

277

her home I met her aged mother and father, her little brothers and sisters, and I took them gifts of army supplies, candy, and cigarettes.

I wrote Dad and Evelyn to ask them to send me an American dress, underwear, and shoes for Una. I estimated her size (she was taller than I) and drew a picture of one of her feet with splayed toes to show what a wide shoe she would need. The Okinawans ordinarily wore nothing but sandals. A letter from Dad came with the package. It implied that he thought Una must be my mistress, but, in fact, I had never been even flirtatious with her. Indeed, I never heard of *any* soldier sleeping with an Okinawan woman, and I wonder now whether this was merely because of my naïvety. Perhaps Holloway found sex as well as two-stringed instruments in the Okinawan villages. At any rate, Una was surprised and delighted, though she seemed worried that her family might think what my father thought. The clothes fit all right, but I never knew of her wearing them after she tried them on to show me that they fit.

I also tried out my Japanese on prisoners. Gangs of POWs would be sent from their barbed-wire fenced compounds to harvest yams near our camp, and I was assigned to guard duty, wearing a massive .45 strapped to my chest. Friendly, curious about the book I was using, the prisoners ganged around me, looked over my shoulder, laughed and chatted. They might easily have overcome me and stolen my pistol, but I didn't think of that at the time.

Such pistols were called "persuaders" because we also wore them to chaperone officers on dates. The few American women on the island—Red Cross girls, nurses, and WAAC officers—all lived in a fenced compound (like those of the POWs). An armed enlisted man was required to be along when officers took them out on dates. This was supposedly to prevent them from having sex, but there wasn't much they could do on a date but go drink at the officers' club and then park somewhere and take off into the woods— leaving the guard, of course, with the jeep. I sneered. Women and officers were of another world, mysterious and irrelevant to those of us acting out our cowboy and Indian game in enlisted uniforms.

278

Our roles, our responsibilities, our function as Occupation Forces all seemed made up as play. My pistol was never needed to persuade.

✦ ✦ ✦

I was having a beer in the day room tent when a young man from another outfit came in asking for me by name. He looked haunted. "You been to collitch?" he asked.

"Yes, I had a couple of years of college."

"You know about Freud?" He hit the *d* hard; I knew enough about German that I pronounced it as a *t*.

"Well, I've never read Freud, but I've read some *about* him."

"A guy in my outfit told me Freud wrote about dreams. I want to tell you this dream."

He and some buddies had been out driving in a weapons-carrier, all of them rather drunk, and they were on their way back to their camp, overdue. He said they passed an ambulance that had overturned, and stopped. Several bodies were on the ground, and a nurse, her uniform and hands bloody, was standing by them. Afraid they would get in trouble for being late, the soldiers in the weapons-carrier sped away. Or so he said.

Since that experience this soldier had been having a recurring dream. In his dream he was standing beside the road, and the nurse approached him. Each night she got closer, lifting her bloody hands, he said, and now he was afraid to go to sleep again because, he said, "She'll get me."

I guessed, but didn't say, that the weapons-carrier crew had a greater responsibility for the wreck than he let on. Perhaps it had forced the ambulance off the road. His dream might result from his sense of guilt. "I can't interpret your dream," I told him, "but I agree that it may not be a good idea to go back to sleep until you can get some help. You need a psychiatrist." He had never heard the term, so I explained what a psychiatrist was, and then I took a jeep and drove him to our little field clinic, but there was only a noncom on duty. The noncom advised me to go to the base hospital and told me how to get there. The soldier insisted on waiting in the jeep while I went in to inquire about a psychiatrist. There was, I was told by the orderly at the desk, no psychiatrist assigned to the island at all. "There's a neurologist," he said, "but he's in the Philippines playing golf this weekend." A neurologist would be irrelevant, anyway, I thought, so I went back to the jeep, told the fellow I didn't know what else to do, and drove him back to his outfit.

I never heard what happened to that soldier, but the story stayed with me. In my imagination it fused with another experience. After a long evening at the craps table at the NCO club, I went staggering back to my tent, already very drunk. From my barracks bag I pulled out a bottle of bourbon one of the officers had given me in return for a favor. So rare was whiskey, I hoarded such bottles. I had read that alcohol had a much stronger effect if one absorbed it slowly, dipping with a toothpick and letting the drops permeate one's tongue. Mostly I saved the liquor I came by for private hours of slow toothpick dipping. This night, though, I swigged—and was soon in a deep sleep. I was wakened by a loud crash of metal and shatter of glass. On the highway outside the tent there must have been, I thought, a serious wreck.

I believed I should get up and see what I could do in this emergency. I was, after all, the noncom in charge of the unit. But I found that I couldn't get myself out of bed. My body simply wouldn't work. I lay there for what seemed hours hearing screams, sirens, shouts, and more sounds of crashing metal, feeling guilty but paralyzed, horrified. The next thing I knew the dim gray light before dawn filtered into my tent. I got up, overwhelmed with guilt, and shuffled my bare feet into the woven grass slippers we customarily wore (which Okinawans made and sold for a dollar a pair) and went out into the still morning. I remember climbing up the embankment to the highway and looking up and down for signs of an accident. Nothing. No skidmarks, no glass, no wreckage. The dream, if dream it was, had been so vivid that I suspected someone was playing tricks on me.

Some eighteen years later these two experiences combined to emerge in fiction: the opening of The Fell of Dark. The hero,

Harry, accidentally forces a jalopy off the road, and its driver, a young black man, is killed. Harry stops, looks back, and sees what happened, then jumps into his car and flees. The rest of the novel is devoted to working out his guilt.

✦　✦　✦

I detested Captain Bland—a career cavalry man misplaced as commanding officer of our photo unit. He was a thin, short, slumped Texan who appeared to be in his fifties, though he was probably younger. He had the kind of accent I was trying to out-grow. I tried to conspire to get rid of him. One day he assembled our unit in the day room to warn us about visitors from a black regiment down the highway. Though the services had recently officially been desegregated, there were still units of all blacks. "The plain truth is," he said, "they're just a bunch of dirty niggers, and we don't want them around here." Lieutenant Sirocco had re-turned to the States, and our adjutant was now Warrant Officer Corrigan, who seemed to be an intelligent, cultured playboy. After being dismissed from the day room, I took a jeep and went hunting for W. O. Corrigan, whom I found in a Quonset hangar at the field making a fiberglass top for his jeep.

"How would you like to be commanding officer of our outfit?" I asked him.

"What do you mean, Peewee?"

I told him what Captain Bland had said and reminded him of the General Order we had recently received from President Tru-man desegregating the services. "What Bland said was against the law. We could report him to his superiors. . . ."

"Get the hell out of here, Peewee, and don't ever say anything like that again!"

✦　✦　✦

I was drafted in July. We landed on Okinawa in November, and the following November I was shipped home for discharge after sixteen months' service. But before I went home I was granted five days of R&R in Shanghai. Because of weather conditions that pre-

281

vented flying, the leave was extended again and again, so I was there a total of ten days. In October of 1987 I was in Shanghai again, with my wife on a tour sponsored by the Writer's Guild, and we looked up many spots I remembered, including the Park Hotel where we were billeted, which was right across the street from a majestic racetrack. (Now the racetrack is a paradeground in People's Park, the former grandstand a reviewing stand.) We saw Suchow Creek, which at that time was solid bank to bank with houseboat junks, squalid homes with babies and pets crawling from boat to boat, people who cooked on braziers on deck using filthy water dipped from the side of the boat. They dumped their waste into the same water.

Shanghai is a relatively clean city now, and one sees few signs of dire poverty, though there is still much air and water pollution. But you can walk safely at night down any alley. No more bars, nightclubs, and brothels. No more begging babies running after rickshaws with extended hands crying, "No mommee, no poppee, no sistee, no brudee." Indeed, there are now over a million bicycles and no more rickshaws and only a few pedicabs. No more sidewalks crowded at night with people sleeping on mats. The Shanghai of the era I first saw is recreated in the film *Empire of the Sun*. The Japanese had occupied it since 1937, and it was just beginning to recover.

By this time my pose was bitter, sensitive, world-weary. I bought a copy of Andrè Malraux's *Man's Fate*, which is set in Shanghai, in a bookstore on Bubbling Well Road. That book opened my eyes for the first time to the meaning of communism. I decided that I was a revolutionary. I traveled the clamorous streets in a rickshaw, contemplated the human condition, cultivated a heavy-lidded, urbane mien, with cigarette bobbing on my lips, eyebrow arching. But it could all be belied in an instant by, say, a laugh, which would make my eyes pop and my cheeks crack into a boy's glad grin.

I had with me two rolls of film for aerial cameras that were past their expiration dates. These huge cartridges, a foot long and about three inches in diameter, could be sold on the black market, where they would be cut up into smaller rolls to be sold on the street. An officer had advised me to take a rickshaw to a particular bar on Bubbling Well Road, leave the film in the rickshaw, go in and privately tell the bartender what I had, and to follow his instructions. All went smoothly. The bartender told me to bring in the film. He swiftly put the cannisters under the bar and gave me twenty dollars—a good thing, because, having planned to be there only five days, I was running out of money.

Some of my money had gone for a pair of boots handmade for me by a craftsman in the street of shoemakers. Each of the narrow lanes feeding into Bubbling Well was devoted to a specialty—silk, ivory, metalworking, and so on. The oxfords I had with me had holes in the soles. After picking up my new boots I took the oxfords down on the street to sell them, as I had seen other soldiers selling personal property to the Chinese. I sat there on the steps of the Park Hotel one night bargaining with a poor man who went up to two dollars in his offer, but when I refused that, wanting more, he shoved two dollars into my hand and ran. Nothing prevented his having taken the shoes without paying me.

But the boots were too tight, I found, after a day's walking around the city, and my feet ached. That evening several of us went to a movie (an American film with Chinese subtitles), sitting on a row of hard chairs with folding seats. The chairs were attached to one another but not to the floor. I slipped my boots off for comfort, but the sailor next to me started feeling up my leg, and though I roughly put his hand aside several times, he wouldn't stop. I decided to leave—but couldn't get my boots back on, struggle as I might, jostling the whole row of chairs, so I walked out with my heels riding up a couple of inches from the soles. The sailor followed me and jumped behind me into a rickshaw. I fought him all the way to the Park Hotel.

I had a message and a gift from an officer to deliver to Madame Elaine Bohune. This White Russian lady had an apartment in the International Quarter (now merely a fashionable subdivision, but then a quite distinct, protected neighborhood) and entertained various officers, including generals, who showed up in Shanghai for R&R. I found her address, delivered my goods, and was invited

283

in for tea, soon to be joined by a sprightly English colonel in a pith helmet, khaki shorts, and high-laced boots. I was enchanted by the view from the kitchen of Madame Bohune's daughter—a beautiful blonde teenager reading while lying on her stomach in her negligee on a white bear rug in the living room, but I was not introduced. Shortly after I returned to Okinawa I learned from *Stars and Stripes* that Madame Bohune had been picked up as a Communist spy who had been prying military secrets from the officers she dated.

I learned about B-girls in Shanghai's bars. These gorgeous little women would sit on one's lap and nuzzle if you bought them drinks—tea disguised as cocktails. I kept returning to one bar in particular where a B-Girl who called herself Rosie—my age and smaller than I—tried every means she could to lure me to her room after the club closed, and I much enjoyed her efforts to persuade, and relished caressing her smooth brown thigh, though I wouldn't dream of risking my neck in Shanghai's dark alleys in the wee hours of the morning.

Less sexual but more satisfying were dates with Jian. She was a woman of about twenty who worked in a haberdashery off the lobby of the Park Hotel. In her company I went to fine restaurants, movies, and fancy nightclubs with floorshows. She took me to her home to meet her wizened little father, a violinist. I never even kissed Jian. I had too much respect for her. I wonder now how *she* felt about such respect. We couldn't dance in the nightclubs because my boots hurt and I didn't know how. I was a pathetic world conqueror.

Before leaving Shanghai I applied for jobs, upon discharge, at the offices of Associated Press and of the *Shanghai Daily News,* an English-language paper. Once back on Okinawa, however, shipping orders in hand, I found the prospect of returning to the States too tempting, and when a job offer came from Associated Press, I turned it down. I have often wondered where life would have taken me had I accepted that job. The Nationalists still held most of the southern part of China, and their battle with the Communists was along a wide front in the North. I cannot imagine Peewee as a war correspondent.

15

Go East, Young Man

On the night before I was discharged I went with buddies on a one-night pass to the Barbary Coast in San Francisco. I thought of myself as seasoned and savvy at nineteen, but was knocked back to youth by a *hsst.* I had gotten separated from my buddies in the busy streets of that entertainment district. When I looked to see where the sound came from there was an incredibly striking woman looking at me—a six-foot mulatto, gorgeous, wearing a turban and a large gold ring in one ear. "Want to have some fun, soldier?" she asked huskily. I looked around for a soldier and discovered that she could mean no one but me. "No, ma'am," I gasped (home from the War, top sergeant, self-proclaimed roué) and dashed for the safety of the pack.

Yet I wore my pride like a boil. In civvies, with a ruptured duck (insignia indicating honorable discharge) worn even on my T-shirt to distinguish me from the other little boys, I nurtured my Weltschmerz, endeavoring to be dissolute. When bartenders accused me of youth I was bleakly haughty and stalked out in indignation, flinging myself upon the night. I would cut them off without a penny.

✦ ✦ ✦

285

After visiting ex-army buddies in Sacramento and Los Angeles for a few days, I took a train East. My vague plan was to visit family in Oklahoma and Texas, then to return to Norman and reenter the University of Oklahoma. About the only college friend I had been corresponding with while on Okinawa was Clarence, who lived in Guthrie, and I stopped off there before going to Oklahoma City. Clarence had not been drafted, and I wasn't sure why, though I was to find out. He had, instead, left college and gone to his home town. His parents had died, and he had inherited the family home. He was working as a clerk in the county courthouse.

Clarence was even smaller than I was, but he looked much older, having a badly pockmarked face with dark complexion. He was a quiet, intellectual fellow, much interested in literature and writing, though I believe he never pursued either its study or practice. It was Clarence who had suggested the name for the last series of my radio programs: *Know Thou This Land.* He had studied German and knew the poetry of Goethe. I remember one rather poignant scene with Clarence. For my eighteenth birthday he gave me a copy of what he assured me was a great book: *Joseph and his Brothers* by Thomas Mann. I had never heard of Mann or the book, but I was continually awed by Clarence's erudition, and I began reading the book reverently. But after the first page I threw it aside in disgust, and it happened that just then Clarence knocked and entered my bedroom (at that time in a rooming house). "He has no *right* to write like that!" I exclaimed indignantly.

"What do you mean?" Clarence asked, obviously appalled.

I picked up the book and read the first sentence: "Deep is the well of the past." Then I threw the book down again. "That is pretentious, obvious. He's trying to sound profound and is just uttering what everyone knows in orotund tones. . . ."

"Jud," Clarence protested in his quiet, authoritative way, "you simply can't make that kind of judgment on the basis of reading one page."

He was right, and I was wrong, and I knew it, but I sounded off with another tirade, and we parted, for the time being in anger. Later, much later, I read the book and was enthralled, and I don't know whether I ever told Clarence about that. Probably not. It was probably after I left campus.

At any rate, my friendship with him was the one relationship of substance that seemed to survive my being drafted, and I wanted to see him. We had a pleasant dinner and evening together, and when it was time to go to bed, I didn't question the fact that only one double bed seemed to be available. During the night, however, I woke to find myself erect and Clarence playing with me. I gently moved his hand away and rolled over, and that was the last of it. We parted on good terms the next morning, but I didn't hear from him again except once—after I was married and in graduate school at the University of Chicago. Somehow he located me by telephone. I don't remember much of the conversation except that he said, in his soft drawl, "Why, Jud, you have an English accent." I hadn't realized that I had lost most of my Southwestern twang.

◆   ◆   ◆

After brief family visits in Oklahoma I headed for Houston—and Janet. I had met Janet, daughter of friends of Mother and Ott, shortly before I went into the army, and we had been corresponding steadily while I was overseas. Her perfumed letters arriving with her buxom handwriting in purple ink on the envelope would invariably stir envy among the other soldiers, and the letters inside were full of suggestive and sensuous phrases. She had become officially my girl, and we veterans were mighty intent on seeing our girls. Ten years later I wrote:

Janet

i

Green, though I was what they called a veteran,
and home a week, I found I had become
transformed from something of a scrawny boy
to something of a flag and fife and drum.
But Janet had an instinct for symbols. She

287

knew Mother, Nation, Church, would find me fit
and sinless. Meanwhile I would serve. She was
lascivious as a banana-split,
this camellia cloud who at eighteen condensed—
vapor of Texas oil. A cumulus thickness

of limb and lip and tongue were her decoy
for a hairspring heart of deadly summer quickness.
A beauty! As one says of a horse that seems
impossibly nimble and sleek. And my embrace
scarcely contained her shoulders. My neck was stiff

from too much reaching for her cloudy face.
Too bad to kid the kid, after such sadness
and drizzly Houston winter nights, the hours
lighted by yellow radio dial, coffee
in drive-ins, smoking, talking, parking—hours

in which, as for a child, she peeled life down
to its core of sudden horror: Nothing had
prepared me for sordidness, not Hitler,
nor any more intimate ways of knowing bad.
Nursery cruelty, adolescent animality,

gave no such vision of deliberate meaninglessness.
I think, to have survived, I must have found
some meaning life cannot make me confess.
That she survived, and how, is all the horror,
the rain of grief, the unfathomable source.

ii

It went like this: Her father lent his car;
and nightly we would scour the spitting course
of wet and flat roads round the glistening city.
Always she came as fresh as advertised,
and always, before the night was gone, her tears

and loving left her pulpy, realized,
as a product bought and used. Harmless necking,

288

true, as I worked slowly—thinking of the sweet
family-type and round-eyed girl in socks
I knew before the spoil of war. To meet

a Post-office mind on its own terms was my
strategy. I had read the way to change
a libido was by talk. The first week I
elaborated on the passing strange
and wondrous pitiful. Then she began

her tale, which was somewhat to disarrange
my Boy Scout Manual seduction. I slept
in the guest room of her home, which went its juice-
and-coffee, vacuum-and-Godfrey way as though
the sun in a kitchen window made a truce

between God and Texas: there was nothing
to forgive. But Janet tiptoed in at ten
and kissed me under a canopy of hair,
and we were back in sunless lives again,
among the shapeless ogres of the heart.

iii

Her parents sent her, innocent and just
sixteen, away to a state-supported prep
school in a flatland town, Beaumont, her bust
having already burst like dough, with large
allowance and wardrobe: College Girl, they thought

her, but amusing, as little girls who scuff
around the house in grown-up shoes. She sought
a Beaumont Corydon and found one with
a car. Oh, *tempora* and *mores* there
conjoined. The pimply squeak for whom a flower

was something to dig pollen from, this Ben,
gave her a towel to sit on so as not
to stain his car seat, said in his insect way
she should stop whimpering. Done. Nothing more
to *that* than an incision, nothing gay

or very passionate, and Janet stared
at the whirling roadside raked by white sealed beams.
In her lap lay all the seeds of consequence,
the pencil point of pain, and high, like dreams,
throbbed phosphorescent stars: no heat, no hurt.

This thing went on. What reason *not* to could
she give to Ben, who went at reasons like
a rat? Thunder of tailpipes nightly would
echo outside the dorm, and she would go—
on a library pass. The Ford would hurtle down

the road like rocks in a chute. What *reason* was
there not to? Janet asked me, and my frown,
like a pupil's figuring a sum, was always
silent, as I still hoped to follow Ben
before she thought of reasons. Sighing, she

went on. A month took pain away, and when
she heard that explosive summons, nerves would race
beneath her skirt, and pleasure was but one
of her pleasures. Sitting in algebra, she said,
she had something to think about. An endless stun

settled like honey in her head, a vague
superiority to all the girls
to all the teachers, too, to all flat-chested
people in the world. Her neck was touched by curls
like fingers, her thighs bellied one another,

and the mirror of her senses thus supplied
all questions and all answers. Even Ben,
the secret piston creature, seemed outside
her orbit of sensation. But he must
have intervened, for at the end of the term

disaster came like grades. There were sure signs
that something grew within her like a worm.
Well, then, confusion—how she wired home she
would have a holiday in Dallas, how
she drew her money, extorted more from Ben,

290

went to a friend who had a friend, and now
losing and gaining weight to contending forces,
she found a fellow who said he could do
it all by chemicals, and went to him—greasy,
thin, pale, no more than twenty—and she knew

this was not working, as he looked her over,
with his curling comma mouth, his smile of scum,
gave her some powder, water in a rusty
glass, said there was danger of a numb
feeling (she said she felt it)—then the dirty

pictures for stimulation (as he said)
and finally, of course, told her that they,
for medical reasons, would have to go to bed.
She did. At the moment this seemed logical,
and, too, she was afraid. His breath was brass.

iv

At last, and soon enough, she found the mill,
run like a Heaven by Dr. Corliss Glass,
who, thirty years before, began a practice—
young, thorny, feminine, a budding rose—
but who, they say, out driving with her lover,

in a bad smash lost him and—joke—her nose.
What future was there for a female doctor
hideous to see? In bitterness she bought
an old stone mansion near the heart of Dallas
with pillared porch two stories high. She fought

her fight out with the law, now offered clean
cheap service scraping women with her skill,
contempt, and high morality. Janet, shrouded,
limp as a sheath, came to her, looked with ill
and liquid eyes at the hairy triangle hole

in her grim face, winced when told how murder
was worse than fornication, and the knife
came as a soothing cold caress. She heard her

291

child flushed away. Outside the city glared
like a griddle. Janet, by instruction, found

a chilly cavern where she saw life squared
in black-and-white. She left on dizzy knees,
returned on dizzy streets, as she was told,
for Dr. Glass made sure her patients left
her sound. The dormitory, which of old

was no less than a ballroom hung with velvet drapes,
now held some thirty beds, though that grey night
that Janet slept there only twelve scoured vessels
lay in the dark on white sheets starched and tight
under the tall open windows. Dallas

breathed in its summer air, its honks, neon
reflections. Down the aisle of beds could just
be seen tomb-statue-resting forms, the wan
and passionless who bore what they could bear.
No sound until after midnight, when a groan

came lipless from the distance, a tentative
social tentacle. Another, a frog tone
testing the silence, answering secret roll,
and Janet, when her turn came mysteriously,
responded a clear sigh. Next cigarettes

appeared like rubies in a line. A knee
moved, and an arm. A body turned, inert
forms were inhabited, the probing threads
of mutuality found root. Janet knew
with hollowness that soon these stony heads

would speak. Think of that slow black morning as
anonymous voices told, one after one,
defeats by circumstance. Experience
scabs strangely: One forgets how it was done,
but rubs it absently and picks away.

These spirits fresh from death could hardly piece
together what it was that brought them there

292

but felt some awe of fact and some release
in knowing, saying, every hard detail,
as though one might disown objective truth.

They knitted out the net of money, marriage,
until it held their flesh, their age, their youth,
in cords of intellect—conceived, but strong
and real, reaching into the far recesses
of the room, stretching out over the concrete city,

the fabric of sterility. Each confessed
to the priest of her mind. As Janet heard her own
bodiless voice name nights without reserve
she was grateful and abject to recognize
her freedom from the needle-race of nerve.

The bleaching sun burned in at last: The past
was gone. She shopped a day before she grew
the grin that would get her through, and then went home,
the next year finished high school patiently,
recovered safely. Her parents never knew.

v

She told the last of this when we were parked
three hours in a drive-in. She was holding
a paper cup of coffee—long since cold.
I had a napkin I was folding and unfolding.
It seemed a time to pay a bill. I honked,

we left, rode aimlessly. At last the slow
logic of silence gave her leave to say,
"You get to need and even want it so. . . ."
Depression trickled icy down my spine:
Was I to be the scalpel to her sore?

In short, she had so taken all my heart
that I no longer could have given more.
Was maturity, then, to be like this:
renunciation of what one has won
because the winning must be soiled with knowledge?

293

Hell! Oh, with what acidity is fun
soured in a boy's adventures! Janet eyed
me as a schemer eyes, as one committed
to the scheme. I kissed her brotherly. She sighed.
I heard that some years later she, admitted

to the Church, was innocently married, confined,
and now, no doubt (she must be twenty-eight)
accepts the sun through chintzy kitchen windows.
I am a fellow to whom girls relate
their old abortions, so must learn to grow

the common callouses and now no gory
discussion interferes with appetite,
but all dissolves in grey, like an old news story.
We all learn not to learn. Unfit to bear
the worm of knowing, we flush it out of sight.

I think we must have talked a lot about love on the many dates
we had in December 1946. On the face of the photo I have of her
she wrote, "Yours *Always,* Janet," and, on the back, "And I really
mean it Jud—I'll always be yours—soul or body—even though I
might never say—I Love You." Janet died young—from, I understand, complications in childbirth. I wonder whether they resulted from her abortion.

✦　　✦　　✦

Was it innocence I was fleeing when I took the train from Oklahoma City to Chicago at age nineteen? A year in the Occupation
force on Okinawa hadn't done much to change my physical appearance or level of maturity. All I knew at the time was that it was
time to start living an independent, adult life, time to leave the
Southwest, where I grew up, to leave my parents, relatives, the
friends of my early years, and to cast myself upon the world. The
world, we all know, is corrupt. You have to be corrupt to survive in
it. Okay, I thought, I'll go out and corrupt myself. I think I had
been trying to do that all my life.

294

In Oklahoma City Dad, Evelyn, three-year-old Judy, Evelyn's parents, and her sister, and four cats were sharing a four-room apartment. There was a housing shortage. Obviously I couldn't live with *them*. I took the interurban train over to Norman and found the campus transformed. The university had had few students during the war years, mostly women, and seemed a friendly place. But when I went to visit it again I found it teeming with real men—veterans puffing jaunty pipes, leather cases for slide rules slapping on their massive thighs. I was intimidated, and I couldn't move into the crowded Oklahoma City apartment, so I decided it was time to go East and become a Writer.

The East was to me the land of the pale and literate, the sophisticated and sinful, the Mandarins who, thin and yellow, were familiar with evil and ruled the nation with elegant cynicism and culture. They probably all knew "Prufrock" by heart. My major literary achievement to date had been to learn that poem. While in college I had tried out for a part in a play for an experimental new medium—television. For this I was to memorize a dramatic skit. I chose "The Love Song of J. Alfred Prufrock." I was good at projecting the mournful, jaded tones of one who accepted his failure in life.

I still could not be served in bars. In the East, I figured, everyone was served in bars. They were above Tchaikovsky and Aldous Huxley and Thomas Wolfe, and I was trying very hard to get above such cultural figures. I was trying to get above Gershwin and Kenneth Roberts. I was trying to advance from Will Rogers to Thurber. I didn't know whether they would let me in the East, but I wanted to go there to endure the damnation real writers endure, to answer the Call of the Tame shouting in my heart, "Go East, young man!"

So I went to the Oklahoma City depot and asked the price of a one-way ticket to New York. Sixty dollars. How about Chicago? I asked. That was twenty. Well, Chicago was, from my perspective, East enough for me. I bought a ticket and, a day or so later, boarded a train, the strap of my army duffel bag over my shoulder, its olive-drab canvas stuffed with all my worldly possessions hanging down my back, the old portable typewriter I had used at college banging against my calf. Dad, Evelyn, and Judy waved to me from the platform. Dad had grown a moustache and was wearing a felt hat, looking very dapper. Gangly Evelyn beside him looked worried. And baby Judy was terrified of the hissing, looming train.

I assumed an expression, that, I hoped, looked both brave and tragic. I was pursuing my destiny, after all. This is the sort of thing we writers have to do in pursuit of that stone, that leaf, that unfound door. Thomas Wolfe had made an epic of the great trains roaring across America bearing writers on their sad and lonely missions. I felt the iron wheels begin to roll under me, felt the thrust of the massive pistons, and settled back on the hard woolen upholstery, lighting a cigarette. I had twenty dollars in my wallet—enough. I did not look back.